tableau 9

the official guide

tableau 9
the official guide

George Peck

New York   Chicago   San Francisco
Athens   London   Madrid   Mexico City
Milan   New Delhi   Singapore   Sydney   Toronto

Library of Congress Cataloging-in-Publication Data

Names: Peck, George (George E.), author.
Title: Tableau 9 : the official guide / George Peck.
Other titles: Tableau nine
Description: New York : McGraw-Hill Education, [2016]
Identifiers: LCCN 2015034059 | ISBN 9780071843294 (paperback)
Subjects: LCSH: Tableau (Computer file) | Information display systems. |
  Visual analytics—Data processing. | Industrial management—Data
  processing. | BISAC: COMPUTERS / Database Management / General.
Classification: LCC TK7882.I6 P425 2016 | DDC 006.6/8—dc23
LC record available at http://lccn.loc.gov/2015034059

McGraw-Hill Education books are available at special quantity discounts to use as premiums and sales promotions, or for use in corporate training programs. To contact a representative, please visit the Contact Us pages at www.mhprofessional.com.

Tableau 9: The Official Guide

1 2 3 4 5 6 7 8 9 10   DOC   20 19 18 17 16

ISBN   978-0-07-184329-4
MHID   0-07-184329-9

Sponsoring Editor Wendy Rinaldi	**Proofreader** Paul Tyler	**Illustration** Cenveo Publisher Services
Editorial Supervisor Janet Walden	**Indexer** Karin Arrigoni	**Art Director, Cover** Jeff Weeks
Project Editor Howie Severson, Fortuitous Publishing	**Production Supervisor** James Kussow	**Cover Designer** Jeff Weeks
Copy Editor Lisa McCoy	**Composition** Cenveo® Publisher Services	

For Denise
10 in 27. WOW!

About the Author

George Peck has been involved in various IT pursuits for over 35 years. His consulting and training firm, The Ablaze Group (AblazeGroup.com), recently celebrated 20 years in business. He has trained, consulted, and developed custom software for large and small organizations throughout the United States, Canada, the United Kingdom, and Puerto Rico.

George works with a variety of Business Intelligence (BI) toolsets. In addition to being an accredited trainer for Tableau, he consults on Tableau and Tableau Server, as well as SAP BusinessObjects and Alteryx products. George is the bestselling author of nine other BI books published by McGraw-Hill, including multiple editions of *Crystal Reports: The Complete Reference* and a previous edition of *Tableau: The Official Guide.*

In addition to his software endeavors, George is a broadcaster and voice actor. His voice may be heard on national radio, TV and web commercials, promotions, and documentaries. He programs his own eclectic music radio station and hosts a regular jazz radio program on FM radio and online from Denver, Colorado. He may be reached via e-mail at Author@TableauBook.com.

Contents at a Glance

Contents

Acknowledgments

One would think that writing a tenth book would be easier than the first. One would think. Still, there's an incredible amount of effort involved, including lots of help from some very generous people.

Once again, Francois Ajenstat at Tableau was always there when I had a nagging question or request. You do set the Tableau Software record for fast e-mail response! Elissa Fink at Tableau provided unparalleled enthusiasm and support. Let's hug again soon! And, of course, thanks to Christian Chabot, Chris Stolte, and Pat Hanrahan for coming up with a great idea and founding a wonderful company.

This is my tenth book with various incarnations of the same publisher, starting with Osborne and progressing through McGraw-Hill Education. I clearly remember that day all those years ago when I interrupted a voiceover session to plan my first book project with Wendy Rinaldi. And, here we still are. Who knew how far we'd go? Thanks again to Lisa McCoy, Paul Tyler, and Janet Walden for turning occasional incoherence into understandable prose. Jean Bodeaux and Patty Mon were great again. And I'm looking forward to more work with James Kussow. It was great to "meet" Howie Severson—great work!

Finally, and most importantly, I give my tenth bit of thanks to Denise. It's got to be special that we've been in business together for 20-plus years and married for more than 27. As I always say, "There are no VISIBLE bruises."

George Peck
Author@TableauBook.com
August 2015

Introduction

Tableau 9 is the latest version of the leading data visualization toolset that lets you visualize virtually any kind of data. By connecting Tableau to a variety of databases and data sources, you can answer questions about trends, exceptions, and hidden insights as quickly as you can frame them. At first glance, Tableau appears simpler and quicker to learn than many legacy Business Intelligence tools. And it is. Yet, there's "a lot under the hood" that may not be apparent at first glance. This book is your complete resource to learn not only quick initial visualization options, but also the deeper fine points to really maximize your use of Tableau 9.

There are several approaches you may prefer to use with *Tableau 9: The Official Guide* to maximize your learning. The book is logically organized to start with more straightforward, quick approaches to data visualization, progressing to more complex concepts as chapters progress. If you are just starting out with Tableau, you may prefer to start with Chapter 1 and proceed in order. If there is a particular topic or feature you want to concentrate on, simply locate the appropriate chapter and begin reading. The index will also help you quickly hone in on specific topics you are interested in. There's also TableauBook.com, the companion website that features helpful videos and finished Tableau 9 workbooks that will aid you in learning this powerful tool (videos and companion workbooks are referenced in appropriate chapters). TableauBook.com also includes a complete formula language reference in PDF format that will aid you in mastering Tableau's built-in formula language. For more information, see the "Companion Online Content: Workbooks, Formula Language Reference, Code Samples, and Videos" section at the end of this introduction.

Chapter 1: Introduction to Tableau 9

Chapter 1 is a great overall introduction to Tableau concepts, including the user interface, general data visualization concepts, and quick ways to start getting immediate value from Tableau. If you're just beginning to explore Tableau 9, this is your starting point.

Chapter 2: Basic Visualization Design

More involved visualization approaches are introduced in Chapter 2. You'll find definitions and in-depth coverage of the differences between dimensions and measures and how Tableau determines which is which. You'll be introduced to Show Me, the quick way to create lightning-fast charts. Choosing different types of chart marks, color options, and Tableau formatting is discussed. And Chapter 2 is where you can learn how to create shared axis and dual axis charts and Tableau's unique approach to analyzing more than one measure with Measure Names and Measure Values.

Chapter 3: Connecting to Data

Chapter 3 is all about connecting to data. Whether you need to analyze data in a traditional relational database, such as Microsoft SQL Server; if you want details on Tableau 9's new features for easy analysis of Microsoft Excel spreadsheets; or you are looking for insight into "big data" from cloud-based data sources, such as Google Big Query, this is the chapter to head to. Connecting to data sources, joining multiple tables, and powerful Tableau data blending are all covered here. Providing a complete customized view of your data sources, as well as extracting traditional data into fast, in-memory Tableau Data Extracts, rounds out Chapter 3.

Chapter 4: Top 10 Chart Types

In honor of late-night TV host David Letterman wrapping up his storied career in 2015, Chapter 4 features the Top 10 chart types. Although Tableau will create far more than just 10 types of charts, this chapter concentrates on some of the most popular types of charts, such as bar and pie charts, to more esoteric bullet graphs and box/whisker plots. This chapter is chock-full of visual best practice notations to help you create the most meaningful and audience-friendly visualizations.

Chapter 5: Interacting with the Viewer

Chapter 5 starts with a complete discussion of Tableau filters, an essential part of any visual analysis requirements. Filter interactivity via quick filters follows. More flexible viewer interactivity options are covered via parameters. And the chapter ends with worksheet-based actions, features that allow worksheets to change appearance and display other related worksheets based on viewer clicks and hovers.

Chapter 6: Advanced Charting, Calculations, and Statistics

When you're ready to customize your Tableau 9 worksheet data beyond what comes from your data source, head to Chapter 6. Here, you'll learn how to group data in a custom form with groups and save selected sets of data for reuse in the entire workbook. Binning measures for histogram charts is also covered here. But the real power to customize Tableau comes in calculated fields, which Chapter 6 also discusses. New Tableau 9 approaches for calculating custom data are discussed extensively, as are new Tableau 9 level-of-detail expressions. You'll also learn table calculations and all Tableau's built-in statistical and forecasting options in this chapter.

Chapter 7: Tableau Maps

Chapter 7 delves into Tableau's rich geographic mapping capabilities. You'll learn how to immediately determine which data fields can be mapped and how to customize your data source to permit mapping of additional fields. Creating custom geographic roles and using widely available background map servers are discussed. This chapter wraps up with a compelling example of Tableau's ability to create your own custom x/y coordinate system for plotting data over your own background image.

Chapter 8: Creating Dashboards and Stories

The word "dashboard" has long ago moved from the image of something you see when you get in a car to a combined single view of visualized data. Chapter 8 teaches you how to create Tableau dashboards—combinations of more than one worksheet in the same physical space. Complete coverage of various dashboard design approaches appears first, followed by flexible approaches to dashboard interactivity. The chapter wraps up with details on Tableau stories, step-by-step guided analytics that lead your audience through a screen-by-screen progression of visual analysis.

Chapter 9: Working with Tableau Server

Once you've designed worksheets, dashboards, and stories in Tableau 9 Desktop, you may want to share them on the Web for the world, or just your particular organization, to view. Chapter 9 covers all web-based sharing options, including Tableau Public, Tableau Online, and Tableau Server. How to publish worksheets to these various choices is covered, as are techniques for filtering data at view time to only show various members of your audience data that is relevant to them. Innovative approaches to keeping web-based data current are illustrated here. If you are tasked with implementing Tableau Server in your organization, this chapter concludes with a rich section on various management techniques, including user maintenance and permissions assignment.

Chapter 10: Custom Programming Tableau and Tableau Server

Chapter 10 is just for programmers. Tableau continues to provide more custom integration options with each successive release of its software, and these latest APIs are covered here. The Tableau Server JavaScript API permits you to design your own custom interface for integration into your own custom portal or a web-based application. The Tableau Server REST API permits you to programmatically add, modify, and maintain Tableau Server content, as well as manage users, projects, and permissions. Chapter 10 wraps up with a sample application that demonstrates how to build your own Tableau Data Extracts without using Tableau Desktop.

Companion Online Content: Workbooks, Formula Language Reference, Code Samples, and Videos

TableauBook.com is your resource for associated online content. Most chapters reference a Tableau packaged workbook that may be downloaded to illustrate examples demonstrated in the chapter, as well as additional examples that may not be included in the chapter. Most workbooks contain annotations that explain concepts demonstrated in the workbook. Because these samples are packaged workbooks, they are entirely self-contained and don't require you to connect to any external databases or resources.

A complete formula language reference, including helpful examples of all functions and discussion of R integration with Tableau 9, is available on TableauBook.com. And Chapter 10 references sample code for the Tableau Server JavaScript API, REST API, and the Tableau Data Extract API. Download these samples to duplicate the examples illustrated in the chapter.

Visit TableauBook.com to watch videos that are referenced throughout the book. These helpful videos include narration by the author, as well as step-by-step illustrations on key concepts in each chapter. If you are viewing the enhanced e-book version, videos are embedded right in the text.

And finally, any updates or corrections will also be posted on TableauBook.com. As "dot" versions (for example, Tableau 9.1) are released, new features will be noted in electronic documents and, possibly, videos on the website.

Note *The videos are also available for viewing or download at www.mhprofessional .com/pecktableau9/.*

Tableau Desktop: Windows and Mac

Since version 8.2, Tableau Desktop has been released in both Windows and native Mac OS X versions. Tableau 9 continues this direction. When you purchase a Tableau Desktop license, you are able to use either Windows or Mac versions, as the license key code is recognized, regardless of computer operating system. And if you own both a Windows and Mac computer, you may install on both computers, as the Tableau license agreement permits this.

The look, feel, and behavior of Tableau Desktop are largely identical with both Windows and Mac versions. Drop-down menu options are virtually identical, as are context menus and dialog boxes. The differences between Windows and Mac versions lie in two primary areas:

- **Mac connects to fewer data sources** Because of operating system differences, Tableau Desktop for Mac connects to fewer data sources than its Windows counterpart. You'll notice a smaller set of available sources and servers on the Connect screen. If you have a Windows version of Tableau Desktop available, you can connect to any data source and extract data to a Tableau Data Extract (this is covered in Chapter 3). The extract can then be used by Tableau for Mac. Or, if you have Tableau Server installed in your organization, you may publish the data source to Tableau Server from Tableau Desktop for Windows. Because Tableau Server is also Windows based, it will connect to all supported data sources and act as a "proxy" data server to Tableau for Mac, enabling a live connection to an otherwise unsupported data source. Saving data connections to Tableau Server is discussed in Chapter 9.

- **Keyboard shortcuts are different**   Tableau Desktop shortcut key combinations generally follow operating system standards. As such, you'll encounter some different keyboard shortcuts with Windows and Mac versions. Most common differences include right-click context menus and right-click drag functionality. If you have configured your Mac mouse secondary click option, right-click mouse options to display context menus will behave identically to Windows. Otherwise, use CONTROL-click to display context menus on Mac. Right-click drag options behave differently in Tableau for Mac as well. Whereas Windows permits you to drag a dimension or measure to a shelf with the right mouse button held down, you'll need to use OPTION-drag on Mac for similar behavior. Other keyboard shortcuts differ as well. Tableau online help contains a complete list of both Windows and Mac shortcut key combinations.

Introduction to Tableau 9

Electronic data is everywhere. Whether it's a traditional corporate database that maintains information about a company's Enterprise Resource Planning system, the keywords that are trending on social media sites, or a portable personal device that keeps track of your workout routine, seemingly endless amounts of data are becoming available for analysis. But what good are mountains of data if there aren't nimble tools able to make sense of it all? Enter the Data Visualization tool. Designed to present data visually (as opposed to more traditional text), these leading-edge tools are allowing more and more people to make meaningful sense of the vast amounts of data available to them.

Tableau fits squarely into this data visualization/dashboard realm. Whereas standard business intelligence tools for corporate and enterprise reporting abound, newer visualization tools, such as Tableau, are just coming of age. Now in its ninth major release, Tableau continues to sit at the leading edge of this growing segment of information technology.

Download *At www.tableaubook.com, download and open the* Chapter 1 - First Workbook.twbx *file to see examples that relate to this chapter.*

What Is Tableau?

Tableau Software has its roots in the Stanford University Computer Science Department, in a Department of Defense–sponsored research project aimed at increasing people's ability to rapidly analyze data. Chris Stolte, a Ph.D. candidate, was researching visualization techniques for exploring relational databases and data cubes. Stolte's Ph.D. advisor, Professor Pat Hanrahan, a founding member of Pixar and chief architect for Pixar's

RenderMan, was the worldwide expert in the science of computer graphics. Chris, Pat, and a team of Stanford Ph.D.s realized that computer graphics could deliver huge gains in people's ability to understand databases. Their invention, VizQL, brought together these two computer science disciplines for the first time. VizQL lets people analyze data just by building drag-and-drop pictures of what they want to see. With Christian Chabot on board as CEO, the company was spun out of Stanford in 2003.

Although Tableau 9 improves on the previous eight major releases of the software, the core approach to visual design remains the same: connect to a desired data source, and drag various data fields to desired parts of the Tableau screen. The result is a simple visualization that can then be enhanced and modified by dragging additional data fields to different destinations in the workspace. Beyond this simple visualization approach, Tableau's *Show Me* feature allows quick choices of predefined visualizations by just selecting relevant data fields and clicking a thumbnail. For more advanced requirements, Tableau features a complete formula language, as well as more robust data connection options.

There are two primary Tableau benefits you'll want to keep in mind as you explore the tool:

- **Visualization of data**   Tableau excels at displaying data visually. Whether it's a simple bar chart or a more complex dual-axis, multimark visualization, Tableau's core purpose is to help you draw conclusions from your data visually. Although Tableau can mimic a traditional spreadsheet by analyzing data with rows and columns of numbers, you'll be wasting Tableau's potential if this is your primary focus.

- **Speed of analysis**   Analyzing data in Tableau is incredibly fast (assuming you present Tableau with a well-performing data source). Once you master the basic paradigm of the Tableau Data pane, shelves, and cards, you can literally answer your "what if" and "how" questions as quickly as you can think of them. What used to take traditional Business Intelligence (BI) tools hours to reveal can be discovered in Tableau in seconds or minutes.

When you first start Tableau, you are presented with the *Start Page*. The largest portion of the Start Page is reserved for thumbnails of recent workbooks you have used. Simply click any one of these to open the workbook (like Microsoft Excel, Tableau's format for storing data on your disk drive is in a *workbook,* with a .twb or .twbx file extension). You may also open sample workbooks included with Tableau by clicking the desired thumbnail at the bottom of the Start Page.

Return to existing sheets/ dashboards in current workbook

Connect to data sources

Open previously viewed workbooks. Hover over a thumbnail and click the pin icon to always display the thumbnail on the Start Page.

Connect to Tableau Software resources

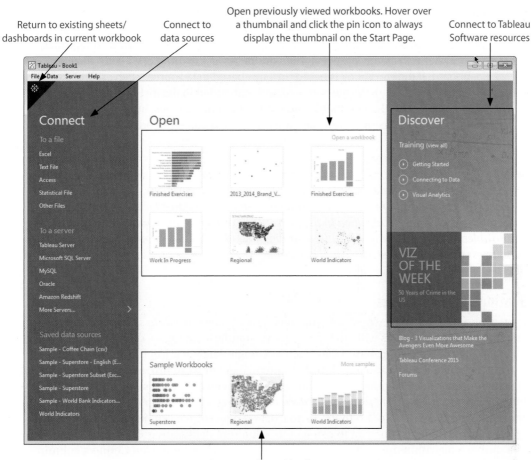

Open sample workbooks

Opening Existing Workbooks

You may open two types of existing Tableau workbooks. Click an existing thumbnail on the Start Page, or use File | Open.

- **Standard Tableau Workbook (.twb file)**   This workbook contains worksheet and dashboard definitions only. Any data sources and external files (custom background images, image files in dashboards, and so forth) are not saved in the .twb file. For example, if the workbook connects to two data sources (such as a standard SQL database server and an Excel file located in a folder on your C drive) and references an image located on a network drive, another Tableau user who opens the workbook will need to be able to connect to the same SQL database, will need to have the same Excel file on their C drive, and must be able to access the image file located on the same network drive.

- **Tableau Packaged Workbook (.twbx file)**   A packaged workbook is a self-contained workbook with any necessary external files embedded in it. It contains worksheet and dashboard definitions, as well as file-based data sources, image files, custom shapes, and any other external files necessary to interact with any sheet or dashboard. If the workbook is based on a file-based data source (such as an Excel workbook or text file), the file is copied and embedded in the .twbx file. Any external files referenced in the workbook, such as background images, images added to dashboards, and custom shape files, are also copied and embedded in the .twbx file.

Caution *If your workbook connects to an external traditional or cloud database, Tableau will not be able to include the data source in the packaged workbook. You may be warned about this and prompted to extract the data source into a local Tableau Data Extract, which is then embedded in the .twbx file. If you want the workbook to be usable in Tableau Reader, you* must *do this, as Tableau Reader will not connect to external data sources (extracting data is discussed in Chapter 3).*

Creating New Workbooks

If you want to create a new workbook, you must first connect to a *data source* (types of data sources Tableau works with include industry-standard databases such as Oracle or Microsoft SQL Server, cloud-based data such as Google Analytics, Microsoft Excel spreadsheets, text files, and so forth). Unlike spreadsheet or word processing programs, Tableau must connect to some existing data before you can create a visualization. Predefined data connections, known as *saved data sources,* will appear on the lower left side of the Start Page. These "pointers" to an existing data source can be selected by simply clicking them. If you want to connect to a different data source, click the desired data source type within the To A File or To A Server section under the left Connect column on the Start Page. Once you've connected to a data source, the Data Source page will appear, where more specific data choices (such as adding and joining tables) are made. Once you've made any data source adjustments, click the Sheet 1 tab at the bottom of the screen to display the Tableau workspace where you can drag and drop desired data fields.

Note *Detailed discussion of the Data Source page and data connections can be found in Chapter 3.*

Tableau User Interface

Once you've made data source choices, click the desired worksheet tab at the bottom of the Tableau screen. You'll notice that Tableau shares the "multiple worksheets within a workbook" paradigm of Microsoft Excel. A workbook can contain one or more worksheets, with each worksheet denoted by a tab at the bottom of the screen. As with most other standard software applications, you'll see a series of drop-down menus and a toolbar. Also, many Tableau functions can be selected from pop-up context menus that will appear when you right-click with your mouse (CONTROL-click with Mac).

The left side of a Tableau worksheet contains the Data pane, which divides fields in your data source into dimensions and measures. You'll find a blank visualization containing a single column, row, and center area, each labeled "Drop field here." The remainder of the worksheet consists of a series of shelves and cards, where you can drag fields to control certain behavior and the appearance of your worksheet.

The Data Pane

Since all Tableau visualizations start with connection to a data source, the first area you'll need to become familiar with is the *side bar*. Comprising the left portion of the workspace, the side bar changes based on selection of either the Analytics pane (discussed in Chapter 6) or the *Data pane*. When you select the Data pane, fields from your data source appear, ready for you to drag and drop to relevant parts of the worksheet. In particular, the Data pane is broken down into two sub-windows: Dimensions and Measures. *Dimensions* are non-number fields that categorize data. *Measures* are numeric fields that are aggregated as sums, averages, and so forth for each occurrence of the categorized dimension. For example, if you want to create a bar chart showing total sales for each continent, the continent dimension will be used to create a separate bar for each continent, with the size of the bar being determined by the sum of the sales measure.

Note *More details on the Data pane, including how to reorganize dimensions and measures, along with detailed discussion of various data types, are available in Chapter 3.*

Shelves and Cards

Once you've connected to data and evaluated available dimensions and measures in the Data pane, you'll need to decide where to drag desired dimensions and measures. You may choose to drag directly on the visualization area where prompted to "Drop field here." You may also choose to drop on a particular shelf or card. To create a vertical bar chart using the sales-by-continent example discussed previously, you would simply drag the continent dimension to the top column "Drop field here" area, or the Columns shelf. You would then drag the sales measure to the left of the continent columns in the visualization, or the Rows shelf.

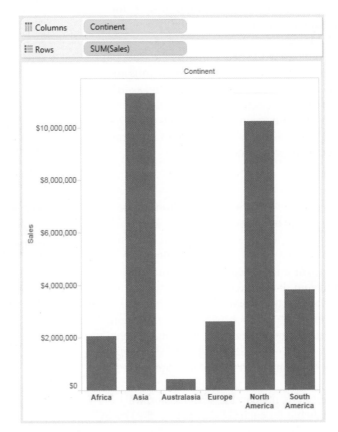

The term *shelf* is unique to Tableau, and refers to a particular part of the worksheet where you can drag and drop a field from the Data pane. The most common shelves are Columns and Rows, as dimensions or measures dropped on these shelves determine the basic layout of your visualization. However, other shelves are used frequently as well. The Filters shelf will narrow down data included in the visualization based on a field that you drag to it. The Pages shelf acts as a modified Filters shelf, allowing you to "page" through values within a dimension or measure to quickly see changes in data.

Some parts of the workspace allow more than one function to be modified within the same general area. These are referred to as *cards* (also a term particular to Tableau). In particular, the *Marks card* is a single area of the workspace that allows you to customize display of chart "marks" (bars, circles, shapes, and so forth) that make up your chart.

The Marks card contains different parts that you can click to make basic mark changes, or where you can drag and drop fields. For example, you can change the overall size of marks of your visualization by clicking the Size icon on the Marks card and dragging the slider. Or, you can drop a field onto the Size icon on the Marks card, which will set mark size variably based on the field you dropped. You can also make basic color changes by clicking Color on the Marks card, or change colors based on a field by dropping the field on Color. Once you've dropped fields on the Marks card, the fields will appear below the original icons where you dropped them. You'll be able to tell which part of the Marks card the field was dropped on by the associated icon appearing to the field's left.

Note *It's easy to confuse the terms "shelf" and "card" in Tableau. For example, the Pages and Filters shelves include a "Hide Card" option on their pop-up context menus. And the Rows and Columns shelves include both "Clear Shelf" and "Hide Card" options on their context menus.*

Three Ways to View Sheets, Dashboards, and Stories

Tableau breaks the contents of workbooks into three types of objects: worksheets, dashboards, and stories. A worksheet contains a single chart. A dashboard combines two or more charts into a single physical screen. A story combines two or more worksheets or dashboards into a step-by-step guided analytic.

By default, each object is displayed in a tab at the bottom of the Tableau workspace. However, Tableau provides three ways to display contents of a workbook.

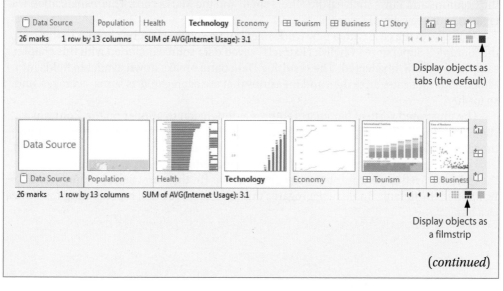

(*continued*)

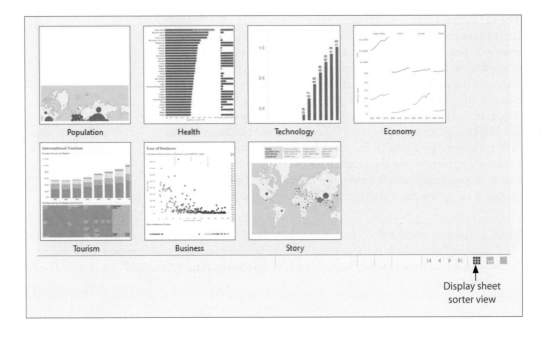

Display sheet
sorter view

Basic Tableau Design Flow

Consider the simple bar chart illustrated in Figure 1-1. This is a fairly meaningful visualization, illustrating a comparison of sales by continent, broken down by department. Notice the various portions of the worksheet discussed previously, such as the Data pane, the Columns and Rows shelves, the Filters shelf, and the Marks card. This visualization was created with a few simple steps.

As is always the case with a new worksheet, a data source must be chosen. In this case, the "Sample - Superstore - English (Extract)" saved data source included with this chapter's sample workbook is selected. The resulting Data pane breaks down available fields into dimensions that categorize data and measures that are aggregated as sums, averages, and so forth.

The illustrated vertical bar chart requires a dimension to appear on the Columns shelf and a measure to appear on the Rows shelf. Re-creating this chart involves simply dragging Continent from the Dimensions portion of the Data pane to the Columns shelf. This will create one "column," or bar, for each dimension value, or each continent. Then the measure used to determine the height of the bar (in this case, Sales) is dragged to the Rows shelf. By default, Tableau aggregates this measure as a sum, representing total sales as a bar.

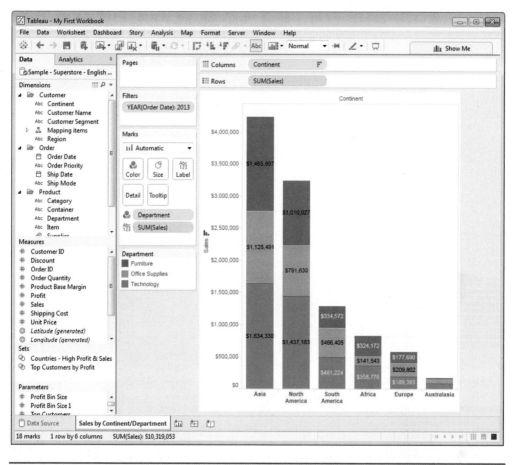

Figure 1-1   Basic Tableau visualization

You may also begin this bar chart by using Tableau's double-click options. If you initially double-click the desired measure, it will automatically be placed on the Rows shelf. Then the desired dimension can be double-clicked, which will place it on the Columns shelf, resulting in the same bar chart. Note that the order in which you double-click is significant. If you double-click the dimension first and the measure second, the result will be a text table and not a bar chart.

The data in the sample data source spans several years. As the desire is to only include products ordered in 2013, data must be *filtered* to include only a specific year. This is accomplished by dragging the Order Date dimension to the Filters shelf and specifying a year date level. The resulting dialog box allows only 2013 data to be selected.

Notice that the continent bars are broken down into three different colors (this is often referred to as a *stacked* bar chart). This is accomplished by dragging the Department dimension onto Color on the Marks card. Note that this field now appears toward the bottom of the Marks card with a corresponding icon indicating that it was dragged onto Color. The resulting color legend appears on its own card.

To help annotate the values represented by each bar stack, the Sales measure is dropped onto Label on the Marks card. The resulting sales amount appears on each stacked bar. As with the Department dimension, the Sales measure is aggregated to a sum and appears toward the bottom of the Marks card with the corresponding label icon appearing to the left.

You may notice that the continents are not appearing in alphabetical order (which is the default behavior when initially creating a visualization). Instead, they are appearing in high to low order, based on sum of Sales. Although there are several ways to accomplish this, the Sort Descending toolbar button is a quick way to sort a visualization on its primary value.

And, last but not least, don't forget to give your worksheet a meaningful name. As with Microsoft Excel, Tableau's default sheet names are the word "Sheet" followed by a number. This is hardly meaningful when dealing with a workbook containing many worksheets. Just right-click the sheet tab at the bottom of the screen and choose Rename Sheet from the context menu (you may also just double-click the tab and type the desired sheet name). You may also choose to highlight the tab with a chosen color. Just right-click the tab, choose Color from the context menu, and choose one of several colors to assign to the tab.

Tip *Make sure you save Tableau workbooks early and often. Unlike some other applications, there is no auto-save or recovery option in Tableau. If the power fails or your computer experiences a freeze or hang and you must reboot, you will lose any unsaved work.*

Video *Introduction to Tableau 9*

Basic Visualization Design

One of the compelling benefits of Tableau is how easily and quickly you can visualize your data. By providing a combination of automatic visual best practices, along with quick shortcut approaches to visual design, you can create meaningful Tableau visuals in literally minutes. And the more familiar you become with Tableau, the quicker it becomes to create more sophisticated and advanced charts as well.

One of the first choices you'll make for many visualizations is which basic design method to use. The first option, briefly introduced in Chapter 1, simply involves dragging fields to shelves or double-clicking fields in the Data pane. The second option, *Show Me,* provides a quick way of choosing from a list of predefined visualization types after selecting desired fields in the Data pane.

Download *At www.tableaubook.com, download and open* Chapter 2 - Basic Visualizations .twbx *to see examples that relate to this chapter.*

Using Show Me

Any time you're editing a new or existing worksheet, you'll notice the Show Me tab at the upper right of the screen. Clicking that tab will expand the Show Me dialog box (to close the Show Me dialog box, just click the title bar of the dialog again). Show Me will display a series of thumbnail images representing the different types of charts you can create with just a few clicks. You can use Show Me anytime you want—whether you've already created an existing visualization or not. If you've already created a chart, Show Me will replace the existing chart with the type you choose in the Show Me dialog box (and the undo toolbar

Exactly What's a Dimension and What's a Measure?

One of the first decisions you make when you create a Tableau visualization is which fields from your chosen data source you'll use to compose the chart. The Data pane at the left of the Tableau screen automatically places these fields into one of two categories: dimensions and measures. This may raise the question, "What's the difference?" or "What determines whether a field becomes a dimension or measure?"

There's no designation in the original database or data source (unless it's a cube data source, such as Microsoft SQL Server Analysis Services) that indicates "dimension" or "measure." Instead, Tableau makes a fairly basic distinction when examining the incoming fields from your data source: whether the field is numeric or non-numeric. With limited exceptions (for example, if the fieldname contains the characters ID), numeric fields are automatically assigned as measures, and non-numeric fields (text, date, and so forth) are automatically assigned as dimensions.

A *dimension* is a field that organizes data in Tableau in categories, or "buckets" (Tableau uses the term *member* to refer to different dimension values). For example, if your data source contains U.S. data and includes a State field, "State" would become a dimension (it's not numeric) and would potentially contain 50 members…one for each state. Even if the data source contains lots of records (far more than 50), there would still only be 50 unique state values, or "members," of the State dimension.

A dimension creates distinct divisions on a chart, such as separate bars for all 50 state members. These divisions typically display labels (Tableau refers to them as *dimension headers)* for each dimension member. Furthermore, Tableau typically treats dimensions as *discrete* values, consisting of specific, categorical members. You may notice light blue coloring for dimensions in the Data pane and field indicators on shelves. Although you may think this blue coloring indicates a dimension, it actually indicates a discrete value.

As the name implies, a *measure* is a field that returns a numeric value for measuring something, such as a sales amount or order quantity. Expanding on the previous U.S. data discussion, a Sales Amount measure in the same data source could return far more than just 50 distinct values. In theory, many records could contain a variety of small sales amounts correlating to the smallest items your company sells (maybe even one cent), up to very large amounts for high-priced items. As such, the Sales Amount measure isn't considered by Tableau to have "members," but instead contains a range of values, from the very minimum (potentially one cent) to the very maximum (potentially millions of dollars or more) and every value in between.

A measure is usually aggregated to a single value (by default, measures are summed) for each corresponding dimension on a chart. So, using the previous Sales Amount by State example, a bar chart might consist of 50 bars, one for each state dimension member, with the size of the bar represented by the sum of Sales Amount for that state. And, while it's easy to distinguish discrete dimension members, a measure can have a much larger variety of values. As such, Tableau treats measures as *continuous* values, consisting of a minimum, maximum, and everything in between. You'll notice a light green coloring on continuous measures in the Data pane and on shelves.

button or CTRL-Z/COMMAND-Z key combination will undo Show Me and redisplay the original chart). If you haven't created a chart yet, Show Me will create one for you in the current blank worksheet.

Although Show Me is designed to be a simple, quick way to create a chart, there are a few fine points you'll need to know to make the best use of it:

- If every thumbnail in Show Me is dimmed and unable to be selected, you probably are creating a new worksheet and no fields have been selected in the Data pane. Select fields you wish to include in your chart, and associated thumbnails in Show Me will be enabled.

- If fields are selected, or you already have a chart created that you wish to change, Show Me will only show chart types that are appropriate for fields that are in use with your current chart or that have been selected in the Data pane.

- Depending on the number and type of fields selected, Show Me will highlight the recommended thumbnail with a blue box (this is yet another example of Tableau's attempt to employ visual best practices for you). To use this recommended chart type, just click the thumbnail. If you prefer to use another chart type, just click the desired thumbnail.

- If you hover your mouse over a Show Me thumbnail, the bottom of the dialog box will show the name of the chart type you are hovering over, as well as the number of dimensions and/or measures that are required for that chart type. If you want to use that chart type, just CTRL-CLICK (COMMAND-CLICK on Mac) the desired dimensions/measures in the Data pane until the desired thumbnail is enabled. Then, click the thumbnail to create the new chart.

Choosing Mark Types

Video *Using the Marks Card*

No matter which approach you use to initially create a visualization (the drag-to-shelves approach or Show Me), Tableau will make some default assumptions about the type of chart created or, more specifically, the *mark type* that will be used. For example, if you initially use a date dimension for a chart, you will find a line chart (and thus, a line mark type) being chosen by default. Use of a geographic dimension (a dimension with a small globe icon next to it) will typically result in a circle mark type placed on a map background. If you choose no dimensions but instead choose more than one measure (resulting in a scatter plot), you'll find the mark type defaults to an open circle. And a bar mark type will typically result in other combinations of nondate, nongeographic dimension/measure combinations.

In all these cases, a mark type of "Automatic" will appear on the *Marks card* (the dialog box that appears to the left of your finished chart). Again, this is Tableau's approach to visual best practices: estimating the proper chart type and mark type based on the number and type of dimensions and measures chosen. However, there may be situations where you prefer to alter Tableau's automatic choices.

A common requirement comes with date or date/time dimensions. As discussed previously, Tableau will choose a line mark type if you choose a date or date/time dimension. Line charts lend themselves to "trend over time" visualizations for a range of dates or date/times—this is a visual best practice. However, if you have a small number of distinct date dimension members you wish to compare (perhaps a "this year versus last year" or "four previous quarters" requirement), you may prefer an alternative to a line chart, such as a bar chart. Accomplishing this is as simple as changing the mark type on the Marks card from Automatic to Bar.

Depending on the mark type you select, other parts of the Marks card may change and require your attention. For example, if you choose a Pie mark type, an additional Angle option will appear on the Marks card. By placing a relevant measure on Angle and a desired dimension on Color, a pie chart wedge will be created for each member of the dimension placed on Color, with the wedge size based on the measure (with the largest aggregated measure value resulting in the largest "piece of the pie").

Maps also have interesting additional Marks card choices. Although the default automatic mark type is a filled circle, you may desire some other mark type on a map background, such as a square or shape (a hollow circle being the default shape displayed). You may even prefer to display a filled map, whereby Tableau shades the entire area of a geographic region, such as country or state, by using the Filled Map mark type.

Choosing different mark types can result in some interesting (but sometimes ineffective) charts. Feel free to experiment, but keep visual best practices in mind. Remember that you want to effectively convey information about your underlying data. Think about what combination of mark types and chart organization will accomplish this.

Color, Size, Shape, and Label Options

In addition to mark types, the Marks card provides other options to customize the appearance of your chart. The first is color. Again, Tableau builds in visual best-practice adherence with default colors that are chosen for you (in fact, Tableau has hired experts in human visual interpretation to help identify the default color palettes and behavior built in to the product). You may choose your own colors, however, by using the Color portion of the Marks card.

Choosing Color Options

If your visualization consists of only one color (a single-dimension bar chart, a map, or so on), clicking Color on the Marks card will display a color palette dialog. Choose a different color from the palette, or click More Colors to display the standard Windows color palette dialog with precise color choices. You may also set transparency options and choose colors for borders of marks. A halo option is even available that provides a way of shading the edges of certain mark types to make them easy to distinguish (typically, this is useful for large numbers of marks in a chart, such as a map with a large number of circles or a busy scatter plot).

You may also drag a dimension or measure to Color on the Marks card to color your chart based on relevant data. Coloring on a dimension will create distinct color values for each dimension member. As such, you'll probably want to use a dimension with a small number of members for color (trying to color a "sales by year" bar chart based on a 50-member state dimension will probably prove to be of little use—a four-member region or five-member product type dimension may be more useful). Dragging a measure onto Color will create a shaded-variance color result based on the "continuous" behavior of numeric measures. For example, a profit measure that ranges from negative to positive values will color the mark in a shaded variation based on whether profit is negative or positive—highly unprofitable bars may appear in a heavy shade of red, while very profitable bars appear as deep green. Moderately profitable bars will appear with a lighter shade of green, and bars that represent products sold at cost will appear with a neutral gray shade. The heat map illustrated in Figure 2-1 is another example of a mark colored via a measure.

Regardless of whether you drag a dimension or measure to Color, a color legend will appear below the Marks card. Clicking the small arrow on the legend and choosing Edit Colors from the resulting menu, or clicking Color on the Marks card, will present options for customizing color behavior. Depending on whether a discrete dimension or continuous measure is on Color, the set of available colors in the current color palette will be reduced to those maintaining visual best practices. Furthermore, a set of predefined color palettes will be available for you to use as alternatives. For example, the automatic red/green color palette discussed earlier used to distinguish profit may be better replaced with a blue/orange palette more appropriate for a color-blind audience.

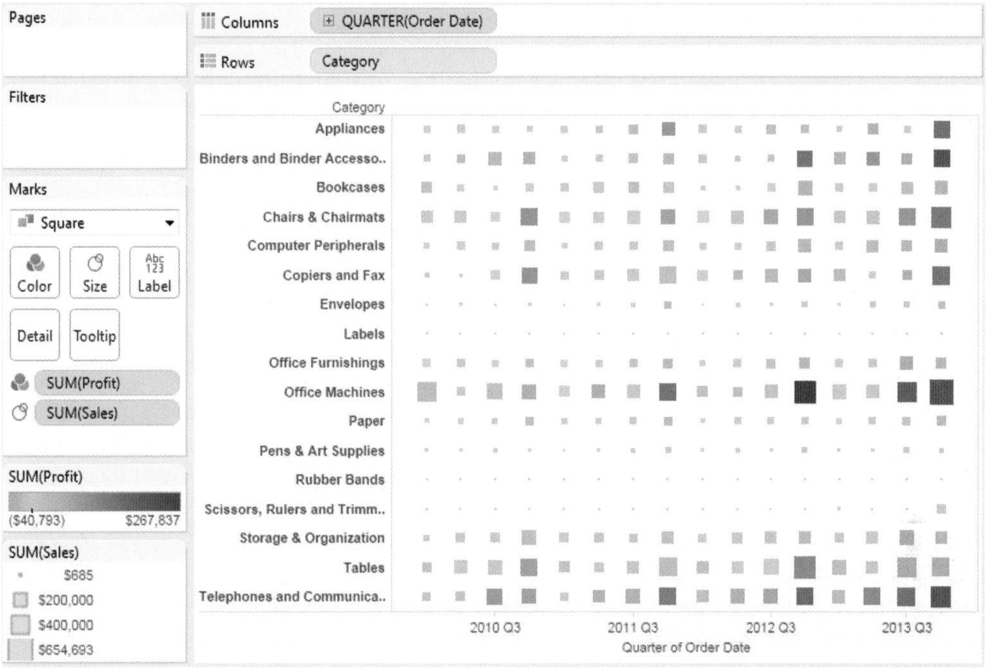

Figure 2-1   Heat map

Tip   *You may add more than one dimension to Color on the Marks card to create combined color variations. Just CTRL-CLICK or SHIFT-CLICK the dimensions you wish to add in the Data pane. Then drag the group of dimensions to Color. Tableau will create a unique color for every combination of dimension member (because of this, you'll probably want to use dimensions that have a relatively small number of members to avoid too many colors on the chart). You'll notice that all dimensions you dragged will appear on the lower portion of the Marks card, each with a color icon. If you later wish to reduce the number of color dimensions, simply drag the desired color dimensions off the Marks card.*

Setting Mark Size

Depending on the mark type, you may wish to change the size of the mark, either consistently across all marks or variably, based on another dimension or measure. Clicking Size on the Marks card simply displays a size slider that you may use to adjust the mark size. This is handy if you want to reduce or increase the white space between bars, make circles on a map larger, and so forth.

However, by dragging a dimension or measure on Size, you can vary the mark size based on another field. This is handy when you wish to size-encode a mark—perhaps vary the size of a circle on a map based on sales, population, or something similar. Some chart types are based on variable mark sizes by design. The *Heat Map* is available in Show Me, or it can be designed manually. This alternative to a cross-tab or text table (similar to a spreadsheet) helps analyze a large number of measures in a row/column matrix. However, rather than showing the actual measure value at the intersection of each row and column, the Heat Map displays a shape (typically a square) that represents the value of the measure. By placing a measure on Size, you can make quick comparisons by simply glancing at the size of a mark. Figure 2-1 illustrates the benefit of variable mark sizes.

Choosing Shapes

As discussed earlier, Tableau provides an automatic mark type based on the types of fields you drag to shelves or the type of chart you choose in Show Me. One chart type, the *scatter plot* (available in Show Me, or resulting from initially using measures on rows and columns in your chart), results in a shape being chosen for the automatic mark type. If you don't create a scatter plot, you may find certain situations where changing the mark type to *Shape* may be of benefit.

By default, an open circle will appear as the initial shape and an additional Shape area will appear on the Marks card. If you click it, a default shape palette will appear, where you can choose an alternative shape. Clicking More Shapes in the shape palette will display the Edit Shape dialog box, where additional shape palettes are available for selection. The default open circle will be replaced by the selected palette/shape combination. The true power of shapes, however, becomes apparent when you drag another dimension or measure onto Shape on the Marks card (generally, you'll find the most benefit from adding dimensions instead of measures). Tableau then assigns a different shape to each mark to delineate different dimension members or measure ranges. In addition, a shape legend will appear, showing assigned shapes.

To further customize shapes, click Shape on the Marks card, double-click the shape legend, or click the small arrow on the shape legend, followed by Edit Shape. The Edit Shape dialog box will appear with the currently assigned shapes displayed, as well as palette choices. If you wish to assign a different shape from the current palette to any existing dimension or measure range, select the dimension/measure range under Select Data Item and click the desired shape from the palette. If you wish to use a different palette, select it from the drop-down list. If you wish to assign all new shapes from the just-selected palette, click Assign Palette. Or, you may just choose one shape from a new palette for a particular dimension/measure by clicking the value and then the desired shape; shapes from more than one palette may be assigned this way.

Edit Shape [Customer Segment]

Select Data Item:

● Consumer
■ Corporate
✚ Home Office
✖ Small Business

Select Shape Palette:

Filled

● ■ ✚ ✖
★ ◆ ▲ ▼
◀ ▶

Assign Palette   Reload Shapes

Reset   OK   Cancel   Apply

Tip *You're not limited to just using the available shapes in the palette drop-down list. To add your own custom shapes, obtain or create a series of image files in .png, .gif, .jpg, .bmp, or .tif formats. Generally speaking, you'll benefit if the images are "icon size," or around 32 by 32 pixels. And, if you want to color-code the shapes with Color on the Marks card, you'll benefit from using .png or .gif format with background transparency enabled. Place the images in their own folder (the folder name will be used to name the palette in Tableau) within your operating system's Documents\My Tableau Repository\Shapes folder. If Tableau is running when you add shapes, click Reload Shapes in the Edit Shape dialog box to read the new shape folder.*

Text Tables and Mark Labels

Although Tableau is designed to present graphical representation of your data, sometimes plain text comes in handy (as proven by the continued popularity of the ubiquitous spreadsheet program introduced in the early 1980s). For these cases, Tableau provides the *text table* (also known as a crosstab). A text table is available in Show Me, or is created automatically if you just double-click two dimensions and then one measure, in that order. The key to a text table is the Text area of the Marks card, which appears automatically with the two-dimension, one-measure scenario just discussed. Text will also appear on the Marks card if you change some nontext mark type in the Marks card, such as bar or circle, to Text (Label appears in place of Text on the Marks card for nontext mark types, as discussed later in this section).

By default, the field displayed at the intersection of each text table row and column is placed on Text on the Marks card. A field appears in the lower portion of the Marks card with the associated text icon. If you wish to display a different field on Text, simply drag the existing field off the Marks card and drag the new one onto Text (or just drag a new field directly on top of the existing field to replace it). You may also click Text on the Marks card and adjust the alignment of the text, as well as customize the actual text displayed. More than one measure can be displayed in a text table. Simply drag additional fields onto Text, and they'll appear next to previously chosen ones. You may also invoke Measure Names and Measure Values to display multiple measures on a text table, as described later in the chapter (this typically is more visually appealing than just dragging multiple measures to Text).

When using a graphical mark type, such as a bar or line, you may find it helpful to still show text around a mark indicating the actual value it represents (to show the value of a bar or point on a line, for example). This is possible using *mark labels.* Basic mark labels can be turned on with the Analysis | Show Mark Labels drop-down menu option or the Mark Labels toolbar button. As mentioned previously, nontext mark types will also display a Label option on the Marks card. Placing a field on Label will add a mark label to the corresponding mark. Using Label on the Marks card provides additional flexibility beyond the toolbar button option.

`Abc`

Multiple labels may be placed on a mark. For example, you may wish to annotate a pie chart with not only the dollar value of the measure represented, but also the percentage each wedge contributes to the total. Or, you may choose to hide the standard color legend and add the dimension name to Label to place the label on top of each bar of a bar chart, as well as the value the bar represents. Simply drag more than one field onto Label. Changing the order in which fields display is as easy as dragging and dropping the order of fields in the lower part of the Marks card.

You may also click Label and customize the mark label display in a number of ways. An edit box allows customization and formatting of all chosen labels. And you may choose which marks to label (all, minimum/maximum only, and so forth) and when to display labels (always or only when marks are selected or highlighted). In addition, an option appears allowing labels to overlap adjoining marks.

Tip *You may reassign any field on the Marks card to a different property. For example, if you mistakenly drop a field on Color but actually want it on Label, there are two quick options. First, you may just drag the field from the lower portion of the Marks card onto the desired area. Or, you may click the icon to the left of the desired field on the lower portion of the Marks card. A pop-up menu of available Marks card properties will appear. Choose the desired property you wish to move the field to. The icon next to the field, and the visualization, will change accordingly.*

Customizing Tooltips

Tooltips are small pop-up text boxes that appear when you hover your mouse over a mark. By default, tooltips show values for all relevant fields included somewhere on your visualization. With Tableau 9 "responsive" tooltips, a click on an existing tooltip will provide additional action links to create inclusion or exclusion filters, create a group or set (groups and sets are discussed in Chapter 6), and view the underlying data making up the mark.

There are several ways of customizing tooltip appearance. First, you may right-click any field used on the worksheet (on a shelf, on the Marks card, and so forth) and toggle the Include In Tooltip option (this option will not appear if you have customized the tooltip in the Edit Tooltip dialog box, described next). You may also choose the Worksheet | Tooltip drop-down menu option, or click Tooltip on the Marks card to display the Edit Tooltip dialog box. You may format various parts of the tooltip text, add more fields (including an All Fields option), choose how tooltips behave when you hover over a mark, and choose whether or not to include the previously described command button/action links in tooltips.

Formatting Options

So far, customized formatting has been limited to options available in text edit dialog boxes. These dialog boxes permit you to select various parts of text and change font and color formatting. However, Tableau also includes complete formatting options for other parts of your visualization, such as marks, headers (column or row headings that appear for each dimension), axes, and so forth.

There are several ways to initiate formatting in Tableau. You may choose options from the Format drop-down menu. You may also right-click virtually any kind of Tableau element (fields on shelves, marks, labels, legends, axes, and so forth) and choose Format from the context menu. The Data pane will be replaced with a Format pane, as illustrated in Figure 2-2.

You'll notice several small icons at the top of the Format pane. Click the desired icon to change font, alignment, shading, borders, and lines on your worksheet. These icons equate to the first five options on the Format drop-down menu. Below the icons are three tabs: Sheet, Rows, and Columns. Click the desired tab to format either the overall worksheet or just row and column items.

A small Fields drop-down arrow appears at the upper-right area of the Format pane. Clicking this arrow will expose a list of all dimensions and measures in use on the worksheet.

Figure 2-2   The Format pane

Selecting an individual dimension or measure will allow you to format just occurrences of that field, as opposed to overall formatting for all fields. The previously described Sheet, Rows, and Columns tabs will be replaced with Header/Axis and Pane tabs. Header/Axis formatting applies to dimension labels (or headers), which appear for each member of a dimension. Axis formatting applies to a numeric axis that is associated with a measure. Pane formatting applies to the actual graphical or text items within your chart. In particular, charts based on more than one dimension will create a series of "panes" within each other, which are formatted via the Pane tab.

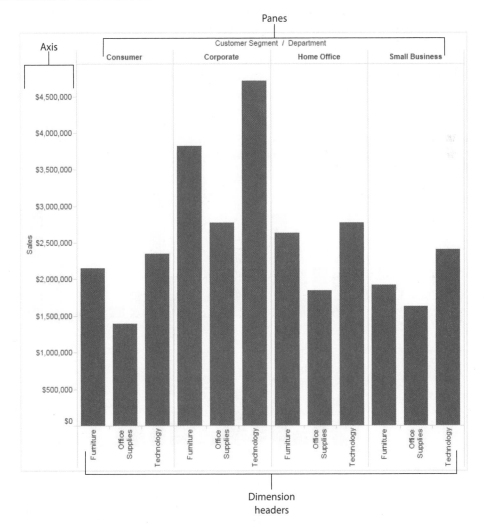

Formatting in Tableau may require some getting used to, as the organization of the Format pane is different from many other standard applications. Just experiment—if you don't see the expected outcome, try choosing other combinations of tabs or formatting icons until you achieve the proper results. There is no OK confirmation button in the

Format pane, so formatting happens on-the-fly as you choose options. You'll be able to see the results of your choices immediately and reverse them if they're not correct. And you can always resort to the Clear button in the Format pane or the Undo button on the toolbar.

Evaluating Multiple Measures

With most basic visualizations illustrated so far, a single measure has been analyzed (with the exception of the scatter plot, which analyzes the relationship between two measures). However, it's often helpful to compare more than one measure—either comparing two measures on two opposite axes in a visualization or side-by-side using the same axis.

There are several ways of comparing more than one measure. The first is accomplished by simply dragging two or more measures onto the Rows or Columns shelf. The result will be multiple rows or columns, with each representing one measure. Consider the chart shown in Figure 2-3. Here, category is contained on the Columns shelf, with the sales measure and

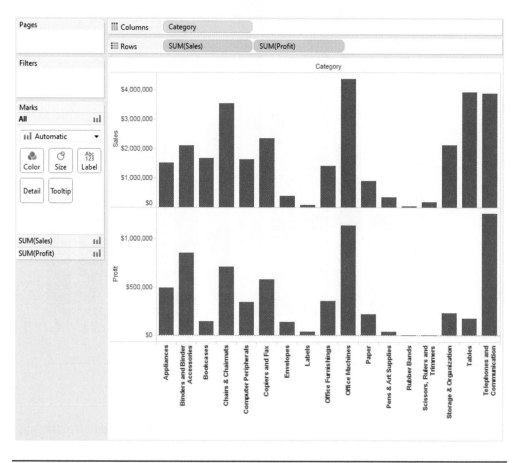

Figure 2-3   Multiple measures on a shelf

profit measure appearing on rows. This creates two different rows, with a separate axis for each measure. This approach provides several benefits: each measure can be compared across a single row, and the measures can be compared to each other by evaluating the two bars within each product category column. This type of chart is helpful if the two measures are drastically different in values or minimum/maximum scale, as each axis is automatically scaled to accommodate its specific measure.

Shared Axis Charts

Although the example presented in Figure 2-3 may be appropriate for certain measure comparisons, you may prefer a more direct comparison of multiple measures in the same "pane," using the same axis. The *shared axis chart,* illustrated in Figure 2-4, accomplishes this. Here, both sales and profit share the same axis. This provides for a more direct comparison of not only the trend that sales and profit follow over time, but how profit and sales compare.

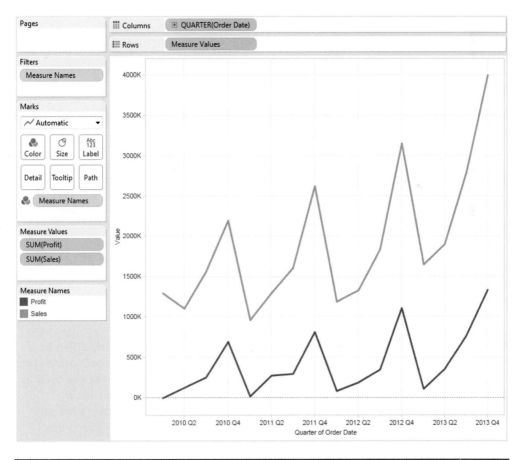

Figure 2-4   Shared axis chart

Creating a shared axis chart, while simple, requires a specific approach. After creating a chart with the first measure, drag the second measure from the Data pane *onto the existing axis in the work area.* Look carefully—you'll see a "double ruler" icon (two side-by-side green bars) appear in the existing axis. When you see this icon, drop the second measure. Both measures will now appear on the visualization sharing the same axis. You may do this as many times as necessary (as long as too many measures don't render the chart unusable). Just drag additional measures onto the shared axis.

Double ruler icon to create shared axis chart →

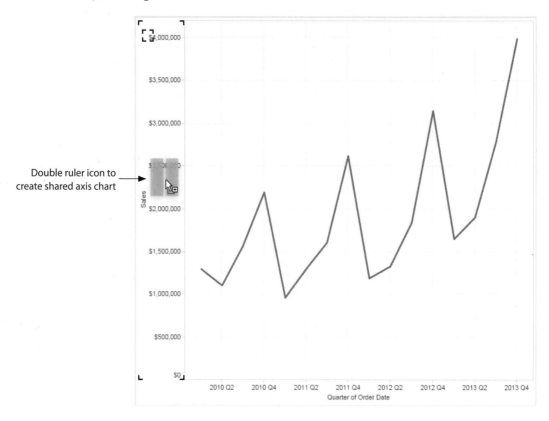

Best Practice *Although Tableau permits multiple measures of drastically different values and scales to share a single axis, you'll probably find these visualizations to be of limited use. The drastic difference will require Tableau to scale the shared axis for the larger measure, which may make comparison to the smaller measure difficult. As such, you should only use shared axis charts if the measures are not dramatically different in scale.*

Measure Names and Measure Values

Shared axis charts are simple to create—simply drag another measure to an existing axis. However, various shelves and cards in the Tableau workspace suddenly show lots of changes based on this simple drag-and-drop. You'll now notice several Measure Names and Measure Values fields appearing in various parts of the workspace.

In summary, *Measure Names* and *Measure Values* are a way of allowing more than one measure to appear in the same place. Measure Names exposes the names of multiple measures (in the example shown in Figure 2-4, there are two names: the word "Sales" and the word "Profit"). Measure Values exposes the actual values of the measures. In the example shown in Figure 2-4, the two values are sum of sales and sum of profit. You'll notice that Measure Names is automatically placed on the Filters shelf, even though no data is actually being filtered from the underlying data source. Instead, the Measure Names filter is limiting the measures exposed to just sales and profit—all other measures in the data source will appear in the Measure Names filter, but only sales and profit are checked. And, you'll notice Measure Values is placed on a shelf to place multiple measures on the same shelf, without creating a new row or column for each measure. Furthermore, Measure Names has been placed on Color on the Marks card in the example illustrated in Figure 2-4 to create different colors for sales and profit.

Filters

    Measure Names

Marks

    Automatic

    Color   Size   Label

    Detail   Tooltip   Path

    Measure Names

Measure Values

    SUM(Profit)

    SUM(Sales)

Measure Names
    Profit
    Sales

Another helpful use of Measure Names and Measure Values is when you wish to use more than one measure in a text table/crosstab (text tables are discussed earlier in this chapter). Although you may drag more than one measure on Text on the Marks card to add multiple measures to a text table, you'll probably prefer the results when you double-click to add more measures. For example, if you drag desired dimensions to Rows and Columns shelves and then simply double-click a measure, the measure will automatically be placed on Text and will appear at the intersection of the row and column dimensions. Instead of dragging a second measure to Text, simply double-click the second measure. Tableau will invoke Measure Names and Measure Values, placing Measure Values on Text to show multiple measures in the same place, and Measure Names on Rows to create a separate row for each measure. The added benefit of this approach when compared to dragging individual measures to Text is that a single set of headers appears containing the names of the measures. No special effort is required (such as a calculated field or manual editing of the text value) to properly label multiple measure rows or columns.

Shelves:

- Pages
- Columns: Region
- Rows: Customer Segment, Measure Names
- Filters: Measure Names
- Marks: Abc Automatic
  - Color, Size, Text, Detail, Tooltip
  - Abc 123 Measure Values
- Measure Values: SUM(Profit), SUM(Sales)

Customer Se..		Central	East	Region International	South	West
Consumer	Profit	$64,281	$61,174	$866,929	$26,558	$54,547
	Sales	$404,292	$480,805	$4,075,355	$329,780	$620,338
Corporate	Profit	$210,126	$144,866	$2,084,506	$23,243	$127,303
	Sales	$1,042,483	$818,102	$8,035,475	$569,904	$838,901
Home Office	Profit	$136,231	$78,402	$1,157,495	$40,036	$29,201
	Sales	$709,259	$506,332	$5,087,195	$427,010	$526,351
Small Business	Profit	$109,187	$93,124	$1,296,110	$14,364	$99,799
	Sales	$384,308	$617,565	$4,284,500	$270,652	$405,849

Note *Although you'll see Measure Names and Measure Values items in the Data pane, it's typically better to let Tableau invoke them automatically with drag-to-axis or double-click functionality described earlier. You may drag them to shelves and cards directly from the Data pane, but you'll probably find lots of additional (and often confusing) effort will be required to achieve the desired end results.*

Dual Axis Charts

One of the potential pitfalls with shared axis charts discussed earlier is an unacceptable difference in scale of values of the compared measures. Sharing a single axis becomes useless in these cases, as the axis scale required for the larger measure renders comparison to the smaller measure impractical. Tableau solves this problem with *dual axis charts,* charts that can display separate left and right axes.

Figure 2-5 shows such an example. Here, sales and shipping cost can be reasonably compared in the same physical space. However, there are two separate axes on the chart: the sales axis appears on the left, the shipping cost axis on the right. Note the two different scales of the axes, which avoids the issue of comparing dissimilar measures on the same axis. As with shared axis charts, creating a dual axis chart is simple, but requires one of two specific steps. First, drag the second measure from the Data pane *onto the right side of the existing chart in the work area.* Look carefully—you'll see a "single axis" icon (one green bar and a dashed line) appear on the right of the chart. When you see this icon, drop the second measure. You may also drag the second measure to the Rows or Columns shelf directly after the first measure. This will initially create a second row or column for the new measure. Now, right-click or select the drop-down menu arrow on the second measure indicator and choose Dual Axis from the context menu. This will place the second measure on its own axis on the right side of the chart.

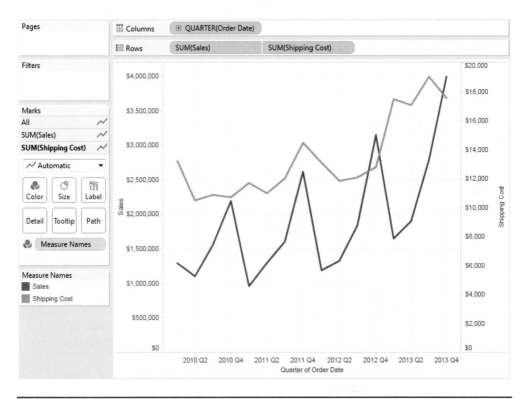

Figure 2-5   Dual axis chart

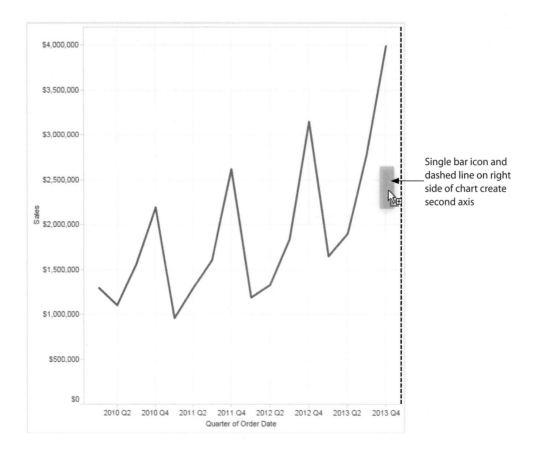

Single bar icon and dashed line on right side of chart create second axis

---

Note *As mentioned earlier, dual axis charts allow dissimilar measures to be analyzed in the same physical space. There is a potential pitfall, however. Since the different measures are displayed using separate axes, data "confusion" may result when comparing them. For example, if the scale of the left axis is showing millions of dollars, while the scale of the right axis is showing thousands of dollars, it may appear that shipping costs being displayed is in the millions or sales being displayed is in the thousands. Although you may right-click the right axis and choose Synchronize Axis to set the scale for both axes to be identical (both measures must be the same data type for you to synchronize), you have then eliminated one of the benefits of a dual axis chart by scaling both measures' axes identically. You'll need to consider the benefit of a dual axis chart against the possible data confusion of different axis scales in the same physical space.*

Multi-Measure Marks Card Fine Points

In the dual axis example presented earlier, you may have noticed invocation of Measure Names but not Measure Values. In this case, Tableau automatically placed Measure Names on Color on the Marks card to set individual colors for the two measures. However, a closer look at the Marks card in this example reveals something new: a *Multi-Measure Marks card.*

When multiple measures are used on a visualization (with the exception of a shared axis chart), the Marks card will expand to show an All option, as well as options for individual measures. Click All or the desired measure you wish to modify. A separate Marks card will appear for your choice. All measures will be affected by choices you make in the All card (Measure Names sets separate colors if used on the All card). However, only the chosen measure will be affected when you select its corresponding Marks card.

Multi-Measure Marks cards come in handy for creating a variation of the dual axis chart known as a *combination chart.* Like a dual axis chart, a combination chart displays more than one measure on separate axes. However, each measure uses a different mark type. For example, by selecting the Marks card for the second measure and choosing something other than an automatic mark type, you may maintain the default line chart for the first measure on the left axis, but display a bar chart for the second measure on the right axis. Color options may be set separately as well.

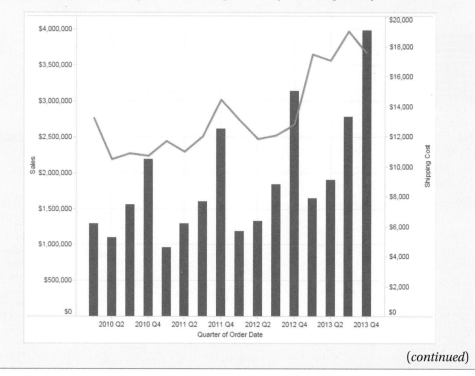

(continued)

You can also make use of a Multi-Measure Marks card for multirow or multicolumn charts using different measures. As with the combination chart, more than one measure will be selectable in the Marks card. Just be careful—consider visual best practices when using different mark types with a multirow or multicolumn chart so as to not confuse your audience.

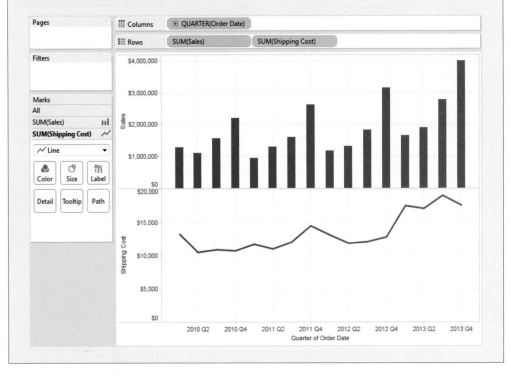

Tip *You may also choose a different mark type for individual measures by right-clicking the relevant axis or clicking the drop-down arrow or right-clicking the field on a shelf. Then select the Mark Type context menu option and make a mark type choice.*

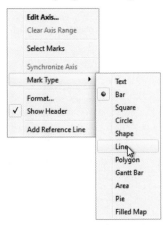

Connecting to Data

A s discussed in Chapter 2, the very first requirement when creating a new Tableau workbook is choosing a data source. Unlike traditional spreadsheet and word processing programs, Tableau can't start with a "blank slate"; it must connect to some existing database, data file, or data source before you can begin to design a chart or graph. Tableau's entire paradigm is visualizing data—the first thing you have to do is pick the data!

Download *At www.tableaubook.com, download* Chapter 3 - Data Connections-Blending.twbx *to see examples that relate to this chapter.*

Connecting to Various Data Sources

When you first start Tableau, you are presented with a wide array of "places to start," including the ability to pick a previously used workbook from a series of thumbnails; open an existing workbook from the list of recent files on the File menu, the "Open a workbook link" on the start page, or the Open entry on the File Menu; or select existing sample workbooks from the bottom of the Start Page.

There are several approaches to creating a new workbook as well. The File | New drop-down menu option will display a new workbook in an additional Tableau window, but without any fields appearing in the Data pane—you will have nothing to drag to shelves. In this instance, there are lots of options. You can click the Connect To Data option at the top of the Data pane, use the corresponding Data | New Data Source drop-down menu choice, click the Add New Data Source toolbar button, or click the Go To Start Page button to redisplay the start page for data source selection.

You may also create a new workbook based on a chosen data source directly from the Tableau Start Page. Just select the desired data source under the Connect column.

Tip *If your version of Tableau only presents the "In a file" selection of data sources and not the "On a server" selection, you have probably acquired Tableau Personal Edition or Tableau Public Desktop. This version of Tableau is designed specifically for analysis of a limited set of PC-based "local" data sources, such as text files, Microsoft Excel and Access, and Tableau Data Extracts. If you need to analyze data located in standard corporate databases, such as Microsoft SQL Server or Oracle, or web-based data sources, such as SalesForce.com or Google Analytics, you'll need to purchase Tableau Professional Edition. Only Professional Edition presents the "On a server" list of data sources.*

Tableau supports connections to many different databases and data sources, including standard corporate databases; newer "big data" data sources, such as various versions of Hadoop and Google Big Query; and web-based data sources, such as Salesforce.com and Google Analytics. Even if the particular database you wish to connect to isn't in the list of existing data sources, Tableau will connect to data via Microsoft's Open Database Connectivity (ODBC) connection type. If your data source includes a standard ODBC driver, Tableau can probably connect to it.

Select the type of data source you wish to connect to. An associated connection dialog box will appear, prompting you to choose various data source properties. Depending on the data source, you'll need to provide a user name or e-mail address, password, server location, database name, and so forth. For example, to connect to Microsoft SQL Server, you'll need to specify a server name, user ID and password (if not using Windows Authentication), and database name.

A different type of connection dialog will appear when you connect to web-based data sources. For example, connecting to Google Analytics will present a significantly different dialog (provided by a web connection). You are still prompted for a user name and password, but additional SQL database options presented by a standard corporate database don't appear.

Although a data source may appear in the list, connecting to it may require downloading additional drivers from the Tableau website. If a driver download is necessary, a dialog box indicating such will appear when you attempt to connect to a data source. Visit Tableau.com/drivers to find additional drivers and try the connection again after the proper driver has been downloaded and installed.

Tip *Probably the biggest difference between the Windows and Mac versions of Tableau is available data sources. Because of the generally larger set of database drivers available for Windows, you'll notice a smaller set of available databases (mostly in the More Servers category) on Mac. However, because Tableau Server is Windows based, it supports all drivers and can act as a data server "proxy," providing full connectivity to Mac clients. Just create the data source on Tableau Server and use it on Tableau Mac to connect. (Chapter 9 has more information on Tableau Server-based data sources.)*

Video *Connecting to Data*

The Data Source Page

Once you select the desired data source and provide any necessary login credentials, Tableau displays the Data Source page. Here, you may select one or more tables to add to your workbook, join the tables, modify the "metadata" that will be viewed in the Tableau workspace, and accommodate Microsoft Excel data that contains extraneous nondata rows, as well as "pivot" columns in Excel or text files to make data analysis easier. All these features are described later in this section.

Virtually all data source types, whether traditional relational databases, Microsoft Excel workbooks, or cloud-based data sources, break down data into "tables." Choosing the desired set of tables is the first task you'll undertake in the Data Source page. A *table* consists of a single set of data items that relate to one particular function or category of data. For example, in an inventory database, there may be tables dedicated to ReorderLevel, OnHand, MasterInventory, and similar inventory-related functions. A payroll database may present Employee, Paycheck, Deduction, and PayPeriod tables. Choosing the proper table or tables is key to getting the right data for your charting need.

Although it may be possible to create meaningful charts and graphs with a single database table, it's not uncommon to require several (and sometimes many) tables to gather all the necessary data for your visualization. For this purpose, you must add more than one table and *join* the tables together on one or more common fields. Figure 3-1 illustrates the Data Source page and various options for adding and joining tables.

Begin by dragging the first (primary) table you want to use to the top part of the screen (known as the Join area). When you drag the next table, Tableau will attempt to join the tables automatically, based on common field names and data types. Tables that Tableau auto-joins will be connected by a "two-bubble" icon. If Tableau can't find common fields to join on, the two-bubble icon will appear with a broken line border and exclamation point. When you click the bubble icon, the Join dialog will appear. The first column will provide a drop-down list of fields in the first table, with the second column providing a drop-down list of fields in the second table. Select the proper matching fields in each column. If the tables require more than one set of fields to be specified to properly join, select additional sets of fields in the following rows. When you are finished selecting common fields, click the small red X on the Join dialog to close it.

Depending on the type of data source you're connecting to, you may see a New Custom SQL option within the table list. Clicking this will present a dialog box whereby you may type or paste in a custom SQL query specific to your data source. If you've created a parameter (discussed in Chapter 5), you may insert the parameter into the custom SQL to allow variables to be passed to the query at time of execution. The resulting query will appear as a separate table in the middle of the Data Source page. If you wish, you may add and join other regular tables (or even other tables resulting from more custom SQL).

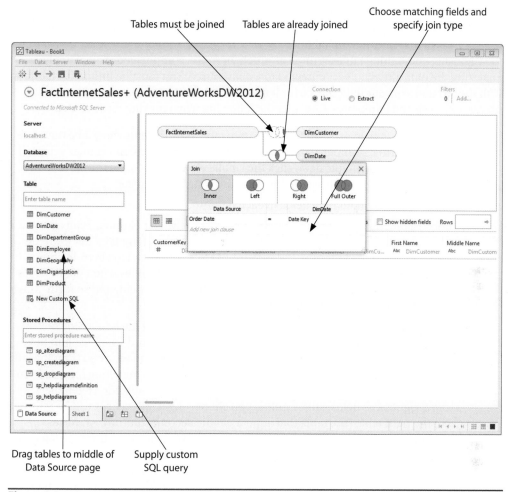

Figure 3-1   The Data Source page

Caution   *Tableau creates and modifies its own SQL queries "on the fly" as you drag and drop dimensions and measures. As such, using custom SQL queries may result in degraded performance, as Tableau may not be able to generate the most efficient queries for your data source. If you notice degraded performance, consider other options that may not require custom SQL, such as creating custom views on the database itself. Another option to mitigate slow performance with custom SQL is Tableau Data Extracts, discussed later in this chapter.*

As you add more tables, you may find table names to be confusing or in conflict. It's easy to change the "alias" of a table (the name that Tableau uses to refer to the table, even if it's not the true table name in the data source) by double-clicking a table that's been dragged to the Join area. For example, if you have to add the same table more than once (perhaps a lookup table that is used many times to join to various other fields) double-click the table name and type a more meaningful alias name to help distinguish it from other occurrences of the same lookup table.

Choosing and joining tables is often as much, or more, complicated than actually analyzing the data after you've connected to a data source. You must be intimately familiar with the structure of your data source (or it must be thoroughly documented) in order to properly choose and join tables. Consider the following when making these choices:

- What common field exists between the two tables? Both fields should be the same data type (string, number, date, and so forth) and should contain similar values. If you need to browse table data, click the small "view data" icon to the right of the desired table in the table list on the left of the Data Source page.
- Select the correct matching fields in each column.
- Choose a join operator from the drop-down list between columns. Typically, you'll leave the default equal sign as the join operator, which will match data from the two tables when the common fields are equal to each other. However, in some specialized cases, you may need to return data from the tables when the first join field is less than the second field, greater than the second field, and so forth. Make the desired choice from the drop-down menu.
- Select the type of join with the bubble buttons at the top of the Join dialog box. By default, Inner is chosen, which will return a combined record when the join field matches in both tables. If you choose Left, all records will be returned from the left table (the table that appears in the first column), as well as matching records from the right table. If there is no matching data from the right table for a left table record, right table fields will be null. If you choose Right, all records will be returned from the right table (the table that appears in the second column), as well as matching records from the left table. If there is no matching data from the left table for a right table record, left table fields will be null. Full, which is not supported for all data sources, will return all combinations of matches from both left and right tables. If there is no match from one table to another, fields from the mismatched table will be null.

Caution   *Even if Tableau joins tables automatically, you should click the bubble icon to double-check the join that Tableau made. It is not uncommon for Tableau to misinterpret fields and join incorrectly (for example, fields such as LastUpdateDateTime and LastUpdatedBy often exist in multiple tables and will be selected as join fields by Tableau, even though they are not the proper fields to match related tables).*

Once you add and join tables, you may click any of the sheet tabs at the bottom of the screen to display either an existing or new sheet. The Tableau workspace will appear with the Data pane breaking down fields from the chosen data source as dimensions and measures (a complete discussion of dimensions versus measures and how Tableau chooses them appears in Chapter 2).

Special Features for Microsoft Excel Data Sources

Although Microsoft Excel is not a database product in the true sense, it is so widely used in both small and large organizations, it has become a de facto "database" time and time again. As such, Tableau includes special features to ease your use of Excel-based data sources.

The Data Interpreter Generally speaking, Tableau (and other analytic tools that make use of Excel as a data source) works best when Excel sheets are organized in a contiguous, consistent row-and-column format. Extraneous rows, subtotals, titles, blank rows or columns, or other sheet organizations that break the "contiguous row-and-column" approach are misinterpreted as data by the analytic tool and often prevent accurate analysis. Tableau features a Data Interpreter that attempts to intercept these types of Excel sheet layouts, rendering otherwise unusable Excel sheets into meaningful data sources.

Consider a sample Excel sheet illustrated in Figure 3-2, which presents formatted data, blank columns, and blank rows. When Tableau initially connects to this sheet, it immediately

TABLE 3. PRELIMINARY POPULATION FORECASTS BY COUNTY, 2000 - 2040

COUNTIES	SDO Est. July, 2000	SDO Proj. July, 2005	SDO Proj. July, 2010	SDO Proj. July, 2015	SDO Proj. July, 2020	SDO Proj. July, 2025	SDO Proj. July, 2030	SDO Proj. July, 2035	SDO Proj. July, 2040
North-Adams	351,736	395,384	443,711	487,576	542,245	599,718	659,900	716,576	768,312
South-Alamosa	15,099	15,395	15,474	16,199	17,521	19,041	20,643	22,283	23,900
North-Arapahoe	490,722	528,214	574,819	627,055	677,047	725,839	771,537	812,528	851,200
West-Archuleta	10,043	11,402	12,060	12,526	13,851	16,029	18,476	20,789	22,950
East-Baca	4,499	4,098	3,795	3,707	3,806	3,920	4,038	4,157	4,276
East-Bent	5,967	6,261	6,506	5,941	6,142	6,312	6,391	6,413	6,426
North-Boulder	276,255	282,910	295,605	317,341	335,076	356,711	374,394	386,919	396,163
North-Broomfield	38,547	48,251	56,107	62,758	72,013	81,998	92,263	94,579	95,868
West-Chaffee	16,312	17,022	17,797	18,939	21,272	23,851	26,074	27,665	28,989
East-Cheyenne	2,216	2,041	1,834	1,937	2,038	2,121	2,204	2,266	2,334
North-Clear Creek	9,361	9,392	9,108	9,022	9,568	10,636	11,709	12,808	13,907
South-Conejos	8,408	8,500	8,282	8,306	8,499	8,738	9,086	9,363	9,625
South-Costilla	3,674	3,695	3,532	3,596	3,734	3,870	3,984	4,081	4,189
East-Crowley	5,130	5,437	5,838	5,338	5,717	6,166	6,612	7,089	7,623
South-Custer	3,520	4,045	4,272	4,534	5,205	5,924	6,631	7,264	7,869
West-Delta	27,909	29,412	30,889	30,937	33,664	38,304	43,277	48,027	52,669
North-Denver	556,738	559,459	604,879	676,282	732,085	768,007	800,605	830,429	857,074
West-Dolores	1,849	1,888	2,060	2,085	2,263	2,481	2,702	2,947	3,208
North-Douglas	180,510	244,442	287,124	317,253	352,675	390,196	424,383	454,518	480,452
West-Eagle	43,289	47,278	52,057	53,655	59,284	67,821	76,203	84,630	92,645
North-Elbert	20,104	22,259	23,107	25,487	33,842	41,094	46,767	51,439	55,503
East-El Paso	519,802	569,322	627,232	675,509	728,610	786,284	844,549	901,006	955,871
West-Fremont	46,370	46,447	46,854	47,239	50,677	54,323	57,708	60,738	63,583
West-Garfield	44,240	49,256	56,150	58,961	66,558	76,687	87,300	97,804	108,000
North-Gilpin	4,809	4,892	5,463	5,795	6,315	6,836	7,349	7,882	8,411
West-Grand	12,853	13,897	14,790	14,929	16,848	19,206	21,520	23,708	25,703
West-Gunnison	13,989	14,473	15,309	15,954	17,190	18,250	19,248	20,186	21,052
West-Hinsdale	792	813	843	851	951	1,037	1,134	1,216	1,296
South-Huerfano	7,827	7,823	6,655	6,586	7,112	7,570	7,970	8,138	8,143
West-Jackson	1,576	1,492	1,387	1,387	1,473	1,531	1,581	1,636	1,681
North-Jefferson	526,718	523,517	535,651	565,535	595,037	617,933	635,263	646,134	651,486
East-Kiowa	1,614	1,543	1,399	1,427	1,475	1,533	1,601	1,671	1,741
East-Kit Carson	7,975	7,998	8,267	8,159	8,395	8,646	8,886	9,101	9,294
West-Lake	7,940	7,284	7,282	7,753	8,928	10,134	11,190	11,844	12,284
West-La Plata	44,578	47,713	51,441	55,920	63,480	71,267	78,487	85,261	91,422
North-Larimer	253,088	275,873	300,532	326,803	356,900	388,866	418,814	446,263	471,612
South-Las Animas	15,286	15,570	15,407	14,757	15,997	17,506	19,090	20,151	20,898
East-Lincoln	6,163	5,787	5,474	5,450	5,792	6,188	6,615	7,048	7,480
East-Logan	20,655	22,088	22,293	22,097	23,237	24,726	26,329	27,940	29,476
West-Mesa	117,651	128,999	146,587	150,987	165,695	182,007	197,574	212,468	226,773
West-Mineral	837	806	705	757	823	880	912	935	957
West-Moffat	13,182	12,965	13,806	13,275	13,981	14,791	15,591	16,372	17,108
West-Montezuma	23,852	24,603	25,532	26,785	29,707	32,927	36,080	39,069	41,957
West-Montrose	33,577	36,997	41,188	42,096	48,274	55,510	62,560	68,378	73,547
East-Morgan	27,251	27,947	28,196	28,733	30,309	32,211	34,084	35,991	38,029
East-Otero	20,244	19,370	18,838	18,798	19,418	19,721	19,828	19,886	19,849
West-Ouray	3,776	4,084	4,446	4,830	5,411	5,596	5,726	5,831	5,921
West-Park	14,729	16,061	16,262	17,085	20,547	25,146	28,727	30,457	30,850
East-Phillips	4,451	4,548	4,465	4,309	4,328	4,417	4,494	4,556	4,604
West-Pitkin	15,764	16,136	17,156	17,658	19,190	21,286	23,478	25,624	27,656
East-Prowers	14,453	13,510	12,531	12,460	12,992	13,546	14,020	14,425	14,770
South-Pueblo	141,854	149,969	159,496	162,891	169,682	181,180	192,429	202,854	211,843
West-Rio Blanco	5,969	5,818	6,617	6,826	7,400	8,078	8,925	9,425	9,767
West-Rio Grande	12,429	12,696	12,001	12,124	13,165	13,982	14,777	15,337	15,736
West-Routt	20,123	21,453	23,439	24,485	27,201	30,467	34,811	39,135	43,302
West-Saguache	5,983	6,284	6,144	6,469	7,065	7,611	8,067	8,487	8,865
West-San Juan	574	645	709	705	728	749	753	765	787
West-San Miguel	6,615	7,045	7,356	8,145	9,385	10,625	11,660	12,601	13,518
East-Sedgwick	2,744	2,578	2,367	2,344	2,354	2,446	2,545	2,635	2,722
North-Summit	25,709	26,623	28,073	29,355	32,940	37,540	41,713	45,480	48,917
South-Teller	21,068	22,505	23,441	23,895	26,420	28,859	31,015	32,904	34,565
East-Washington	4,942	4,995	4,815	4,670	4,675	4,811	4,954	4,986	4,941
North-Weld	183,076	223,432	254,230	283,767	329,759	386,651	446,517	507,221	568,954
East-Yuma	9,815	9,892	10,032	10,255	10,721	11,191	11,624	12,007	12,335

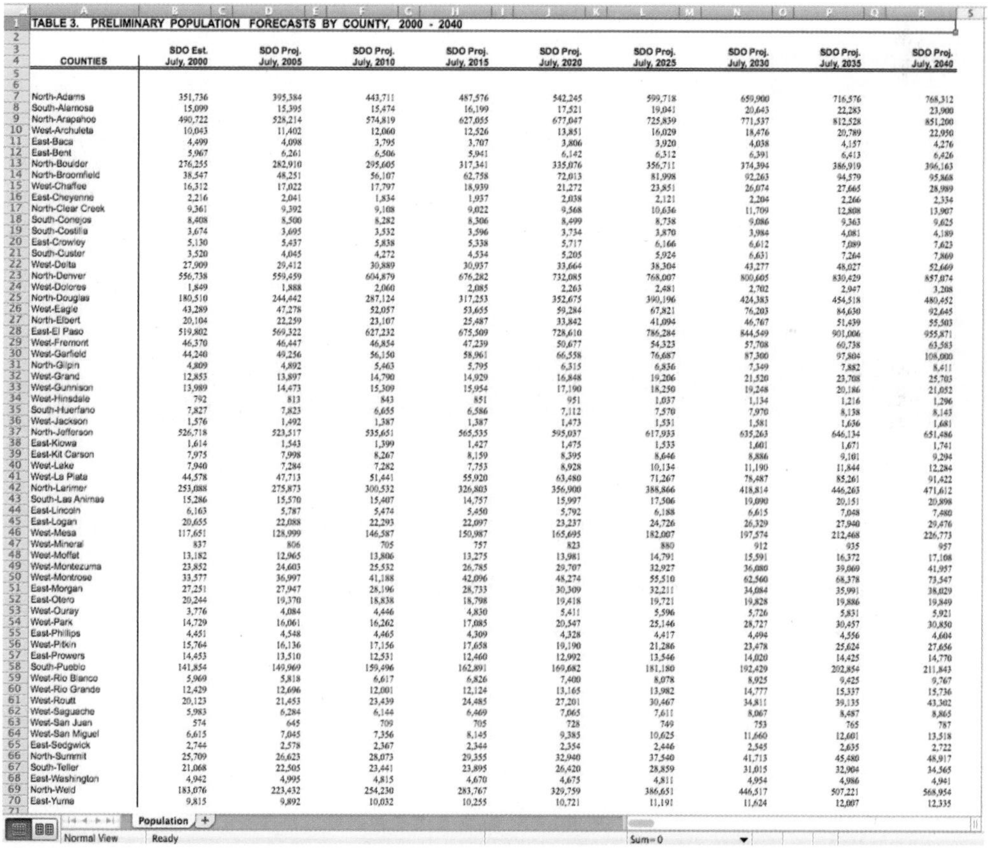

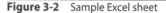

Figure 3-2 Sample Excel sheet

ignores some blank rows. However, the formatted sheet title is still interpreted by Tableau as data, as are extra blank columns. As a result, Tableau can't properly interpret the column headings as field names and interprets both rows of field headings as separate extraneous data rows. The preview portion of the Data Source page shows the results.

Population

Data doesn't look right? Tableau Data Interpreter might be able to help.   [Turn on]

[☐] [☰]   [Copy]   ☐ Show aliases   ☐ Show hidden fields   Rows 67   →

F1 Abc	F2 Abc	F3 #	F4 Abc	F5 #	F6 Abc	F7 #	F8 Abc	F9 #	F10 Abc	F11 #	F12 Abc
TABLE 3. PRELIMINA...	null	null	null	null	null	null	null	null	null	null	null
null	SDO E...	null	SDO Proj.	null	SDO Proj.	null	SDO Proj.	null	SDO Proj.	null	SDO Proj.
COUNTIES	July, 2000	null	July, 2005	null	July, 2010	null	July, 2015	null	July, 2020	null	July, 2025
North-Adams	351,736	null	395,384	null	443,711	null	487,576	null	542,245	null	599,718
South-Alamosa	15,099	null	15,395	null	15,474	null	16,199	null	17,521	null	19,041
North-Arapahoe	490,722	null	528,214	null	574,819	null	627,055	null	677,047	null	725,839
West-Archuleta	10,043	null	11,402	null	12,060	null	12,526	null	13,851	null	16,029
East-Baca	4,499	null	4,098	null	3,795	null	3,707	null	3,806	null	3,920
East-Bent	5,967	null	6,261	null	6,506	null	5,941	null	6,142	null	6,312
North-Boulder	276,255	null	282,910	null	295,605	null	317,341	null	335,076	null	356,711
North-Broomfield	38,547	null	48,251	null	56,107	null	62,758	null	72,013	null	81,998
West-Chaffee	16,312	null	17,022	null	17,797	null	18,939	null	21,272	null	23,851
East-Cheyenne	2,216	null	2,041	null	1,834	null	1,937	null	2,038	null	2,121

Tableau discovers the inconsistency and prompts you to turn on the Data Interpreter. If you click the Turn On button, Tableau will attempt to determine where extraneous rows and columns exist and remove them. The preview will be updated to show the results.

Population

Data Interpreter is on. | Review results... | | Turn off |

| | | | Copy | | | | Show aliases   Show hidden fields   Rows 64 →

COUNTIES Abc	SDO Est. July, 2000 #	SDO Proj. July, 2005 #	SDO Proj. July, 2010 #	SDO Proj. July, 2015 #	SDO Proj. July, 2020 #	SDO Proj. J #
North-Adams	351,736	395,384	443,711	487,576.46	542,245.22	
South-Alamosa	15,099	15,395	15,474	16,198.51	17,521.02	
North-Arapahoe	490,722	528,214	574,819	627,055.49	677,046.88	
West-Archuleta	10,043	11,402	12,060	12,525.83	13,850.87	
East-Baca	4,499	4,098	3,795	3,706.73	3,806.01	
East-Bent	5,967	6,261	6,506	5,940.86	6,142.00	
North-Boulder	276,255	282,910	295,605	317,341.22	335,075.56	
North-Broomfield	38,547	48,251	56,107	62,757.61	72,013.16	
West-Chaffee	16,312	17,022	17,797	18,938.92	21,272.25	
East-Cheyenne	2,216	2,041	1,834	1,937.03	2,038.39	
North-Clear Creek	9,361	9,392	9,108	9,022.20	9,568.04	
South-Conejos	8,408	8,500	8,282	8,305.56	8,498.85	
South-Costilla	3,674	3,695	3,532	3,596.42	3,733.75	

Notice that the formatted heading is now ignored, blank columns have been eliminated, and the two column heading rows have been combined and interpreted as actual column heading/field names. When the Data Interpreter is used, click the Review Results button to launch an instance of Excel showing the resulting raw data in a separate sheet, along with a descriptive sheet describing the changes the Data Interpreter made. If the results are not what you desire, you can click the Turn Off button to return the Excel data to its original form. If the Data Interpreter won't properly discern the core data from your Excel sheet, you'll need to manually edit out the extraneous items, save the Excel workbook, and reconnect within Tableau.

Column Pivot   Another occurrence that is often encountered when using Excel sheets as data sources is a data organization that places a large number of numeric measures in separate columns. Although this lends itself to more typical spreadsheet "wide columns view" applications, it is often more difficult to analyze with an analysis tool that expects more traditional relational database organization.

In the spreadsheet illustrated in Figure 3-2, notice separate columns for projected population values for various years. The result is a separate measure for each year range. Although this certainly doesn't make the data set unusable, it does require potential use of Measure Names and Measure Values (discussed in Chapter 2) to compare multiple years on a single axis. And if you need to combine data from multiple years together for higher-level analysis, calculated fields will be required (discussed in Chapter 6).

Measures
\# SDO Est. July, 2000
\# SDO Proj. July, 2005
\# SDO Proj. July, 2010
\# SDO Proj. July, 2015
\# SDO Proj. July, 2020
\# SDO Proj. July, 2025
\# SDO Proj. July, 2030
\# SDO Proj. July, 2035
\# SDO Proj. July, 2040
\# *Number of Records*
\# *Measure Values*

Tableau permits the data to be "pivoted," whereby each column measure is combined with a dimension and replicated to an individual dimension/measure row. To do this, select the column header for the measure or measures you want to pivot. You may select more than one column measure with CTRL-CLICK (COMMAND-CLICK on Mac). You may also select a contiguous set of columns by dragging across the small rows at the top of column headings. Once you've selected desired measures, hover over a column heading and click the down arrow. Choose Pivot from the menu. You may also right-click (CONTROL-CLICK on Mac) a column heading and make the same choice. If you don't initially choose all desired measure columns, you may select additional columns in a similar manner and choose the Add Data To Pivot context menu option. The result is the addition of *Pivot field names* and *Pivot field values* columns to the data source (used as a dimension and measure, respectively), which replicate each previous combination of column/row.

| COUNTIES | SDO Est. July, 2000 | SDO Proj. July, 2005 | SDO Proj. July, 2010 |
Abc Population	\# Population	\# Populati Hide	Population
North-Adams	351,736	395,3 Pivot	443,711
South-Alamosa	15,099	15,395	15,474
North-Arapahoe	490,722	528,214	574,819
West-Archuleta	10,043	11,402	12,060
East-Baca	4,499	4,098	3,795
East-Bent	5,967	6,261	6,506
North-Boulder	276,255	282,910	295,605
North-Broomfield	38,547	48,251	56,107
West-Chaffee	16,312	17,022	17,797
East-Cheyenne	2,216	2,041	1,834
North-Clear Creek	9,361	9,392	9,108

Dimensions
Abc COUNTIES
=Abc County
Abc Pivot field names
=Abc Region
Abc *Measure Names*

Measures
\# Pivot field values
\# *Number of Records*
\# *Measure Values*

This permits more flexible analysis. By using filters with Pivot field names to limit the chart to only certain values (in the case of the population example discussed in this section, specific projected year ranges), simpler and more flexible results may be achieved without use of Measure Names/Measure Values or calculated fields. The Chapter 3 - Data Connections-Blending.twbx sample workbook, available for download from the companion website, illustrates the simpler approach with comparative worksheets.

Customizing Your View of the Data

It can be said that there are two fundamental requirements to successful data analysis in Tableau: learning to use Tableau to its fullest potential, and understanding the underlying data source or database. Whereas you may be very familiar with Tableau's features and capabilities, a new database that you haven't worked with before can be very daunting and complicated. A standard corporate database may consist of hundreds of underlying tables, each containing a significant number of fields. Depending on how the database is designed, the table and field names may be cryptic and unfamiliar. And required fields for joining tables may be ambiguous. This complexity can cause even the most experienced Tableau analyst to shy away from a visualization project, as the underlying database may prove too complex.

One of the ways that database designers and vendors simplify the organization of complex database structures is through the use of metadata. *Metadata* is a broad term that generally covers a simplified view of a complex database. By reducing the number of database tables to only those required for typical analysis (and by renaming them to be more intuitive), by pre-joining tables in advance, and by only including fields necessary for typical analysis (and renaming them to be meaningful), metadata can make complex databases easy to understand and analyze. Although you may consider Tableau to be primarily a data visualization tool, it features many metadata capabilities that can greatly simplify the complexity of an underlying data source.

Tableau 9 provides two methods of modifying database metadata: Data preview or Metadata view on the Data Source page, and in the Data pane in a worksheet. When you initially connect to a data source, add and join tables, or pivot columns (with Excel data sources), you may perform metadata tasks on the lower portion of the Data Source page, either when viewing sample data or from Metadata view (accessed by clicking the second small Manage Metadata button above the data preview portion of the Data Source page). Either view permits metadata manipulation.

If you navigate to a worksheet, you may customize data source metadata by hovering over a dimension or measure and clicking the small drop-down arrow or by right-clicking (CONTROL-clicking on a Mac) on a dimension or measure in the Data pane. Choose the desired option from the context menu.

Dimensions
Abc Category
⊕ City
⊕ Country
Abc Customer ID
Abc Custome...
🗓 Order Da...
Abc Order ID
⊕ Postal Co
Abc Product I
Abc Product I
Abc Region
Row ID
Abc Segment
🗓 Ship Date
Abc Ship Mod
⊕ State
Abc Sub-Cate
Abc *Measure*

Context menu:
- **Add to Sheet**
- Duplicate
- Rename...
- Hide
- Aliases...
- Create ▶
- Transform ▶
- Convert to Measure
- Change Data Type ▶
- Geographic Role ▶
- Default Properties ▶
- Group by ▶
- Folders ▶
- Hierarchy ▶
- Replace References...
- Describe...

Measures
Discount
Profit
Quantity
Sales
⊕ *Latitude*
⊕ *Longitud*
⊹# *Number*
Measure

 Video *Creating Your Own View of Data*

Note *Metadata modification capabilities will vary, depending on the type of data source you are using. For example, fewer features will be available when using online analytical processing (OLAP) or "cube" data sources, and other features will vary for cloud-based data sources and Tableau Data Extracts.*

Changing Data Type

When a database designer creates a traditional relational database table, each field is given a data type, such as string, number, date, and so forth. And columns and fields in other data sources, such as text files, cloud data sources, and Excel worksheets, are interpreted by Tableau to have specific data types as well. Ultimately, Tableau relegates any field or column from any data source into a limited set of data types. Icons next to dimensions and measures indicate the data type Tableau has interpreted.

Data Type	Icon	Usage
String/Text	Abc	Letters, numbers, spaces, and special characters
Geographic	⊕	Interpreted by Tableau to contain geographic data (see Chapter 7)
Integer/Float	#	Numeric values only. Integer contains no decimal places, and Float interprets up to 15 decimal places of precision
Date	📅	Date, including month, day, and year
Date/Time	📅	Date/time, including month, day, year, hour, minute, and second
Boolean	T|F	Only two values are returned, either True or False

Tableau may misinterpret data types in the data source, which will require data type reassignment for more appropriate usage. For example, Tableau may assign a numeric column in an Excel worksheet as text because of blank rows, column formatting, or one errant row that contains non-numeric data. Or data may be stored in a data source as text, but the text contains a consistent series of date values separated by common delimiters, such as a dash or slash. In these cases, you may reassign the data type to properly use the Excel column as a numeric measure and the text dates as "real" dates in order to take advantage of Tableau date analysis features.

- **Data Source page**   Click the icon next to the field name and choose a different data type from the context menu.
- **Data pane**   Pick the desired data type from the Change Data Type submenu on the context menu.

Modifying Dimension/Measure Assignment

As discussed in Chapter 2, Tableau uses a field's data type to determine whether to categorize a field as a dimension (non-numeric field) or measure (numeric field). Although this automatic assignment is usually appropriate, there are times when you'll need to override Tableau's defaults. For example, a numeric key field may be more appropriately categorized as a dimension instead of a measure, as you will mostly probably not want to sum or average a key field. This reassignment is done in the Data pane.

Recategorizing a measure as a dimension is as simple as dragging it from the Measures area in the Data pane to the Dimensions area. Recategorize a dimension as a measure using the same approach. Just drag it to the Measures area. The dimension will be moved to the Measures section of the Data pane with a default aggregation of Count Distinct.

Hiding, Renaming, and Combining Fields

It's quite possible the default field name from a data source may be confusing. For example, a field with the same name may appear in more than one table and, as such, may be annotated with the table name to avoid ambiguity. Or field names may simply be unintuitive, as database designers may not always keep simple field-naming concepts in mind when databases are initially designed. And, fields may have been added en masse with a number of tables that later are not required for common analysis tasks. These unneeded and hard-to-understand fields don't lend themselves to common data analysis tasks.

In even the most basic data structure, there are probably fields you have no desire to use and prefer to hide from view.

- **Data Source page**   Hover your mouse over the desired field and click the small drop-down arrow. Or right-click (CONTROL-click on Mac) and choose Hide from the context menu.
- **Data pane**   Choose Hide from the context menu. The field will simply disappear.

You may hide as many fields as necessary, even CTRL- or SHIFT-clicking multiple fields and choosing Hide from the combined context menu. If you're editing a worksheet and the Data pane is visible, you may even hide all fields that aren't being used in a worksheet once you've completed your chart. Just right-click a blank portion of the Data pane (make sure no fields are selected) and choose Hide All Unused Fields. Fields not in use on any worksheet in the workbook will be hidden (remember that some fields may not be in use in the current worksheet, but will be in use in other worksheets).

You may wish to later redisplay fields that were previously hidden.

- **Data Source page**   Check the Show Hidden Fields box in the upper right. Display the context menu on hidden fields and select Unhide.
- **Data pane**   First, right-click a blank portion of the Data pane (make sure no fields are selected) or click the drop-down arrow to the right of the Dimensions box. Choose Show Hidden Fields. All previously hidden fields will now appear in the Data pane, but will be dimmed. Select one or more hidden fields, right-click, and choose Unhide from the context menu.

Renaming fields is very straightforward.

- **Data Source page**   Hover your mouse over the desired field and click the small drop-down arrow. Or right-click (CONTROL-click on Mac) and choose Rename from the context menu. If displaying Metadata view, just hold the mouse button down on the desired field name. It will appear as editable text.
- **Data pane**   Choose Rename from the context menu. A Rename Field dialog will appear. Just type in the desired field name and click OK. If you later decide to restore a field to its original name, repeat the original rename process and click Reset in the Rename Field dialog.

If you need to combine the contents of more than one dimension into a single value (sometimes referred to as *concatenation*), you must be editing a worksheet and make the choice in the Data pane.

Just CTRL-click (CONTROL-click on Mac) or SHIFT-click the dimensions that you wish to combine. Then hover over one of the fields and select the drop-down arrow (or right-click) and choose Create | Combined Field from the context menu. A new dimension will appear in the Data pane, initially named based on the field names of the combined fields. If you wish to rename the new dimension, right-click it and select Rename from the context menu.

When the combined dimension is used in your worksheet, every combination of members from the source dimensions will result in a new combined member.

Splitting Fields

Depending on how fields are organized, you may benefit from splitting (sometimes known as *parsing*) a field into two or more parts. For example, if a product part number contains three letters constituting the product type, followed by a dash (known as a *separator*), followed by a part number, you'll probably benefit by splitting the field in two to permit analysis by product type without having to manually create a calculated field to extract the first three letters. Or, you may wish to split a city/state combination, separated by a comma, into separate city and state fields.

In addition to the basic split option, which attempts to automatically detect separators, you may choose a custom split option. If you choose custom split, the Custom Split dialog box will appear. Here, you may leave the default list of separators or type in one or more custom separators. You'll need to specify how many splits to perform in the columns box, as well as whether to split from the beginning of the source field, the end of the source field, or throughout the entire source field.

- **Data Source page**   Hover your mouse over the desired field and click the small drop-down arrow. Or right-click (CONTROL-click on Mac) and choose Split or Custom Split from the context menu.

- **Data pane**   Choose Transform | Split or Transform | Custom Split from the context menu.

Tableau will split the original field into multiple separately split fields, in addition to leaving the original source field in place. You may delete or rename any of the additional split fields using techniques outlined elsewhere in this section. Note, though, that you can't use split results to join to other tables (although you can blend on split fields—data blending is covered later in this chapter).

Note that using the split feature will actually create a calculated field (described in Chapter 6) and place it in the Data pane. If you aren't satisfied with the way the initial split process worked, you may edit the calculated field and customize split logic. Also, you may create new calculated fields using the Split function without returning to the Data Source page.

Note   *Split is not available for all data sources. If your data source doesn't support Split, it won't be available on menus or in calculated fields.*

Using Clipboard Data Sources

When you look at the list of available data sources on the Start Page, you may be under the impression that the only way to make use of data is to ensure that it is in one of these formats. In fact, it's possible to cut and paste data directly into Tableau via the Windows or Mac Clipboard.

Consider the World Population web page illustrated here. Note that a standard "table" organization exists, with each country comprising a row, and a country name and population for four years spread across five columns. Notice that the table has been highlighted, including the first row containing labels for the country and year columns.

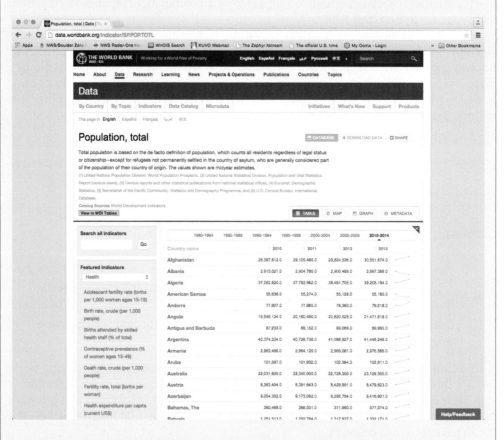

Making use of this data in Tableau is as easy as copying the highlighted data to the Clipboard via the browser's Edit | Copy drop-down menu option or CTRL-C/COMMAND-C keyboard shortcut. Then choose an existing workbook where you wish to use the data, or just display the Tableau Start Page. Then choose Data | Paste from the Tableau drop-down menu, or simply press the CTRL-V/COMMAND-V keyboard shortcut. Tableau will create a new data source in the Data pane (labeled Clipboard, followed by a number based on the current date and time) and display all pasted fields in a new worksheet, as illustrated here.

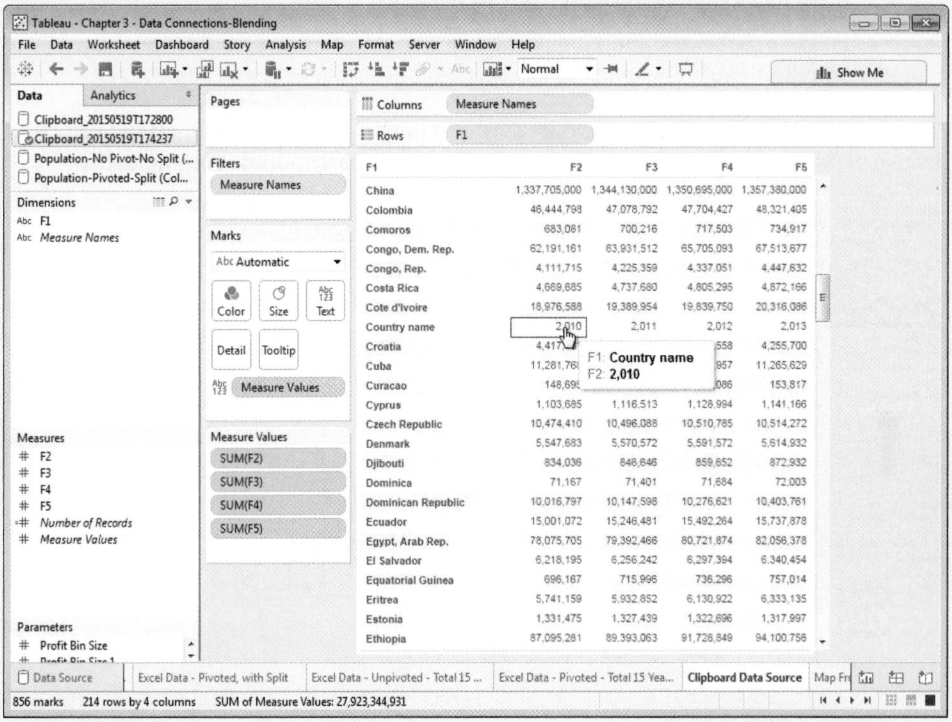

In some cases, Tableau may perfectly interpret data in the pasted table and properly identify data types and dimension and measure assignments. However, in other cases, misinterpretation may occur. In this example, notice that although the general row-and-column format of the pasted data is intact, there are several issues that will prevent the data from being properly used in Tableau:

- The first row in the pasted chart was interpreted as data and not as column headings. As such, field names are meaningless "F" values, and an extra row of data for Country Name appears in the data source.

- Years appear as columns, which may cause difficulty in analyzing data across multiple years, or require calculated fields, for the most flexible analysis.

Fixing these issues is fairly straightforward, making use of previously described techniques for customizing a data source:

- As with any data source, field names and data types may be changed in the Data pane. Fields have been renamed as intended.

(*continued*)

- Filters may be added to remove data rows that are misinterpreted as data.
- Columns may be pivoted to create a more flexible data source arrangement. Pivot fields may be renamed appropriately.
- Fields may be assigned a geographic role if not done so automatically with Tableau.

The result is a far more usable data source, allowing a population map to be created by use of the geographic country field and one of the yearly population measures.

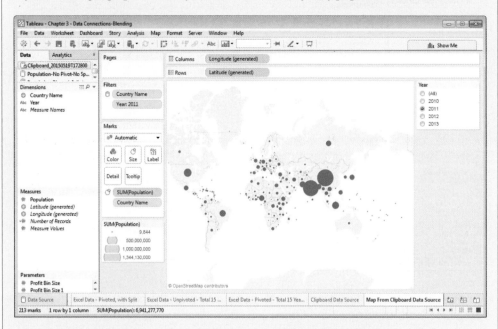

Once you've done any necessary data source modifications and saved the associated workbook, the Clipboard data source will be saved in a tab-delimited file. You may then reuse (or extract) that file for further use in other workbooks. A dialog box will confirm saving of the Clipboard data source.

Changing the Default Field Appearance

Tableau provides several default properties and behaviors for a field, depending on its data type. For example, numbers take on a certain default number format, dates are automatically formatted with a certain month/day/year organization, numeric measures are automatically summed when added to the worksheet, and dimensions are assigned default colors based on Tableau's built-in visual best practices.

If you wish to change any of these defaults, make choices from a field's context menu Default Properties option in the Data pane (you can't modify these properties in the Data Source page). For example, you may change the default colors that Tableau will assign dimension members. Or, if you prefer a different default date format, choose Date Format. If you'd rather display the average for a numeric measure by default instead of a sum, select a different Aggregation option. And you may add a descriptive comment that will appear when you hover your mouse over the field in the Data pane. The Comment option is helpful for providing descriptive background information for a field.

Organizing Dimensions in Hierarchies

A *hierarchy* is a from-the-top-down organization of related dimensions. By default, Tableau displays date or date/time fields in a hierarchy. So if you drag a date field to a shelf, the date will initially be rolled up to year. You can then click a plus sign on the date field indicator to expand the date hierarchy from year, to quarter, to month, to week, to day, and if time is included, from hour, to minute, to second.

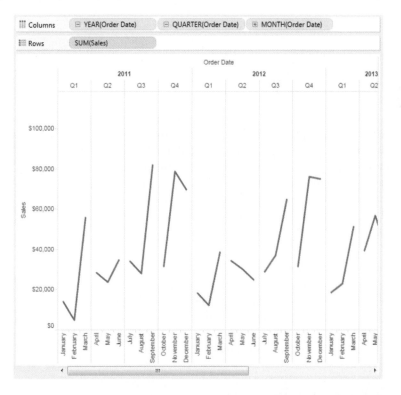

You may have other related nondate dimensions that lend themselves to a hierarchy. For example, you might have a series of separate product-related fields, such as category, subcategory, and product name, that lend themselves to a natural hierarchy. Or you may prefer to create a hierarchy to navigate from country, to state, to city, to ZIP code.

Creating your own hierarchies in Tableau is easy. In the Data pane, simply drag the "inner" dimension on top of the "outer" dimension. For example, if you are creating the product hierarchy discussed previously, drag Subcategory on top of Category. The Create Hierarchy dialog box will appear, prompting for a name for the hierarchy (with the default name being the fields you dragged and dropped). Give the hierarchy a more meaningful name (such as "Products") and click OK. Notice that the Data pane now contains the hierarchy you created, preceded with a plus sign. Click the plus sign to expand the hierarchy and expose the dimensions within it. Drag additional dimensions inside the existing hierarchy. If you happen to drag the dimensions in the wrong order, simply drag and drop within the hierarchy to reorder dimensions properly. If you drag a dimension into the hierarchy by mistake, just drag it back out. To completely erase a hierarchy, right-click the hierarchy name and choose Remove Hierarchy from the context menu.

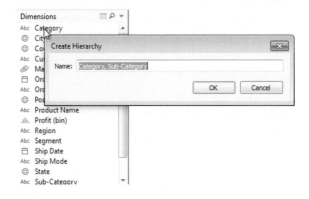

Once you've created your own hierarchy, drag the hierarchy name onto a shelf. Notice that the top-level dimension in the hierarchy is displayed on your visualization and that a plus sign appears on the field indicator on the shelf. As with the previously illustrated date hierarchy, plus and minus signs on the field indicators can be used to navigate through the hierarchy. You may also drag an inner field from the hierarchy to a shelf. Navigation will be available from that field on down.

Using Table or Folder View

If you add and join more than one table in a data connection, dimensions and measures will be organized by table in the Data pane. This may be preferable to help you determine which source table a dimension or measure comes from, especially if there are similar field names in more than one table.

However, in other cases, a large number of cryptically named database tables may just confuse an analyst looking to just find the appropriate dimensions and measures to use. And although the field-to-table relationship a database designer uses may make sense for the core database purposes, it may not be the most logical for analysis. As such, you may turn off the database table view and instead use Tableau's *folder view* to create your own folder/field organization.

Either right-click (CTRL-click on Mac) a nonfield portion of the Data pane or click the small down arrow to the right of the dimensions box. Select Group By Folder. Then, from the same context menu, choose options from the Folder submenu, such as Create Folder or Add To Folder. You may also just drag dimensions or measures to the desired folder. You may also display the context menu on an existing folder and rename or remove it. This process allows you flexible control over how you organize dimensions and measures, regardless of underlying data table organization.

Note *All the techniques discussed in this chapter to modify your "view" of the data do not change the underlying data source in any way. Only the way Tableau presents the data structure is customized—the underlying database structure is untouched.*

Saving and Sharing Metadata

So far, this chapter has discussed myriad ways of modifying the "view" of your data source (the metadata). When you save the workbook, this metadata is saved within it—the next time you open the workbook, the Data pane will appear just as it was when the workbook was saved. However, once you've expended a fair amount of effort customizing this metadata, you very probably would like to save it for use with new workbooks you create in the future. In fact, if more than one person in your organization uses Tableau, you may want to share it with them as well. Enter the *Tableau Data Source File.*

A Tableau Data Source File is a separate file saved on your hard disk with a .tds extension. This .tds file contains the "view," or metadata, you have created, including renamed fields, hierarchies, and custom folders. The original data source file, or database, that the .tds file is based on remains unchanged in its original location. You may then open the .tds file in the future to reconnect to the original data source or database it references, but with your customized view of the data.

To save a .tds file, right-click the data source name at the top of the Data pane and choose Add To Saved Data Sources from the context menu. You may also use the Data | <*data source name*> | Add To Saved Data Sources drop-down menu option. A standard Windows Save As dialog box will appear, prompting you for a filename. Notice the default .tds extension. By default, the directory will be My Tableau Repository within your personal operating system folder.

Tableau Data Source Files placed in My Repository will automatically appear on the Tableau start page from that point forward. However, since others in your organization will be using their own personal repository folders, you may choose to save the .tds file in another shared location, such as a shared network drive. In that instance, you (and others in your organization who want to use the shared .tds files) will need to use the Other Files option in Tableau to open .tds files not in their repositories.

If your organization has access to Tableau Server, you may also save .tds files there for sharing among your other Tableau users. Right-click the data source name at the top of the Data pane, or use the Data drop-down menu option, and select Publish To Server. You'll be prompted to log on to Tableau Server. Supply the necessary logon credentials and click OK. The Publish Data Source To Tableau Server dialog box will appear. Choose the desired project, name, and other values, and click OK to publish the .tds file to the server. Anyone who has access to Tableau Server may now use the custom data source by selecting Tableau Server in the "On a server" category of the Connect To Data screen, just as they would select another data source.

Tip   *You may also save a packaged Tableau Data Source with a .tdsx extension by choosing the appropriate file extension when saving a data source. Similar to a packaged Tableau workbook (.twbx), a packaged data source will bundle any local data files, such as text files and Microsoft Excel or Access files, with the saved data source so that the entire .tdsx file may be distributed as a stand-alone data connection.*

Extracting Data

If you use standard corporate databases, such as Microsoft SQL Server or Oracle, you may find situations where it's inconvenient (or impossible) to perform data analysis. The first potential issue may be poor performance. If the database is very large or has not been fully optimized by the database designer, real-time analysis with Tableau may be difficult. Or, you may wish to continue to work with a centralized database when you're away from your office (perhaps on an airplane) and connection to the database isn't practical. Also, you may want to share a workbook with another Tableau user who doesn't have access to your data source (perhaps they are outside your organization or don't have access rights to your corporate database). Finally, if you wish to provide your workbook to a viewer using the free Tableau Reader read-only product, you must provide a packaged workbook (.twbx file) that is entirely self-contained, as Tableau Reader won't connect to a live data source by design.

These are the types of situations that call for a Data Extract. A *Data Extract* is a Tableau-proprietary file that contains the imported contents of another database or data source. A Tableau Data Extract file (you'll notice the .tde file extension) consists of a very compact, high-speed, optimized data file. As such, analysis with an extract is typically very, very fast.

Note   *Some data sources, such as Salesforce.com and Google Analytics, will create extracts automatically when they are first accessed. This is because these web-based data sources may perform slowly if interacted with natively. Also, frequent web-based data source interactivity may exceed service limits placed on users by the data source vendor.*

Your first opportunity to create an extract is when you initially connect to most data sources. On the Data Source page, notice the Connection radio buttons on the upper right of the page. If you click the Extract radio button, the chosen data source will be extracted in its entirety when you select a sheet. If you want to specify more granular options for the extract, click the Edit link next to the Extract radio button. The Create Extract dialog box will permit you to narrow down your extract to a limited set of data from the underlying data source.

To create an extract from an existing data source in your workbook, right-click the desired data source in the top portion of the Data pane and choose Extract Data from the context menu. You may also use Data | <data source name> | Extract Data from the Tableau drop-down menu. The Extract Data dialog box appears.

To simply extract all data from your underlying data source, just click OK. But if you want to narrow down the extract to only include a subset of the original data source's data, select various options in this dialog box:

- To narrow down your extract to a limited set of data (perhaps only for the past year or only for your region), add one or more filters. Filters are specified similarly here as they are in Tableau when dragging a field to the Filters shelf.

- If you check the Aggregate Data For Visible Dimensions box, Tableau will summarize (or "roll up") the underlying data based on the dimensions that have not been hidden. This will reduce the size of the resulting extract file. You may also choose to roll up dates. If you choose this option, select the level of date detail you wish to retain in the extract. For example, if you select Month, the underlying data source will be summarized ("rolled up") to the month level. Using the extract from that point will allow you to display dates at the month, quarter, or year level, but not the week or day level.

- You may choose to extract all rows from the underlying data source (any filters or roll-ups you specify will still be applied) or select an incremental extract. Checking Incremental Refresh will permit the extract to be updated at a later time with only new data that's been added to the underlying data source. For large extracts, this may significantly speed up extract updates in the future. Select either a date dimension or unique numeric ID/key in the underlying data source to base the incremental refresh on. The next time you refresh the extract from the Data pane context menu or Data drop-down menu, only rows that contain a date or key later than that of the last refresh will be imported.

- If you select the Top (or, depending on the data source, Sample) radio buttons, you may further narrow down to a number or percent of rows from the underlying data source. This type of extract may be helpful when you wish to use a limited set of data from the underlying data source for "on the road" or initial development, with the expectation that you will eventually return to the full underlying data source for production analysis.

Once you've completed the dialog box, click OK to create the extract. You'll be prompted for a location to save the Tableau Data Extract (.tde) file. Specify the location and filename and click Save. The extract file will be created, and any worksheets in the current workbook using the original underlying data source will be converted to use the extract (you'll notice a checkmark next to Use Extract on the data connection's context menu or the Data drop-down menu and a two-barrel-with-arrow icon next to the data source in the Data pane).

One of the initial concerns you may have about using an extract is the "disconnection" from the underlying data source, particularly in terms of currency of data. For example, if the initial data source is a transactional database that is updated frequently, you may be concerned that you will now be analyzing on an extract that's out of date. Tableau provides a simple way to *refresh* extracts from the underlying data source to update the extract with new data. A full refresh will read all data from the underlying data source again with filters and rolls-ups applied. Although this assures that your extract will fully match the underlying data source, a full refresh can be time consuming. An incremental refresh (discussed previously) will only import new records from the underlying data source into the extract. To perform either kind of refresh, just right-click the data source at the top of the Data pane, or select Data | *<data source name>* from the drop-down menus, followed by Extract | Refresh. If you initially chose to import all rows when the extract was first specified, a full refresh will occur. If you selected incremental refresh options when the extract was first created, you'll notice both Incremental and Full refresh options. Choose the type of refresh you wish to perform.

Tip *If you are using Tableau Server, you are able to store extracts on the server and schedule automatic refreshes at regular intervals. This powerful feature can often bridge the gap between currency of data and speed of analysis that extracts sometimes present. More information on scheduling Tableau Server extract refreshes appears in Chapter 9.*

Once you have extracted data, several menu options are enabled to help you maintain extracts and switch between the original data source and the extract. Right-click the data source at the top of the Data pane, or choose Data | *<data source name>* from the drop-down menu. The first option is to return to the underlying data source by unchecking Use Extract. You may easily return to the previously generated extract by selecting this option again. When an extract is being used, the Extract sub-menu provides additional options:

- **Append Data From File**   You may add data to an existing extract from an external desktop-type file (Excel, Microsoft Access, text, comma-separated values), as well as other existing extract files. The column names and data types in the external file must match those in the extract.

- **Append Data From Data Source**   If another data source in the same workbook is similar in structure to the extract (perhaps you originally extracted from a combined data warehouse but the original transaction database is also connected in your workbook), you may choose it and add data to the existing extract. Fields/columns in the second data source must match extract fields, or the second data source won't be available when you select this option.

- **Optimize**   If you have created any new calculated fields since an extract was created, this option will evaluate the results of the calculations and write them to the extract file. This may improve performance with large extracts, as calculated fields won't have to be reevaluated "on the fly."

- **Remove**   You may remove the extract and return to the underlying data source. When you choose this option, you'll be provided an additional option to delete or retain the .tde extract file.
- **History**   Displays a dialog box indicating dates the extract has been refreshed.
- **Properties**   Displays a dialog box providing overall information about the extract, including location of the extract file, filters used, and so forth.

Best Practice *When you initially create an extract based on an existing data source in a workbook, Tableau will maintain the relationship between the original data source and the extract in that workbook. This will permit you to uncheck the Use Extract option to use the original data source, refresh the extract from the underlying data source, and so forth. However, if you create a new workbook based only on the resulting .tde file, the relationship to the original data source won't be available. You will be unable to switch back and forth between the original data source and the extract, refresh the extract, and so forth. As such, you may want to retain the original "master" workbook to permit extract modification later on.*

Data Blending

▶ **Video** *Data Blending*

It's not uncommon to require data from more than one table within a database/data source, or maybe even more than one database/data source, in a Tableau workbook. Depending on how your workbook is organized and what analysis requirements you have, there are several ways of accomplishing this:

- Join multiple tables from the same database, as discussed earlier in the chapter, and use the joined tables in one or more worksheets in your workbook.
- Create several worksheets, each using various data sources (including joined tables), and combine the worksheets on a dashboard. The dashboard can provide links between the worksheets via filters and so forth (creating dashboards is covered in Chapter 8).
- Tie more than one data source together on a single worksheet using data blending. This is what this section of the chapter will cover.

In traditional relational database analysis, joining tables from the *same* database is a common practice. However, when data needs to be combined from *different* databases, complications often arise. Because most database vendors don't provide easy methods of combining data from other vendors (if they provide it at all), this task is often left to the analysis tool itself. Tableau's approach to this predicament is called *data blending*.

Data blending provides a way to combine data from more than one data source on a single worksheet. In short, Tableau connects to multiple data sources, sends independent queries to those data sources, and then combines (or "blends") the aggregated results of the independent queries on a single worksheet.

Note *It's important to keep the "independent queries/aggregated results blended" paradigm in mind when considering whether data blending will work in your environment. Remember that data blending is not the same as a table join or more common single-database-combining techniques, such as unions. The key to blending is identifying a common dimension in both data sources that can be aggregated to.*

Despite the somewhat-complex concepts of data blending, it's very easy to implement. Consider a fairly common requirement where existing transactional or sales data is contained in one database and goal data is contained in another. For this example, transactional data is contained in the "Sample - Superstore" file that is included with Tableau 9. Because Sales Goal data is absent from this file, a tab-delimited text file has been created that contains goal data. In order to calculate the variance between actual and goal, as well as display everything side by side on the same worksheet, data blending must be used.

Consider the chart illustrated in Figure 3-3. This chart, based on transactional data, is based on a single data source. This data source is considered the *primary* data source, as it

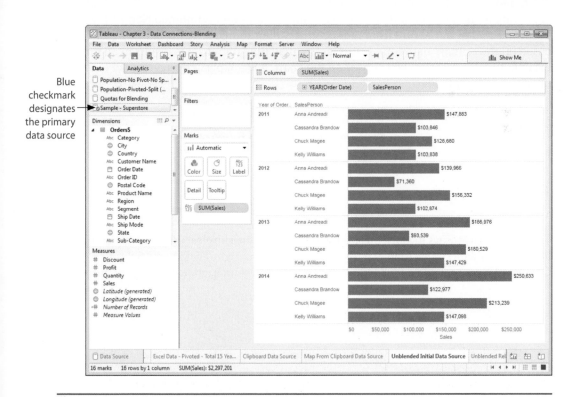

Figure 3-3 Data-blending candidate

was the first data source used to generate the worksheet. This is confirmed by the small blue checkmark that is displayed on the data source name at the top of the Data pane. However, notice that other data sources also exist in the workbook.

Since more than one data connection can exist in a Tableau workbook, another connection can be made to the text file containing the quotas, using already covered approaches. Once the new connection is added, you may view its underlying data to see that goal records exist for each matching sales rep. However, since a primary data source has already been used for the existing worksheet, notice the orange line that appears in the Data pane when the second data source is selected. This indicates that this data source will become a *secondary* data source—primary and secondary data sources will be connected via data blending.

Two other considerations that may not be immediately evident from this example are mismatched data organization and inconsistent field names. While a single dimension containing the salesperson value exists in the transactional data source, the text file breaks salesperson into separate first and last name fields. While this may initially appear to be a serious issue, data blending can make use of calculated fields. As such, a combined salesperson calculation has been created in the text file data source (calculated fields are covered in Chapter 6). Even so, the calculated field name doesn't match the related dimension in the primary data sources (Tableau will automatically create a relationship between identically named fields). Specifically, the dimension illustrated in Figure 3-3 is named "SalesPerson," while the matching calculated field appearing in the secondary data source is named "Sales Rep Combined Name." If you simply try to drag a measure from the secondary data source onto the existing chart based on the primary data source, this lack of matching dimensions results in an error. Even though the measure will appear on the chart, it is not properly aggregated to match up to the primary field.

There are two ways to solve this problem. Probably the simplest is to merely rename the field in either data source to match that of the other. After right-clicking the Sales Rep Combined Name calculated field in the secondary data source, choosing Rename from the pop-up menu and renaming to SalesPerson, examine the Data pane. Note the orange link icon next to the field. This indicates that a matching dimension exists in the primary data source and that this field will be used as the common field between the data sources.

Tip *If multiple link icons appear in the secondary data source, more than one field name matches in the two data sources. "Broken" link icons indicate data-blending candidate dimensions. Determine which dimension you wish to use to blend, and click the link. The icon will change to a "closed" link, and that dimension will be used to match to the other data source.*

If, for some reason, you prefer not to rename a dimension in one data source to match the other, you may specifically tie the two dimensions together by choosing Data | Edit Relationships from the drop-down menus. This will display the Relationships dialog box. First, ensure that the proper primary data source is displayed in the first drop-down list. Then choose the desired secondary data source in the list to the left. If Tableau has performed any automatic by-field-name matches, you'll see them when the Automatic radio button is selected. If Tableau has not been able to do a proper match, click the

Custom radio button, followed by the Add button at the bottom of the dialog box. The Add/Edit Field Mapping dialog will appear.

Select the desired dimensions to match in the left and right lists. Click OK to add the relationship. If you need to add relationships because more fields need to be matched, click Add however many times you need, and choose additional sets of matched dimensions. When you have specified all matching dimensions, click OK to close the Relationships dialog box. The Data pane will return with the orange link icon appearing on the selected dimension (note that if a blend requires more than one matching dimension, you may need to click the broken link icon on unblended dimensions to add them to the blend).

Once you have successfully matched the primary and secondary data sources, simply drag measures from the secondary data source onto the existing visualization. The data from both data sources will be blended. Figure 3-4 shows the resulting actual-versus-quota bullet graph (bullet graphs are covered in Chapter 4).

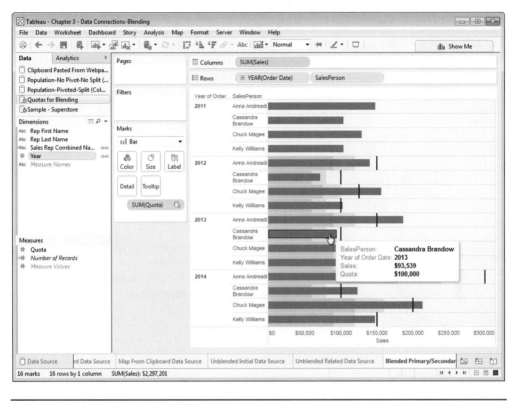

Figure 3-4   Completed data-blending chart

Data blending can sometimes introduce data mismatches when dimension members that exist in one data source aren't matched in the other. By convention (and you are unable to change this), Tableau performs the equivalent of a left join between primary and secondary data sources. The example illustrated in Figure 3-4 shows this, in that all years show an actual "sales" bar, but 2011 shows no quota reference lines (there are no quotas for 2011 in the text file). You'll also notice no data at all for Preston Richards, even though he has quota records in the text file for 2013 and 2014. This is because there is no sales data for Preston Richards in the primary data source.

If, however, the quota text file is used first in a worksheet (it will show a blue checkmark in the Data pane, indicating it is now the primary data source), a blend to the secondary sales data source will result in different results. Figure 3-5 illustrates this. Notice that 2011 sales doesn't appear on the chart, as there are no 2011 quota data in the primary data source. And Preston Richards shows a quota for both 2013 and 2014 with no matching sales (the missing sales figures for the two years result in the null indicator at the lower right). In this type of scenario, you may need to create a third "driver" data source (perhaps copying data to the Clipboard or creating a small Excel workbook) that includes all possible

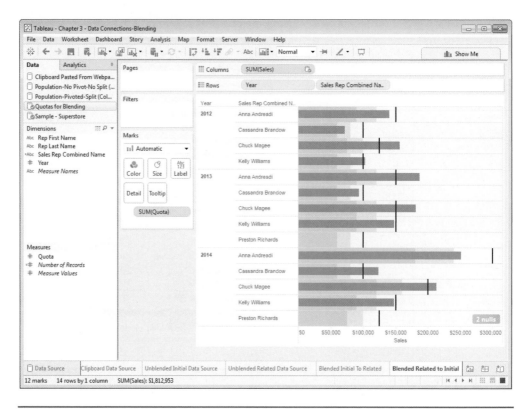

Figure 3-5   Data blend with primary/secondary sources reversed

combinations of dimensions. Add this to your Tableau worksheet as the primary data source, and then blend to the two additional secondary data sources to return all combinations from the two secondary sources.

> **Tip**   *Not only can you resolve data-blending dimension name mismatches by just renaming a field in the Data pane, but you can resolve dimension member mismatches by editing a member's alias. For example, if you are blending on state and one data source returns Colorado while the other returns CO, just right-click the incorrect member name in the worksheet header and choose Edit Alias from the context menu. Change the member name to match the other data source. The two data sources will then properly blend.*

Moving from Test to Production Databases

It's not uncommon to initially develop a workbook using one data source and then eventually need to migrate that workbook to another similar data source. A very common example of this is developing against a test database and then migrating the workbook to a production database. In some cases, these databases may be on similar database platforms.

But, in others, the test database may be a desktop system, such as Microsoft Access, with the production database being SQL Server. Regardless of the underlying types of data sources, Tableau makes it easy to migrate a workbook from one data source to another.

Consider this Data pane based on a Microsoft Access "test" database. In particular, it's significant to note that the current worksheet is using the Country dimension and Order Amount measure.

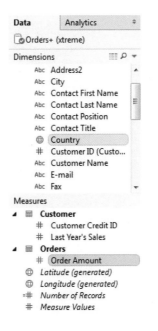

For this example, assume that a "production" database exists on SQL Server. The first requirement is to connect to the SQL Server as you would any other data connection. Add and join any necessary tables. When complete, the SQL Server data source will appear in the Data pane. Then right-click either of the data sources at the top of the Data pane, or choose the Data drop-down menu and select Replace Data Source. The Replace Data Source dialog box will appear, showing drop-down lists where you may choose the existing (test) data source and the data source you wish to replace it with (production). Choose the desired data sources and click OK.

All worksheets in your workbook that were using the original test data source will now be directed to the new production data source. Provided all field names in the new data source match the original data source, all worksheets will immediately reflect the new data source. However, if field names aren't identical, portions of your visualization may be dimmed and an "invalid" icon (an exclamation point) may appear on any fields that aren't found in the new data source.

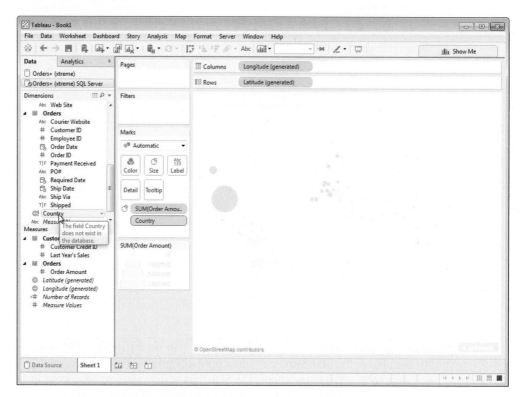

Resolving these field name mismatches is a straightforward process. Right-click the "invalid" field in the Data pane and choose Replace References in the context menu. The Replace Reference dialog box will appear, prompting you to replace all references to the now-invalid field with the field chosen in the new list of fields. Just select the proper field in the new data source and click OK. Any worksheet using the invalid field will now refer to the new field from the new data source. If necessary, right-click the invalid field and choose Delete from the context menu to delete it from the Data pane.

Top 10 Chart Types

T ableau can create many different chart types. Although Show Me (covered in Chapter 2) provides a number of charts you can create very quickly, it's hardly the limit of Tableau's capabilities. Still, there are 10 chart types that you'll probably use more than others if you are performing standard visualization and analytical activities. Some of the charts discussed in this chapter can be created very quickly with Show Me. However, in order to provide fuller knowledge of Tableau, manual steps to create each chart are covered here.

Download *At www.tableaubook.com, download the* Chapter 4 - Top 10 Chart Types.twbx *file to see examples that relate to this chapter.*

Bar Chart

Despite all the visualization possibilities and the plethora of tools to create charts and graphs, the basic *bar chart* is still probably used more than any other type. This is very useful for comparing many different types of measures, including dollars, quantities, number of phone calls, web page hits, and so forth.

In many cases, leaving the mark type on the Marks card set to Automatic will result in a bar chart (charts based on date/time dimensions being a notable exception). Just drag your desired dimension to the Columns shelf and your desired measure to the Rows shelf to create a vertical bar chart (you may also double-click a measure first, then double-click a non-date/time dimension for the same results). If you want to change another chart type to bar (for example, if the default line chart for a date/time dimension isn't what you want), select Bar in the Mark Type drop-down on the Marks card.

Tip *Although you can redrag dimensions and measures to different shelves to change from a horizontal to vertical bar chart, try using the Swap button in the toolbar instead.*

You can enhance a basic bar chart using any number of Tableau features. To create a stacked bar chart, where each bar is broken down by portions of another dimension, drag the second dimension to Color on the Marks card (this is illustrated in Figure 4-1). Or you can create a graduated-color bar chart, where each bar is shaded with a variation of a color range based on a different measure. Drag the desired measure to Color on the Marks card. You can even create some interesting variations of a bar chart by utilizing both Color and Size on the Marks card, as well as unstacking bars by choosing Analysis | Stack Marks | Off from the drop-down menu. This results in two bars appearing on top of each other, but with a different size and color.

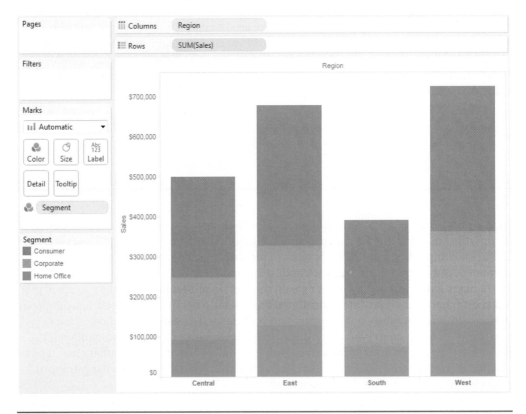

Figure 4-1   Stacked bar chart

Best Practice *If you are charting a single dimension, you may be tempted to add the same dimension the chart is based on to Color on the Marks card to assign each bar a different color. Reconsider this. The different colors may not benefit your audience and may actually confuse them. Ask yourself which is a more effective, less confusing, visualization.*

Line/Area Chart

Another popular chart, the *line chart,* shows a trend over time. For example, sales plotted for the past 12 months or number of web hits by time of day benefit from a line chart. If you initially add a date or date/time dimension to the Rows or Columns shelf and a measure to the other shelf, a line chart trending the measure over time will result. (Though a line chart will be created either way, vertical line charts based on a dimension on the Rows shelf may be of limited use.)

As with other chart types, a basic line chart can expand with placements on Color on the Marks card. If you place another dimension on Color, a different colored line will appear for each member of the dimension. Alternatively, if you add a different measure to Color, the existing line will take on a graduated color indicating the variation of the measure placed on Color. Although you can also place measures or dimensions on Size on the Marks card, you may find the results to be more confusing than useful with a line chart.

Best Practice *It's easy to convert a chart initially created as bar to line or area. Just choose Line or Area from the drop-down on the Marks card. This is helpful if you have a dimension that Tableau doesn't automatically determine to be a date/time dimension but that still can be used to show a trend.*

A variation on the line chart is the *area chart*. Like a line chart, an area chart is best used to trend data over time. However, rather than just showing a single line to represent the path of the trend, the area chart fills in the entire portion of the chart from the bottom of the chart with a shaded color. This often results in a "mountain range" look. Simply select Area from the drop-down on the Marks card to create an area chart.

Like line charts, area charts can be enhanced by dragging a dimension to Color on the Marks card (using a measure on Color will have no usable benefit). This will create a stacked area chart with each member of the dimension placed on Color creating a separate colored stacked area (this is illustrated in Figure 4-2).

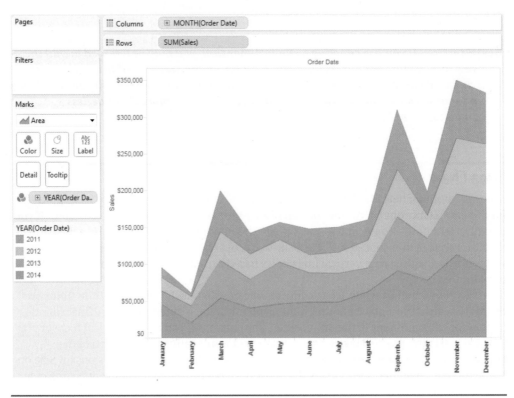

Figure 4-2   Stacked area chart

A variation of an area chart is an unstacked area chart. Create this by dragging a desired dimension (with a minimal number of members) to Color on the Marks card. Initially, you'll see a stacked area chart. Then select Analysis | Stack Marks | Off from the drop-down menu. The areas that were previously stacked will now overlap each other, and Tableau will change the colors to make them easier to distinguish. This may not always be desirable. Even though Tableau displays the color dimension with transparency, it's still easy to miss certain valleys in the "mountain range" if other peaks occlude them.

Discrete Versus Continuous Dates

Tableau is very versatile when it comes to analyzing with date or date/time dimensions (denoted with the calendar or calendar-clock icon in the Data pane) when creating line or area charts. With this versatility, however, comes a certain level of complexity.

Consider the following simple line chart. There are a few quick things to note:

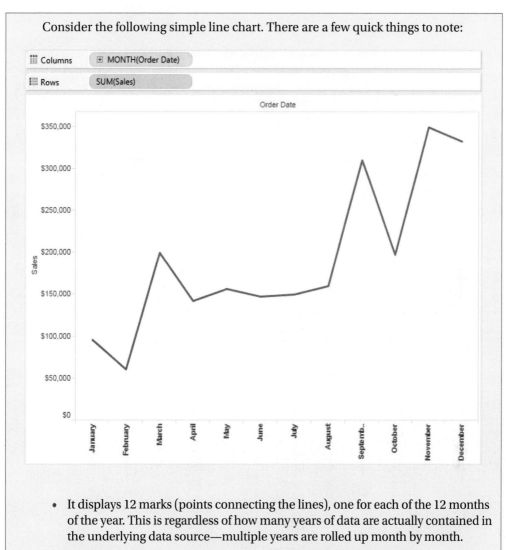

- It displays 12 marks (points connecting the lines), one for each of the 12 months of the year. This is regardless of how many years of data are actually contained in the underlying data source—multiple years are rolled up month by month.

- The Order Date field appears on the Columns shelf at the month level and is colored a pastel blue.

(continued)

This was accomplished by one of several approaches:

- Order Date was dragged to Columns, which initially rolled up the date to the year level. Then, the plus sign was clicked to navigate to the next level in the date hierarchy: quarter. And then the plus sign was clicked again to navigate to month. Then, the year and quarter fields were dragged off the Columns shelf, leaving only the month level.

  Or

- After the initial year level field was dragged to the Columns shelf, the context menu was chosen on the field (with right-click—CONTROL-click on Mac—or the drop-down arrow), and the first occurrence of Month (May) was chosen from the context menu.

	Filter...	
	Show Quick Filter	
F	Sort...	
	Format...	
✓	Show Header	
✓	Include in Tooltip	
	Show Missing Values	
	Year	2015
	Quarter	Q2
⊙	Month	May
	Day	8
	More	▶
	Year	2015
	Quarter	Q2 2015
	Month	May 2015
	Week Number	Week 5, 2015
	Day	May 8, 2015
	More	▶
	Exact Date	
	Attribute	
	Measure	▶
⊙	Discrete	
	Continuous	
	Edit in Shelf	
	Remove	

Now, examine the following variation. Note two basic differences:

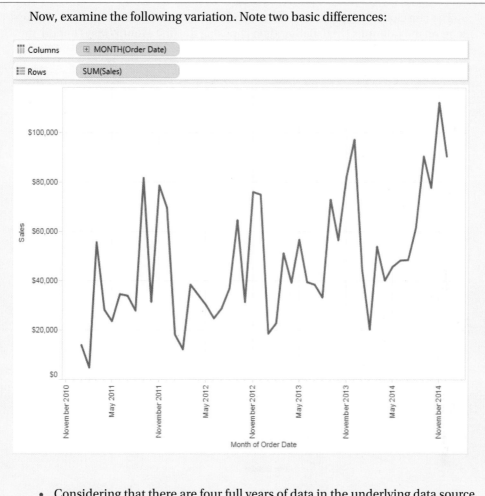

- Considering that there are four full years of data in the underlying data source, there are 48 marks rather than 12, one for each month/year combination.
- The Order Date field on the Columns shelf is still at the month level, but is now colored a pastel green.

(continued)

The one change that results in the second variation comes from the field's context menu on the Columns shelf. Rather than choosing the first Month (May) option, the second Month (May 2015) choice was made.

	Filter...	
	Show Quick Filter	
	Format...	
✓	Show Header	
✓	Include in Tooltip	
	Show Missing Values	
	Year	2015
	Quarter	Q2
	Month	May
	Day	8
	More	▸
	Year	2015
	Quarter	Q2 2015
●	Month	May 2015
	Week Number	Week 5, 2015
	Day	May 8, 2015
	More	▸
	Exact Date	
	Attribute	
	Measure	▸
	Discrete	
●	Continuous	
	Edit in Shelf	
	Remove	

These two charts, while displaying the same underlying data, analyze it in a starkly different fashion. The choice you make will determine whether you see data for any number of years rolled up by month, with only one mark appearing for a month, or displayed across time from one month to the next, over several years. Tableau refers to the different treatment of these dates as "discrete versus continuous."

Discrete dates are treated as date "buckets"—regardless of the amount of underlying data, dates are rolled up to the specific level chosen, with only one mark appearing for each "bucket" of data. *Continuous* dates appear continuously, from beginning to end, spanning the entire data set, with a new mark appearing at each occurrence of the date level chosen. Discrete or continuous date treatment may be chosen for any date level, such as month, quarter, day of week, and so forth. And very different analyses will result based on your choice.

So, while your initial impression of Tableau may have been that dimensions were highlighted in pastel blue and measures were highlighted in pastel green (look on shelves, cards, and icons in the Dimensions and Measures portions of the Data pane), in actuality, discrete values are displayed with pastel blue and continuous values are displayed with pastel green. Although most dimensions and measures, even if not date related, can be treated either as discrete or continuous values, you rarely need to make this choice or distinction. Tableau will make the choice for you, and things will typically (but not always) behave as expected. However, dates are a broad exception, in that they may be treated either way. The choice you make will determine how your date analysis is broken down.

Tip *If you already know the date level (month, quarter, and so forth) you wish to use and have determined whether you want to analyze discretely or continuously, use the right-click drag approach (OPTION-drag on Mac). Right-click the desired date dimension, and while holding the mouse button down, drop the dimension on the desired shelf or card. When you release the mouse button, a Drop Field menu will appear. Choose the desired discrete date option from the pastel blue icon choices at the top of the dialog, or choose the desired continuous date option from the pastel green icon choices at the bottom.*

Drop Field

Which field do you want to drop?

- 🗒 **Order Date (Continuous)**
- 🗒 Order Date (Discrete)

- # YEAR(Order Date)
- # QUARTER(Order Date)
- # MONTH(Order Date)
- # DAY(Order Date)
- # WEEK(Order Date)
- # WEEKDAY(Order Date)
- # MY(Order Date)
- # MDY(Order Date)

- # CNT(Order Date)
- # CNTD(Order Date)
- 🗒 MIN(Order Date)
- 🗒 MAX(Order Date)

- 🗒 YEAR(Order Date)
- 🗒 QUARTER(Order Date)
- 🗒 MONTH(Order Date)
- 🗒 WEEK(Order Date)
- 🗒 DAY(Order Date)

- 🗒 ATTR(Order Date)

OK   Cancel

Pie Chart

Although some authorities in visual design decry them (preferring, for example, stacked bar charts), *pie charts* remain a fixture of the visualization world. They are used to show a single measure for a smaller number of dimension members (probably not more than six or eight) to illustrate what "piece of the pie" each member has. Tableau provides the ability to populate a worksheet with a single pie chart, with multiple pie charts organized for different combinations of dimensions or measures, and even as a chosen mark type for other types of visualizations, such as maps.

To create a pie chart worksheet, choose Pie from the drop-down on the Marks card. Then drag the measure you want the pie to represent onto Angle on the Marks card (Angle will only appear after you choose a Pie mark type). Finally, drag the dimension that you want to use to create pie wedges to Color on the Marks card (again, the dimension should have no more than six to eight members to avoid creating too many pie wedges).

Tip *To add a percentage label to each pie wedge, drag the same measure used on Angle on the Marks card to Label on the Marks card. Then choose Analysis | Percentage Of Cell Or Analysis | Percentage Of Table from the drop-down menu. Tableau allows multiple items to be included on mark labels. For example, you can also drag the dimension used to set pie colors onto Label on the Marks card, along with the measure to show both the percentage and dimension at the same time.*

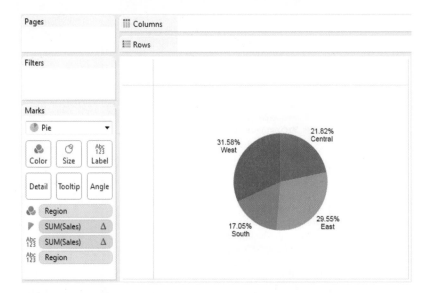

Multiple pie charts can be created by just dragging a dimension you'd like to subdivide by onto the Rows or Columns shelf. Be careful, however, as multiple pies can quickly become difficult to interpret. Consider stacked bar charts or other easier-to-interpret chart types if you find that multiple pie charts are difficult to understand. In the case of a multiple-row or multiple-column pie, another measure placed on Size on the Marks card will change the relative size of each overall pie chart, while the measure on Angle will determine the size of each wedge of an individual pie chart.

Tableau also features the ability to choose the Pie mark type on other visualizations. One example is using a pie on a map. A Pie mark type can add context to a map that would otherwise just show a single circle for a state or country. After creating the map, change the Automatic mark type to Pie from the drop-down on the Marks card. Then drag a dimension onto Color on the Marks card to divide into pie wedges (the fewer dimension members, the better). The result will be individual pie charts on each country, state, or other geographic dimension used to create the map. Again, another measure placed on Size will vary the size of each pie chart on the map.

Text Table/Crosstab

One of the original applications that made personal computers popular was the spreadsheet program. Decades later, spreadsheets are still used widely in all aspects of virtually every type of organization. Even after the introduction of leading-edge visualization tools such as Tableau, numbers organized in rows and columns are still often used when analyzing data. For these requirements, Tableau provides the *text table* or *crosstab* (with the term *crosstab* being used for the remainder of this chapter).

Like a spreadsheet, Tableau displays rows and columns of numbers, with one or more dimensions appearing on the Rows and Columns shelves, and one or more measures appearing on Text on the Marks card. In fact, a crosstab is created automatically using Tableau's default double-click behavior if one or more dimensions are initially double-clicked and a subsequent measure is double-clicked. You can also drag dimensions to the Rows and Columns shelves, and then drag a measure to Text on the Marks card. If you include more than one dimension on the Rows or Columns shelf, a hierarchy of "panes" will be created showing the second dimension organization within the first dimension (make sure the dimensions have a logical hierarchical relationship if you do this).

In the case of a crosstab based on more than one dimension on a shelf, you may want to show subtotals on the crosstab at the end of each outer dimension. Even if you don't use multiple dimensions, you may want to see grand totals for rows or columns in the crosstab. Options from the Analysis | Totals drop-down menu will add these totals.

Note *The Totals option from the Analysis menu, while probably most appropriate for crosstabs, can be used with other visualization types. Just be careful if you use totals beyond crosstabs. For example, a total bar at the end of a bar chart may introduce confusion when trying to compare individual value bars while a total bar appears in the same chart.*

By default, a crosstab will display measures on the Text shelf in black. As with spreadsheet programs, certain numbers may need to stand out based on their value. Tableau facilitates this by allowing another measure or dimension to be placed on Color on the Marks card. If a measure is placed on Color, the range of measure values will create a color range that will automatically color-code cells in the crosstab (typically a graduated color palette will result). A dimension (or perhaps a calculated field that returns only two values) can also be placed on Color to create a more stark "this color or this color" coding for the crosstab.

As discussed earlier, the spreadsheet metaphor of numbers in rows and columns is still popular. A request to "just see the numbers" when viewing a non-crosstab visualization can be easily resolved by right-clicking the worksheet tab. Simply choose Duplicate As Crosstab from the context menu. A new sheet will be created containing a crosstab representation of the dimension/measure organization from the original worksheet. Any worksheet (whether it contains a crosstab or not) can be copied to the Windows Clipboard as a crosstab of numbers in rows and columns for pasting into another application. Just right-click a measure or mark in the visualization and choose Copy | Crosstab from the context menu. The resulting crosstab on the Clipboard can be pasted into another application as a matrix containing rows and columns with numbers. The same option is available from the Worksheet drop-down menu Copy option.

Tip *Crosstabs are particularly useful for "just show me the numbers" types of user requests. Not only can you quickly "just show the numbers" when designing a workbook, crosstabs also provide drill-down capabilities in dashboards. By adding a crosstab to a dashboard with filter actions, you can show related numbers when a user clicks a particular dimension in another portion of the dashboard. Filter actions are covered in more detail in Chapter 8.*

Scatter Plot

Although more esoteric than many of the standard chart types discussed in this chapter so far, the *scatter plot* can provide very meaningful visualization of two related numeric measures. There are, generally speaking, two different analyses that scatter plots help consider: comparison/correlation of the two measures, and concentration of data/existence of outliers. In most cases, one or more related dimensions are also used in a scatter plot.

For example, a scatter plot may be ideal in looking for correlation between the number of web ads placed and number of hits to your website, with further analysis on dimension data, such as where the web ad was placed, the day the ad ran, or known demographics of the person who visited your website. Or your candidate may want to see if the number of outgoing phone calls asking for campaign contributions can be correlated to the number of contributors or the amount of contributions. Certain outliers, such as a few contributors who contributed large amounts, will stand out on a scatter plot, allowing for targeted analysis.

A particular scatter plot example that may be close to home if you've compared other business intelligence (BI) tools to Tableau is the BI Magic Quadrant issued by Gartner. This scatter plot evaluates BI vendors by two measures: completeness of vision and ability to execute. While not all scatter plots share the Magic Quadrant's "both farther to the right and farther up is better" approach, many scatter plots make analysis easy by automatically indicating preference to higher or lower areas on either or both axes.

A scatter plot in Tableau begins with numeric measures placed on both the Rows and Columns shelves. You can either drag them there individually or simply double-click one measure after the other, with the first measure becoming the row and the second the column. Initially, this will simply place one mark (a blue open circle) on the scatter plot indicating where the aggregation of both measures appears. While this may be somewhat helpful for a very quick analysis of how the measures relate, you'll typically want to place additional dimensions "in the mix" to make the scatter plot more useful.

Tip *If you initially add measures to the wrong shelves, you can undo the addition or manually move them to the proper shelves. But you may find it faster to CTRL-click both measure fields on the Rows and Columns shelves to select them. Then right-click and choose Swap from the context menu, or just click the toolbar Swap button.*

Dimensions (or other measures that help broaden scatter plot analysis) can be added to additional areas of the Marks card. For example, to simply add more blue open circles for every member of a desired dimension, drag the dimension to Detail. Although you can change the shape from the default open circle to another shape by choosing a different mark type from the Marks card drop-down, you may prefer to have different shapes appear for different members of a desired dimension. Just drag that dimension to Shape. You can have different colors appear for different dimension members or measure ranges by dragging the desired dimension or measure to Color. Marks can be sized by dragging a dimension or measure to Size. Figure 4-3 shows an example of the effects of these different Marks card options.

Since scatter plots display a mark for every combination of dimensions added to the worksheet, they can quickly become busy with different combinations of marks. In some cases, you may want to show an even denser series of marks if you choose to use a scatter plot to deduce broader generalizations rather than correlations for a smaller number of marks. In that case, you may want to *disaggregate data,* which will retrieve individual values from the underlying data source instead of aggregated sums, averages, and so forth (which Tableau provides by default). To disaggregate, uncheck Analysis | Aggregate Measures from the drop-down menu. You may need to add filters (covered in detail in Chapter 5) to reduce the large number of marks that can result from disaggregation. Hovering your mouse over an individual mark on a disaggregated scatter plot may be of limited use, as no dimension information will appear for the individual mark. Drag desired dimensions to Detail or Tooltip on the Marks card to include that dimension on the tooltip that appears when you hover over a mark.

While not required, trend lines generally add interpretive value to a scatter plot. Just click the Analytics tab to display the Analytics pane and double-click the Trend Line option in the Model box (or drag it to the chart to choose the type of trend line to display). You can also right-click the visualization and choose Trend Lines from the context menu, or choose Analysis | Trend Lines | Show Trend Lines from the drop-down menus (trend lines are covered in more detail in Chapter 6).

And although annotations are available for any visualization type, they come in particularly handy for scatter plots. Add annotations by right-clicking the workspace and choosing Annotate from the context menu. A *mark* annotation will add text and an arrow pointing to a particular mark (a unique combination of measures and dimensions) on the plot. If that particular mark later moves elsewhere on the scatter plot or is eliminated via a filter, the associated annotation will either move or disappear. A *point* annotation will add text and an arrow pointing to a specific x/y coordinate on the scatter plot whether a mark

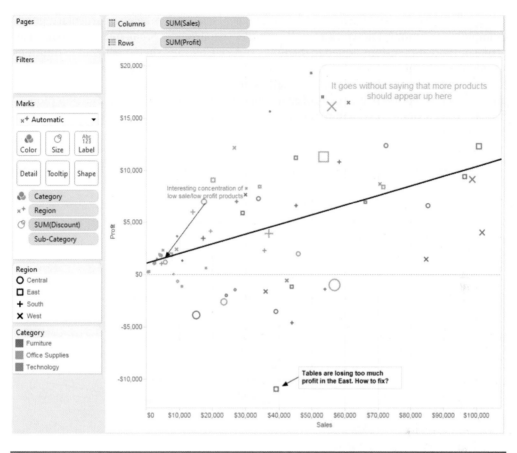

Figure 4-3   Scatter plot with Marks card features, trend line, and annotations

appears there or not. As the scatter plot's axes change with variations in data or filters, the annotation will follow the original x/y coordinate. An *area* annotation, like a point annotation, will add text to a particular x/y coordinate. However, rather than displaying an arrow, an area annotation will draw a rounded box containing the text. You can resize the box to set not only the originating x/y coordinate for the annotation, but the width and height of the annotation as well. Like a point annotation, the area annotation will move as the underlying data changes the dimensions of the scatter plot.

Best Practice *Effective scatter plots include either a small enough number of marks following a general trend to draw quick conclusions about the individual dimensions or a large concentration of marks (perhaps due to disaggregation) to draw general conclusions.*

An effective variation of many Tableau chart types (scatter plots being a particularly good example) is commonly known as a *small multiples* visualization. Small multiples make use of one or more dimensions added to the Rows and/or Columns shelf that result in multiple scatter plots on one or more rows or columns. This allows not only individual conclusions to be drawn from individual scatter plot analysis, but comparisons to other dimension members with identical scatter plots. Best practice dictates that the individual scatter plots display either a small enough number of marks to be easily interpreted at first glance, or a large number of marks (perhaps via disaggregated data) to draw general conclusions at a quick glance.

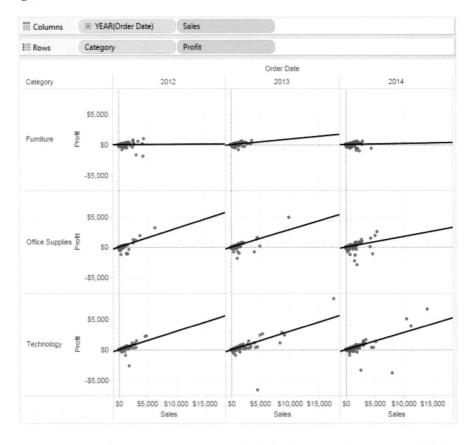

Bubble Chart

Tableau can create two variations of a chart designed to visualize a comparison of size and color of a numeric measure. By displaying varying sizes and colors in filled circles, the *bubble chart* leads to quick comparison and correlation of the chosen metric. One Tableau bubble chart is a variation on the scatter plot (discussed previously). Although this bubble chart variation still plots marks on two numeric axes to exhibit a height/width correlation between values, there are several differences between a bubble chart and scatter plot:

- Marks are designated as filled circles. No other mark types or shapes are used.
- Mark size is increased significantly over a scatter plot to display large circles (hence, the term "bubble chart").
- Smaller numbers of marks are often preferred over the larger mark counts of scatter plots. Because of the larger mark type, a bubble chart starts to lose effectiveness with more than 20 to 25 bubbles. You will probably not disaggregate data with a bubble chart.

To create this form of bubble chart, place measures on the Rows and Columns shelves (double-clicking one measure after the other will automatically place them on the Row and Column shelves, respectively). Choose a circle mark type from the drop-down on the Marks card. Click Size on the Marks card to display the size slider. Size the filled circle to a substantially larger size than the default. Add the dimension whose members you want to create bubbles for to Label on the Marks card. Since this may cause "label overkill" by showing labels on too many marks, click Label and choose Selected to only display a label on a mark when it is clicked. Finally, either CTRL-drag (COMMAND-drag on Mac) measures you used on Rows and Columns to duplicate them on Size (and, optionally, Color), or drag additional dimensions or measures to set the size (and, optionally, color) of the bubbles according to your needs.

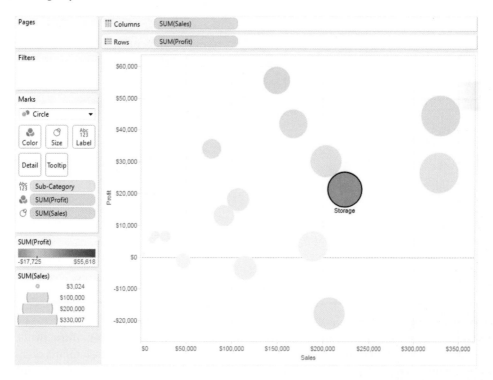

The second type of bubble chart doesn't show a height/width correlation between two measures, but instead just clusters bubbles together, denoting the difference between values based on size and, optionally, color. Show Me offers this choice (choose Packed Bubbles), or you can create it manually.

If you choose to create it manually, begin by choosing Circle in the drop-down on the Marks card. Then add the dimension whose members you want to create bubbles for to Label on the Marks card. Tableau will create a set of identically sized blue bubbles for each dimension member. Finally, drag desired an additional measure to Size (and, optionally, a measure or dimension to Color) on the Marks card to vary the size and color of bubbles as desired.

Here, as in the previous example of a modified scatter plot, bubbles are sized based on sales and colored based on profit. It's fairly easy to compare sales and profit, noting categories that sell similarly (with similar-sized bubbles) but that are far different profit-wise (very different coloring).

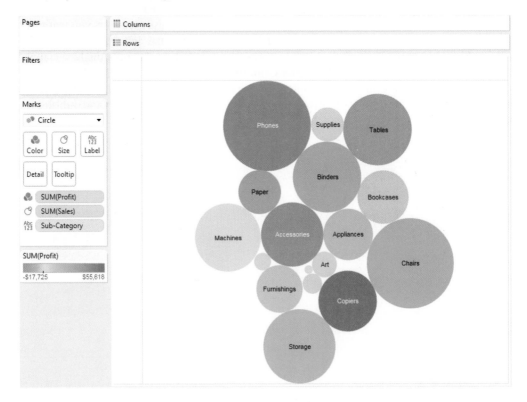

Bullet Graph

A common requirement in visualization is to compare two measures. Often, those two measures are an actual number and a target or goal. Depending on other elements of the comparison, a bar chart (sales versus quota by salesperson) or line chart (sales by month compared to monthly goal) may suffice. However, Tableau includes another option that provides an effective comparison method that takes up a minimal amount of space. The *bullet graph* was created by visualization author and lecturer Stephen Few to provide just such an "actual to target" visualization.

The basic portion of a bullet graph is a bar chart (typically, a horizontal bar chart), which denotes the actual or base measure for comparison. Each bar is then paired with a reference line, which denotes the goal or target. The compact combination of bars and reference lines not only allows a quick comparison of the actual values to each other, but a quick determination of how actual value bars compare to target reference lines. The bullet graph even provides for good comparison of goals/targets by allowing, at a glance, analysis of relative positions of the reference lines. An optional portion of a bullet chart is a reference distribution, which shows a shaded area extending above and below the actual bar to indicate relative comparison of the actual measure to the goal or target.

Note *More detail on reference lines and reference distributions can be found in Chapter 6.*

Because several steps are required to create a bullet graph from scratch, you may prefer to use the Bullet Graph option in Show Me. Simply select the actual measure, the goal/target measure, and the desired dimension in the Data pane. Then click the Bullet Graph option in the Show Me dialog box. Note that Show Me may reverse assignment of the actual and goal/target measures to the proper bar/reference line locations. Tableau provides a quick shortcut to fix this issue. Just right-click the axis for the incorrect measure and choose Swap Reference Line Fields.

If you want to create a bullet graph from scratch or modify some aspect of the one created by Show Me, make use of these Tableau features:

- The dimension used to create individual bars is placed on the Rows shelf (or Columns shelf, if you prefer to create a vertical bullet graph).

- The actual measure is placed on the Columns shelf (or Rows shelf, if you prefer to create a vertical bullet graph).

- The target/goal measure is placed on Detail on the Marks card (in order for reference lines/distributions to make use of the target/goal, it must be in use on the worksheet).

- A reference line is created from the Analytics pane or right-click context menu of the worksheet's axis. Line is chosen, per cell, showing the average of the goal/target measure, with Label set to None, and a black line color.

- If a "range of performance" distribution band is desired, another reference line can be created from the Analytics pane or right-click context menu of the worksheet's axis. Distribution is chosen per cell showing 60%, 80% of the average of the goal/target measure, with Label set to None, and with Fill Above and Fill Below checked.

- If the distribution band is difficult to see, the size of the bar can be reduced by clicking Size on the Marks card and moving the slider to the midpoint.

- Optionally, another dimension or calculated field can be applied to Color on the Marks card to denote actual values that are above and below the goal/target.

Where Are the Gauges?

If you're used to other BI toolsets, you may spend a fair amount of time looking around Tableau trying to find a gauge Show Me option or mark type. Search as you might, you won't find one. Although some people may consider this a shortcoming of Tableau, the gauge is missing for a very good reason: it's generally not a visualization best practice. As Tableau works very hard to help you create meaningful visualizations as you design your worksheets and dashboards (the Automatic mark type being an example of this approach), other visualization types are available in Tableau as replacement for gauges. The bullet chart is an example.

Figure 4-4 shows a comparison of gauges and a bullet chart, with each visualization showing the same set of salespeople, their actual sales, and sales goals. Look closely and ask yourself the same questions a sales manager who was charged with evaluating his or her sales team would ask. Which is a more effective visualization of sales versus goals? Which salesperson is highest and lowest in sales? How close is each salesperson to goal? Which salesperson is over or under goal, and by how much? Which is a more efficient use of precious dashboard space? You'll probably find that bullet charts and other available Tableau visualizations will provide more effective analytics for your audience.

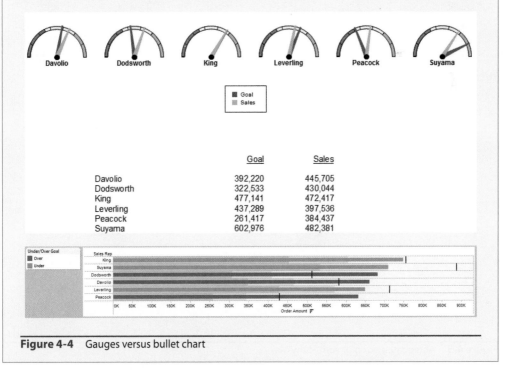

Figure 4-4   Gauges versus bullet chart

Box Plot

Although it may not be found as frequently as bar, line, and pie charts, the *box plot* is a very useful visualization when circumstances demand it. Introduced in the mid-1970s by the statistician John Tukey, the box plot excels at displaying the distribution of data over a range. You can easily determine where the heaviest concentration of data elements is in the range, and optionally, you can easily identify outliers using *whiskers* (small lines that identify where outliers exist). There are two broad ways of creating a box plot: using Show Me, or creating a box plot manually with one or two reference distribution options.

To use Show Me, simply select the measures and dimensions you wish to chart. Selecting more than one dimension will create multiple columns, with one dimension aggregated within the other dimensions' columns. Multiple measures will create multiple rows, one for each measure. Then display Show Me and select the Box Plot icon. Tableau will create a chart using a circle mark type and box plot reference distribution. Figure 4-5 shows an example with aggregated profit plotted as sub-category circles within category columns.

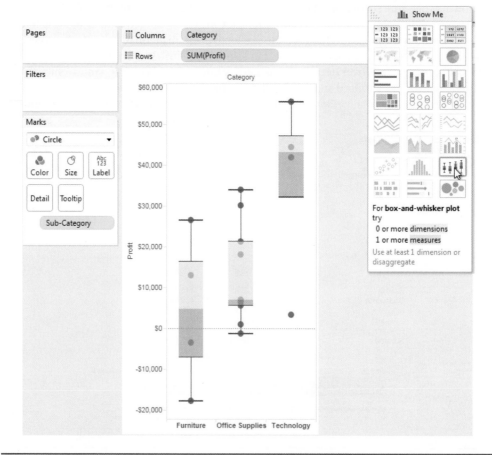

Figure 4-5   Aggregated box plot with Show Me

Because box plots are designed to illustrate distribution of data, as opposed to aggregated values (sum, average, and so forth), you'll often get true benefit of box plot analysis with a large set of data. This can be accomplished by dragging a more granular dimension to Detail on the Marks card or actually plotting individual underlying data records, rather than rolled-up aggregations (uncheck Aggregate Measures from the Analysis drop-down menu). Figure 4-6 shows the same box plot as Figure 4-5, but with data disaggregated.

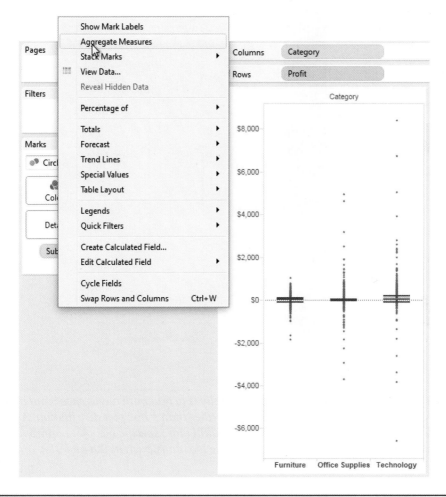

Figure 4-6   Disaggregated box plot

You may also create a box plot manually, typically using a circle mark type (but, theoretically, any mark type that provides a usable chart within visual best practices). You may choose to disaggregate data to display a larger number of marks for better distribution analysis. Then, you may apply a box plot reference distribution from the Analytics pane or by adding a reference line from the axis right-click context menu.

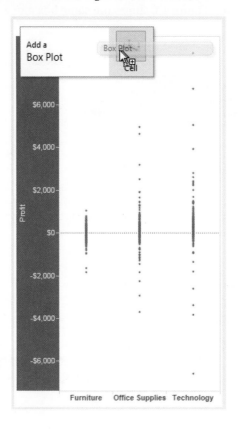

Tip *Another option to create a box plot manually is to add both a reference band and reference distribution to an existing chart rather than a box plot distribution. Although this involves more manual effort, you can fulfill more specific box plot requirements, such as setting whiskers at specific percentile locations, such as 9th and 91st, or 2nd and 98th.*

Tree Map

When faced with identifying the folders that resulted in a full hard disk in 1990, Ben Shneiderman of the University of Maryland began experimenting with a way of visualizing which folders were using up space. Rather than the typical folder/subfolder tree view that is still often used to decode hard disk contents, Shneiderman looked for a more compact way to evaluate hard disk space usage. The *tree map* was born. Despite its origin, it's useful for many other constrained-space visualization requirements. Tableau provides a Tree Map option on Show Me, and permits manual creation of tree maps as well.

A tree map is designed to display hierarchical data as rectangles within rectangles. For each rectangle, two measures can be coded—one will affect the size of a rectangle, and the other will affect color. If a single dimension is used, all dimension members will appear size- and color-encoded together. However, if more than one dimension is used (there should be a logical hierarchy between the dimensions, such as State and City), rectangles will be grouped together by the higher-level dimension, with the overall size of the higher-level group of rectangles encoded by a measure. The resulting tree map can display a large number of dimension members in a relatively small space. A particular rectangle whose color/size combination interests the viewer can be hovered over to show a more detailed tooltip.

If you want to modify a tree map created with Show Me, or create your own, the steps are straightforward:

1. Choose Square as the mark type from the Marks card drop-down (although, if you initially build the tree map without placing anything on the Rows or Columns shelf, you may leave the mark type set to Automatic).

2. Drag one or more dimensions whose members you want to create rectangles for to Label on the Marks card. Ensure that the higher-level dimension appears first (either drag it first or reorder dimensions on the Marks card).

3. Drag the measure you want to size-encode rectangles with to Size on the Marks card.

4. Optionally, drag the dimension or measure you want to color-code rectangles with to Color on the Marks card.

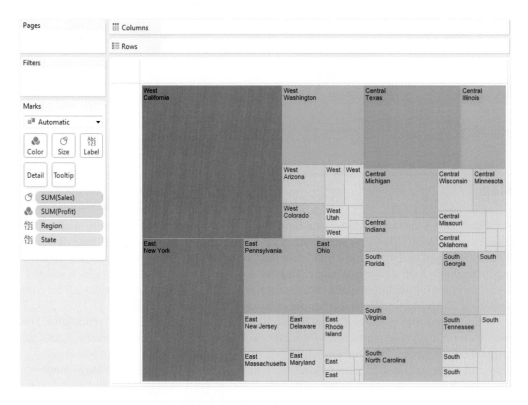

Note several traits of the resulting tree map:

- Member names for both dimensions appear on each rectangle.
- Rectangles for the higher-level dimension (Region) appear together. The overall size of the higher-level rectangles is based on the Size.
- Individual rectangles are color-coded (in this example, low-profit states display varying shades of red, while high-profit states display varying shades of green).

Word Cloud

The *word cloud* (sometimes also referred to as a tag cloud) displays members of a chosen dimension as text, but in varying sizes and colors, depending on one or two measures. A common example of word cloud usage is analyzing the effectiveness of search engine keywords in website visit metrics, or showing the relative popularity of trending social media terms.

The word cloud visualization is not available in Show Me. To create it manually, make use of the following Marks card settings:

- The mark type is set to Text from the drop-down.
- The dimension used to create the words is placed on Text.
- The measure used to vary the size of words is placed on Size.
- The dimension or measure used to vary the color of words is placed on Color.

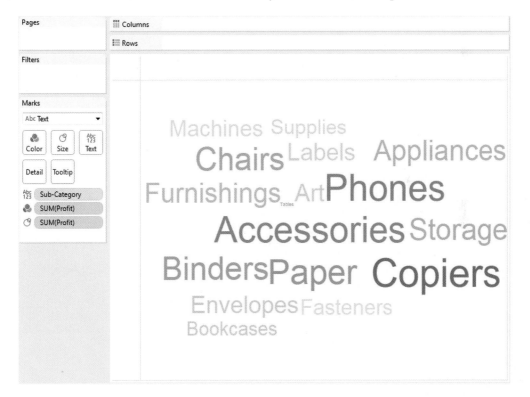

Tableau

98

CHA ... ...

Interacting with the Viewer

T ableau provides a great deal of interactivity as you design visualizations. You can quickly modify visualizations by dragging and dropping different fields to different places on the workspace. Eventually, however, you may want to provide your charts and dashboards to viewers who don't have the full Tableau Desktop product, but who still want to fully interact with your visualizations. By adding interactive features such as quick filters, parameters, and actions, you can still provide an immense amount of flexibility and customizability for your audience without them having to understand the intricate details of Tableau design techniques.

Note *Most of the techniques described here require various Tableau interactive end-user environments, such as Tableau Reader, Tableau Public, Tableau Online, or Tableau Server.*

Download *At www.tableaubook.com, download the Chapter 5 - Interacting With The Viewer.twbx file in Tableau to see examples that relate to this chapter.*

Filtering Data

No matter what visualization or analytical tool you use, one of the first things you'll need to do is filter data. *Filtering* is simply the process of narrowing down your chart or graph to only the data that is relevant to your current need. For example, if you have an historical data warehouse that contains 10 years of data in millions (or more) of records, it's very unlikely that you'll want to include every row in your visualization—you'll almost certainly want to limit your view to a specific year or a few years. Other options for filtering are as numerous as your choice of dimensions and measures: only certain regions, sales that are at least $1,000, and so forth.

Include or Exclude from the Worksheet

The first opportunity to filter presents itself on any existing worksheet. This quick approach is useful for you as you design your initial visualizations, as well as to other viewers if your Tableau workbook is shared with your audience via Tableau Reader, Tableau Online, Tableau Public, or Tableau Server.

Simply select one or more marks, or one or more dimension headers in a visualization, and then make choices from the tooltip or the context menu. Select one or more marks (bars, shapes, and so forth) by CTRL-clicking (COMMAND-clicking on Mac) or drawing an elastic box around multiple marks with your mouse. Or, select one or more dimension headers with click or CTRL-click. Then, just hover your mouse over one of the selected items. A tooltip will appear that includes Keep Only and Exclude options. You may also right-click one of the items and choose Keep Only or Exclude from the context menu. Clicking Keep Only will create a filter to include only the highlighted dimension members. Others will be eliminated from the worksheet. Conversely, clicking Exclude will create a filter to exclude the selected dimension members, retaining all others. You'll notice the dimension now appears on the Filters shelf. You may click the Undo toolbar button or press CTRL-Z (CMD-Z on Mac) to undo the filter.

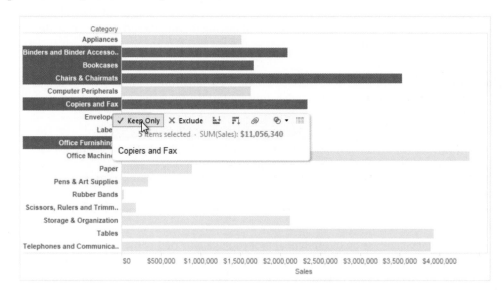

Basic Filtering

The focus point for filtering in Tableau is the *Filters* shelf, which appears at the upper left beside your chart. If you included or excluded dimension values as described earlier in the chapter, you'll notice the dimension you chose appears on the Filters shelf. Like other shelves in Tableau, you may drag dimensions or measures to this shelf. Depending on the type of field (dimension or measure) and the field's data type (string, number, date, and so forth), various filter dialog boxes will result. For example, if you drag a string dimension to the Filters shelf, a filter dialog will appear, showing all members of the dimension.

To only include certain values in your worksheet, check the values you wish to retain (the All and None buttons may be used to select all values if only some are checked and to clear all existing checkmarks, respectively). To exclude certain values in your worksheet, check the values you wish to exclude, as well as the Exclude checkbox in the lower right (the dimension values you select will appear with a line through them). When you click OK, the filter will be immediately applied; the field will be placed on the Filters shelf, and the chart will immediately update to reflect the new filter. Modify an existing filter by right-clicking (COMMAND-clicking on Mac) the field indicator on the Filters shelf or by clicking the small arrow on the indicator, and choose Filter from the context menu. The filter dialog box will reappear, where you may make desired modifications. To remove a filter, simply drag it off the Filters shelf.

A variation of the filter dialog box will appear if you drag a date or date/time field to the Filters shelf. First, you'll be prompted to choose the date level (year, month, and so forth) you wish to use for the filter. Clicking Next will display the standard filter dialog, presenting choices based on the initial date level you select:

- **Relative Date**   This option will filter relative to some specified date (initially, today's date). Relative date filtering is helpful for "yesterday," "last week," "two previous years," and similar types of date ranges that will adjust automatically as your computer's date and time change.

- **Range of Dates**   Allows selection of beginning and ending dates in a date range. Variations of this option allow specification of only a beginning or ending date to provide open-ended date range filters.

- **Date Level** Choose Years, Quarters, Months, and so forth to filter on one or more years, quarters, months, and the like. For example, if you choose Years, the filter dialog will show all years in the filter field. Conversely, choosing Months will display a choice of the 12 months of the year. Select one or more date values to include in the filter.

- **Count or Count (Distinct)** Evaluates the field as a numeric measure, presenting a numeric filter dialog (discussed later in this section).

Dimension and date filters also include options for more advanced filtering. In addition to the default General tab, the filter dialog box will display Wildcard, Condition, and Top tabs (date filters only include Condition and Top tabs). Click one of these tabs for more advanced filtering capabilities:

- **Wildcard** Allows freeform filters using wildcard searches, such as "contains," "starts with," and "ends with" choices. Choose the desired radio button and type full or partial matching text in the Match Value text box.

- **Condition**   Filters the chosen dimension, but not on the actual dimension members themselves. Instead, you may specify a condition based on an aggregated numeric value (the count of another dimension or a numeric aggregation of another measure). If, for example, you only wish to include categories that are unprofitable, click the Condition tab, click the By Field radio button, select Sum Of Profit, and specify a less than (<) operator and zero comparison value. The By Formula option allows specification of a Tableau calculation formula (calculated fields are discussed in Chapter 6) for more advanced filter calculations.

- **Top**   Similar to the Condition tab, the Top tab will filter, not on the actual dimension members, but on an aggregated numeric value. Rather than including all occurrences of dimensions that meet the filter, however, the Top tab will limit the filter to the top or bottom "N" occurrences of the dimension. For example, to see the top 10 selling products, select the Top tab, choose the By Field radio button, choose Top, type a value of **10**, and select Sum Of Sales. The By Formula option allows specification of a Tableau calculation formula (calculated fields are discussed in Chapter 6) for more advanced filter calculations.

Filtering on a measure presents a different type of filter dialog that provides numeric options based on the range of values within the measure. First, you'll be prompted to choose the type of aggregation calculation you wish to use for the filter (sum, count, and so forth). Make this choice and click Next. The resulting filter dialog will allow a range of numeric values (minimum and maximum) to be specified or open-ended numeric ranges (at least/at most). Use the slider control to select beginning or ending range values, or type in the desired values directly.

Sharing Filters Among Worksheets

By default, any filter you specify on the Filters shelf applies only to the worksheet where you add it. If you create another worksheet using the same data connection, any filters you specified elsewhere don't apply to the new worksheet. You may wish to share the filter with additional worksheets that use the same data connection (this is particularly helpful when you plan on placing multiple filtered worksheets on a dashboard).

To make this choice, right-click the desired field indicator on the Filters shelf, or click the drop-down arrow on the field indicator. Click Apply To Worksheets to display a sub-menu where you may choose the desired scope:

- **Only This Worksheet**   This is the default. The filter will only apply to the worksheet where it has been placed on the Filters shelf.

- **All Using This Data Source**   The filter will apply to every worksheet in this workbook that's using the same data source as the worksheet where the filter is applied. You'll notice the filter appear on the Filters shelf on other worksheets with a small barrel icon next to it.

- **Selected Worksheets**   This option, only available when more than one worksheet exists in the workbook, will present a list of all worksheets in the workbook making use of the data connection the filter is based on. Select the worksheets you wish the filter to apply to. The filter will appear on the Filters shelf on these worksheets with a small two-page icon next to it.

Quick Filters

 Video *Using Quick Filters*

The most intuitive filter interactivity in Tableau comes in the form of quick filters. *Quick filters* are customizable dialog boxes that prompt a viewer for filter values. When the viewer chooses values from the quick filter, the visualization is immediately updated to reflect those filter choices. There are two strong benefits of quick filters over filters specified directly on the Filters shelf or interactive filtering by mark/header selection:

- There are many flexible user interface choices for quick filter display, such as drop-down boxes, radio buttons, and so forth.
- They are fully supported in all other Tableau distribution environments, such as Tableau Reader, Tableau Server, and Tableau Online/Public.

You may display a quick filter for existing filters already on the Filters shelf or create one from scratch. Simply right-click (CONTROL-click on Mac) either the field indicator on the Filters shelf or a field in the Data pane (you may filter on dimensions or measures). Choose Show Quick Filter from the context menu. A quick filter dialog will appear on the right side of the chart and, if it wasn't already there, the field name will be added to the Filters shelf.

As with filters directly placed on the Filters shelf (discussed earlier in this chapter), you may remove a quick filter by dragging it off the Filters shelf. You may also remove the quick filter dialog box but leave the filter on the Filters shelf with its last-chosen value by right-clicking the quick filter title or clicking the small context arrow and choosing Hide Card from the context menu. And, as with filters added directly to the Filters shelf, you may choose the filter's scope (apply to just this worksheet, all worksheets using the data connection, or selected sheets) from the context menu, as discussed previously in this chapter.

Depending on the data type of the field the quick filter is based on, the quick filter dialog box will take on an initial default appearance and behavior. For example, if the quick filter is based on a dimension with a small number of members, the quick filter will default to a series of checkboxes, along with an (All) checkbox. If a dimension contains a large number of members, the default quick filter will be a search box. Date dimension quick filters behave in various ways, depending on the date level you chose when first creating the filter. If you create a quick filter directly from a date dimension in the Data pane, it will default to year level and will appear as checkboxes. However, if you first drag a date field to the Filters shelf and choose a different default date level or choose relative dates or a range of dates, the resulting quick filter will display as either a drop-down list of options or a slider. Quick filters based on numeric measures will display a range slider—you may slide either side or type in values directly above the sliders to set minimum and maximum values.

You're hardly limited to this default behavior, though. Right-click the quick filter title or click the small context arrow in the upper right. The context menu will display a bevy of user interface options for your quick filter. Dimension quick filters will present many options for display, such as Single Value (List, Dropdown, Slider), Multiple Values (List,

Dropdown, Custom List), and Wildcard Match. Here's the result of a Multiple Values (Dropdown) choice.

Edit Filter...	
Remove Filter	
Apply to Worksheets	▶
Format Quick Filters...	
Customize	▶
✓ Show Title	
Edit Title...	
Single Value (List)	◉○
Single Value (Dropdown)	▭
Single Value (Slider)	—0—
Multiple Values (List)	☑☑
● Multiple Values (Dropdown)	▭☑
Multiple Values (Custom List)	▭☑
Wildcard Match	▭
Only relevant values	
● All values in database	
● Include Values	
Exclude Values	
✕ Hide Card	

Customer Segment ▽ ▾
(Multiple values) ▾
- ☐ (All)
- ☑ Consumer
- ☑ Corporate
- ☐ Home Office
- ☐ Small Business

Date or date/time quick filters offer a different set of options. You may choose from sliders that present a date range or just a starting or ending date. The Relative Date option will display a rich dialog allowing most of the relative date choices found when initially adding a date field to the Filters shelf. And Browse Periods presents a choice of pre-defined date ranges (1 day, 1 week, 1 month, and so forth) that may be selected. Here's an example using Range Of Dates.

Edit Filter...	
Remove Filter	
Apply to Worksheets	▶
Format Quick Filters...	
Customize	▶
✓ Show Title	
Edit Title...	
Relative Date	⇚⊟⇛
● Range of Dates	▯━━▯
Starting Date	⊲▯⇛
Ending Date	⇚▯⊳
Browse Periods	⌐⊞
Only relevant values	
● All values in database	
✕ Hide Card	

Order Month Range ▽ ▾
August 2010   May 2013
▯━━━━━━━━━▯

Tip *For date and date/time quick filters, you may need to choose date range choices from the Filters shelf context menu before displaying the quick filter. For example, in order to show a quick filter that displays a range of month/year values, you'll need to choose the May 2015 (continuous month) option from the Filters shelf context menu before you display the quick filter. Otherwise, the range-of-dates quick filter will display month/day/ year values instead of just month/year values.*

Quick filters based on numeric measures have the fewest customization choices, but still offer sufficient options for most needs. Range Of Values will display a slider control with both starting and ending points, which may be moved to modify the starting and ending values of the range. At Least and At Most will present sliders to select just the beginning and ending values of an open-ended range. In all cases, you may also type values directly into the boxes above the sliders.

Customizing Quick Filter Appearance and Behavior

There are many options on the quick filter context menu (click the small drop-down arrow on the quick filter itself) for customizing the way a quick filter appears and behaves. Here are some notable choices:

- **Edit Title**   This option will display a text edit dialog box permitting you to change the default title Tableau assigns to the quick filter. You may even format the modified quick filter title, including font, color, and font size choices.

- **Customize | Show "All" Value**   Quick filters based on text/string fields will, by default, display an All choice, permitting the viewer to retrieve all data in the data source for the chosen dimension. If you wish to permit the viewer to only choose a combination of individual dimension values and not all values, the All option may be disabled with this selection.

- **Customize | Show Apply Button**   By default, Tableau executes the filter (which requires a data source query) every time an individual value in a multivalue quick filter is selected or deselected. For example, Tableau will query the database every time you check an individual state in the multistate quick filter, even if the desire is to check multiple states before updating the worksheet. If you enable this option, Tableau won't actually query the database until the Apply button on the quick filter is clicked, even if multiple values are checked or unchecked. This can improve performance (sometimes dramatically) when using particularly slow quick filter fields.

- **Format Quick Filter**   This will replace the Data pane with the Format pane (formatting is discussed more in Chapter 2), providing additional quick filter appearance options for font type, size, and alignment, as well as shading and border choices.

- **All Values In Database/Only Relevant Values**   By selecting All Values In Database, the quick filter will always present all available values in the database for the matching field, even if choices from other filters would render some values invalid. However, choosing Only Relevant Values will apply other quick filters *before* showing available values in this quick filter. This feature (sometimes referred to as *cascading filters*) will permit, for example, a quick filter based on Sales Rep to only show sales reps within a selected region if another quick filter presents region choices.

Parameters

 Video   *Using Parameters*

Although quick filters provide flexible interactivity for filtering data, there are other occasions when you may wish to prompt your audience for a value that's not based on an existing data field. In particular, you may wish to create customized calculated fields (discussed in detail in Chapter 6) that make use of a value supplied by a user. For this, Tableau provides parameters. A *parameter* is a prompt, similar in appearance to a quick filter, that returns a variable value that can be used in many parts of Tableau, such as calculated fields and portions of various dialog boxes, as well as being placed directly on a shelf. As with quick filters, parameters are usable with all Tableau distribution methods, such as Tableau Reader, Tableau Server, and Tableau Online/Public. And parameters are not limited to being used just on the worksheet where they are created—they can be used by any worksheet in your workbook, regardless of the worksheet's data source. A value you supply to a parameter on the first worksheet can be used in any other worksheet in the workbook.

There are three general requirements to make use of parameters in your workbook:

- Create the parameter.
- Display the parameter.
- Use the parameter in a calculated field, in a dialog box, or on a shelf.

Creating a Parameter

There are several ways to create a parameter in Tableau. The first is from another dialog box where a fixed value can be provided, such as the value for a top filter or the value for a reference line. Consider the example of a top filter (discussed earlier in this chapter).

Recall that a top filter permits you to choose whether to see the top or bottom values of a dimension based on a measure. You are also given a choice of how many top or bottom dimension members to see, with the default value of 10 appearing in the dialog box. However, if you wish to parameterize the input value rather than "hard-coding" it, you may expand the value drop-down and choose Create A New Parameter.

You may also just right-click somewhere in the Data pane (either on a field or on a blank area). Or, you may display the Data pane context menu with the small down arrow on the Dimensions box. Choose Create Parameter from the pop-up context menu.

The Parameter dialog box will appear. Depending on where you created the parameter (from a dialog box, from the Data pane, and so forth), the dialog box may already have some values pre-specified. For example, if you create a parameter from the top filter dialog box (where the parameter will be used to replace the numeric N value), the parameter will already be defined with a data type of Integer. You must still give the parameter a meaningful name. You may optionally provide a comment. The remainder of the dialog box will change based on the data type of the parameter. Here, the default value of N is set to 10; formatting of the numeric parameter value will be automatic (if you wish, you may select from a variety of specific formats, depending on the parameter data type); and a range of values will be prompted for, with a minimum of 10, a maximum of 50, and a step size of 5. As such, this parameter will permit entry of integer values between 10 and 50 in increments of 5.

If you create a parameter from the Data pane, the Parameter dialog will be similar, but you must choose a data type as well. This is crucial, as it will determine how the parameter will appear on the worksheet, what properties you can set for the parameter, and how you can use the parameter. Consider your data type choice carefully. For example, you won't want to choose a string data type if you wish to use the parameter to ultimately affect the percent change in a numeric calculation. Also, if you want to create a dynamic reference line based off a date field to call out a reference date, string and numeric options will not even be available as selections from the date range axis.

In this example, a string parameter is being created to prompt for one of four string values. The values are being pre-defined in the parameter so that they will be the only available options when the parameter displays on the worksheet. A default value of "Profit" is being set, which will initially display when the workbook is opened. If an existing database field contains the desired values for a parameter, select it by clicking the Add From Field button. The parameter values will be read from the chosen field. You may also paste values from the Clipboard by clicking the Paste From Clipboard button.

Caution *If you use the Add From Field button to populate a string parameter, new values added to the database later will not appear in the parameter (Tableau does not provide "dynamic" parameter lists). If you wish to add newly created values from the database to a parameter, you must edit the parameter and click the Add From Field button again after the database has changed.*

In all cases, once you create a parameter, it will appear in a new area of the Data pane dedicated to displaying parameters. Even if you add new worksheets or data connections to the workbook, the parameters will still display in the Data pane and will be usable in any worksheet.

Displaying a Parameter

Once a parameter is created, it must be displayed on the worksheet so that your audience can interact with it. If you created a parameter in a dialog box (the top filter parameter discussed earlier being an example), the parameter will automatically appear on the worksheet as soon as you close the dialog box where you created it. However, if you created a parameter in the Data pane, it will not automatically be displayed. You must explicitly right-click the desired parameter in the Data pane or click the small down arrow on the parameter and choose Show Parameter Control from the context menu. The parameter will then appear on the right side of the worksheet next to any existing parameters or quick filters.

Once a parameter appears on the worksheet, its user interface may be customized, much like a quick filter's can. As with a quick filter, right-click the title of the parameter or click the small context arrow to display the context menu. Depending on the parameter's data type and options you chose when you created the parameter, you'll find various choices for how the parameter is displayed (slider, single value list, and so forth). The previously discussed string parameter, for example, will display as radio buttons when the appropriate choice is made.

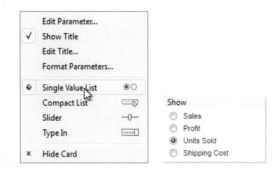

Using a Parameter in a Worksheet

Finally, the effort required to create and display a parameter won't be fully realized if the parameter is not used somewhere on your worksheet. If you created a parameter directly from a dialog box, such as the previously discussed top filter, then the parameter will automatically be placed in the dialog box and will immediately be reflected on your visualization. However, if you create a parameter in the Data pane, you must now choose where to make use of the parameter. You may wish to use it on a shelf (for example, to color some portion of your visualization), use it in a title or caption to annotate the visualization, or use it in a calculated field (you may begin typing the parameter name and choose the full parameter from Tableau's auto-completion capability, or just drag the parameter into a calculated field from the Data pane).

Don't forget that parameters may be used on any worksheet in your workbook. Even though you create them and use them in one particular worksheet, they are available everywhere else in your workbook—they will always appear in the Data pane no matter what worksheet you're currently editing. You may use them differently on different sheets. For example, you may supply a parameter to a top filter in one worksheet but use it in a calculated field on another. You'll soon find that parameters will take you to a whole new level of interactivity and flexibility with Tableau.

Tip *If you created a parameter but it doesn't appear in a variable portion of a dialog box, such as the N value in a top filter or the value to use for a reference line, it's because the parameter doesn't match the required data type for the dialog box. For example, the N value of a top filter will only expose numeric parameters. If a reference line is being created on an axis based on a date value, only date parameters will appear in the reference line value.*

Worksheet Actions

Another way of enabling interactivity is by using worksheet actions. *Worksheet actions* are an interactive feature to control behavior or appearance on either the current worksheet or other worksheets in the workbook, based on some action your viewer takes. There are three types of actions a viewer can initiate from a worksheet:

- **Filter Action**   This action filters other worksheets in the workbook based on marks selected on the current worksheet.
- **Highlight Action**   This action highlights marks on other worksheets in the workbook based on marks selected on the current worksheet.
- **URL Action**   This action launches a web page containing a specified URL based on marks selected on the current worksheet.

Furthermore, worksheet actions can be initiated in one of three ways:

- **Select**   This method initiates the action when a user selects a mark by clicking it, selects more than one mark by CTRL-clicking them, or selects multiple marks by drawing an elastic box around them.
- **Menu**   This method initiates the action when you hover your mouse over a mark and choose the action name from the tooltip. The action may also be initiated on the context menu that appears when you right-click selected marks.
- **Hover**   This method initiates the action when you hover your mouse over a mark.

Note   *Hovering is generally used to initiate actions (typically, highlight actions) on dashboards and not worksheets. While hover works for single worksheets as well, you will want to only select the same worksheet that initiates the action as the target. You won't be able to see the results of the hover action on any other worksheets, unless they have been added to a dashboard.*

All worksheet actions are created from the Worksheet | Actions drop-down menu. The Actions dialog will appear, where you may create new actions or edit existing actions.

Filter Actions

A *filter action* adds a filter to one or more worksheets in your workbook. Although there are many possible uses for a filter action, worksheet "drill-down" is one common popular use. For example, you might create a crosstab worksheet that contains detailed dimension/measure information that you wish to act as a drill-down target for a filter action. When you select one or more marks on a chart, the marks you selected can be used to filter the target text table.

Click the Add Action button in the Action dialog box, and choose Filter from the sub-menu. Complete the Filter Action dialog box:

- First, give the action a meaningful name (leaving the default name doesn't provide detail about what the action does, which makes it difficult to determine its purpose when you create multiple actions).

- In the Source Sheets box, choose the worksheet or worksheets you want to initiate the action from.

- Click the desired Hover, Select, or Menu button to determine what will initiate the action. If you click Select and want the action only initiated when a single mark is clicked, check the appropriate box (multiple mark selections using CTRL-click or drawing an elastic box around multiple marks won't initiate the action).

- In the Target Sheets box, choose the worksheet or worksheets you want the action to take place on. The sheets you select here will be filtered when the action is initiated.

- Select one of three radio buttons to indicate what you want to occur when the original marks that were used to initiate the action are cleared (the original mark is clicked again, or a blank space on the worksheet is clicked to clear previous selections). Leave The Filter will leave the filter in place even when you clear the selection. Show All Values will eliminate the filter and show all data in the target sheets. Exclude All Values will eliminate all data from the target sheets so they appear blank.

- Make choices in the Target Filters box, if necessary, to match fields between the source and target sheets. If, for example, the source sheet is based on one data connection and the target is based on a different connection, Tableau will not be able to determine how to match the field used for selection in the source worksheet to a field to filter in the target worksheet if the fields don't have the same name. In this case, click the Selected Fields radio button and then click the Add Filter button to create one or more matching filters, choosing fields from the source sheet and target sheet that Tableau should match when creating the filter.

Click OK to create the filter action. In this example, a filter action has been created to filter a target crosstab worksheet when marks are selected on a map. Here, drawing an elastic box around five countries in South America filters the crosstab to these countries. When the action is initiated, the target sheet will be displayed and the filter applied.

© OpenStreetMap contributors

Country / Region	State	City	Order Quantity	Profit	Sales
Argentina	Province de Buenos Aires	Buenos Aires	14,789	$286,865	$1,037,812
Brazil	Bahia	Salvador	2,734	$126,331	$230,105
	Ceara	Fortaleza	2,397	$47,294	$209,041
	Distrito Federal	Brasilia	1,062	$14,658	$42,923
	Minas Gerais	Belo Horizonte	513	($1,422)	$36,882
	Parana	Curitiba	364	$367	$9,640
	Pernambuco	Recife	1,245	$14,710	$72,069
	Rio de Janeiro	Rio de Janeiro	10,355	$131,867	$666,902
	Rio Grande do Sul	Porto Alegre	1,108	$18,103	$101,600
	São Paulo	Sao Paulo	8,852	$156,017	$732,718
Chile	Santiago	Santiago	1,716	$22,551	$101,844
Colombia	Antioquia	Medellin	1,810	$97,324	$238,668
	Bogotá D.C.	BogotÁj	2,794	$70,570	$213,671
Peru	Provincia de Lima	Lima	2,592	$11,626	$112,767

Highlight Actions

A *highlight action* highlights particular marks on one or more worksheets in your workbook, based on marks you select on the source worksheet. When you select one or more marks on a chart, the other sheet will match the selection. When you select the other sheet in the workbook, you'll notice matching marks are highlighted.

Click the Add Action button in the Action dialog box and choose Highlight from the sub-menu. Complete the Highlight Action dialog box as follows:

- First, give the action a meaningful name (leaving the default name doesn't provide detail about what the action does, which makes it difficult to determine its purpose when you create multiple actions).

- In the Source Sheets box, choose the worksheet or worksheets you want to initiate the action from.

- Click the desired Hover, Select, or Menu button to determine what will initiate the action.

- In the Target Sheets box, choose the worksheet or worksheets you want the action to take place on. The sheets you select here will be highlighted when the action is initiated.

- Make choices in the Target Highlighting box, if necessary, to match fields between the source and target sheets. All Fields will consider all combinations of dimensions in the source and target sheets when attempting to match what to highlight. Selected Fields will permit you to check specific dimensions in the source sheet that will be used to match marks in the target sheet to highlight. Dates And Times will match date and/or time fields in the target, based on what you select in the source sheet.

Click OK to create the highlight action. In this example, a highlight action has been created to highlight a target bar chart worksheet when marks are selected on a map. Here, selecting China on the map will highlight matching customers from China on the bar chart. After the selection, when the bar chart tab is selected in the workbook, matching customer bars are highlighted.

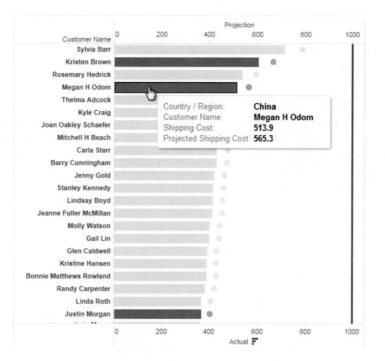

URL Actions

A *URL action* launches a web page based on marks you select on the source worksheet. The web page can contain a static web page uniform resource locator (URL). However, any field on your worksheet (the selected mark, in particular) can be used to customize the URL based on marks you select when the action is initiated. This provides for very powerful customized web pages to be delivered based on selections.

Click the Add Action button in the Action dialog box and choose URL from the sub-menu. Complete the URL Action dialog box as follows:

- First, give the action a meaningful name (leaving the default name doesn't provide detail about what the action does, which makes it difficult to determine its purpose when you create multiple actions). If you wish to customize the action name by using a field from your data source, click the small arrow at the right of the Name text box. You may select a field to be included in the action name.

- In the Source Sheets box, choose the worksheet or worksheets you want to initiate the action from.

- Click the desired Hover, Select, or Menu button to determine what will initiate the action. Be very cautious if you choose Hover—understand that a web page will be launched whenever you just move your mouse over a mark!

- Specify the URL you wish to use when the web page is launched. To customize the URL with data from your worksheet, click the small arrow at the right of the URL text box. You may select a field to be used in the URL.

- If you wish to "URL-encode" certain characters (spaces and so forth) in the URL, check the appropriate box. If you wish to allow selection of multiple marks to launch the URL (with CTRL-click/COMMAND-click or an elastic box), check Allow Multiple Values and type in the delimiter and escape character you wish to use to separate the resulting multiple values in the URL.

Click OK to create the URL action. In this example, a URL action has been created to display a Wikipedia web page when a mark is selected on a map. The URL has been customized with the Country/Region field to display a specific entry relating to the country that is selected. Because this is a menu action, the option to run it appears on the tooltip when the mouse is hovered over a mark.

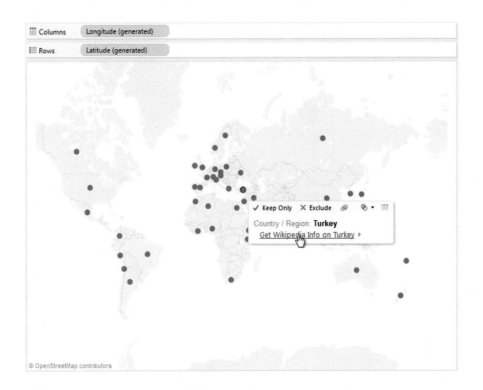

Note   *Worksheet actions are similar to dashboard actions, with the exception that they only apply to other worksheets in your workbook. No dashboards need exist in your workbook for worksheet actions to be used. Dashboard actions are covered in more detail in Chapter 8.*

Advanced Charting, Calculations, and Statistics

Once you feel more comfortable with basic Tableau visualizations using shelves, Show Me, and the Marks card, you're ready to move on to more sophisticated analysis techniques. This chapter will cover more flexible data organization with groups and sets, custom data manipulation with calculated fields and table calculations, and statistical analysis techniques using the Analytics pane and related options.

Download *At www.tableaubook.com, download* Chapter 6 - Advanced Charting-Calculations-Statistics.twbx *to see examples that relate to this chapter.*

Grouping Dimensions

In many cases, the data source you are presented with may not have dimension (categorical) values organized perfectly for the data analysis task at hand. Tableau allows you to reorganize and customize dimensions as necessary using groups. Groups allow you to organize data in a more logical fashion, as well as accommodating certain types of data inconsistencies, perhaps resulting from data entry errors. Any custom groups you create are saved with a custom data connection so that they may be reused and shared within your organization (saving data connections is discussed in Chapter 3).

A *group* is a reorganized collection of dimension members. For example, your data source may contain data broken down by state, but a data entry error places some data in a state labeled CO and other data in a state labeled Colorado. These may be combined into a single dimension member. Or, if you wish to analyze data by salesperson territories and these territories don't exist in your data source, you can create salesperson territory groups based on state. You could highlight Montana, Wyoming, Colorado, Utah, and Arizona and create a "John Doe" group; California, Oregon, Washington, Nevada, and Texas could be placed in a group named "Jane Smith"; and so forth. You may then use either the original state field or the new group to analyze data. And when you save the data source, the group is saved with it for use in other workbooks.

There are two ways to create these kinds of groups: by selecting dimension headers on an existing worksheet, or by using the Create Group option in the Data pane. To use an existing worksheet, CTRL- or SHIFT-click (COMMAND-click on Mac) the group member headers you wish to combine (it's important that you click the names of the members—the headers—and not the actual marks, as you'll see later in this section). Then, with your mouse hovered over one of the selected headers, click the paper clip icon in the tooltip. You may also click the group (paper clip) button on the toolbar. Or, you can right-click (CONTROL-click on Mac) the header and choose Group from the context menu.

The selected dimension members will be combined into a new single member consisting of the names of the original members, and a new group dimension will be created in the Data pane (the group will be named the same as the original dimension with a group designation appended to it). In addition, the original dimension on any worksheet shelves will be replaced by the new group dimension. From this point forward, you may analyze either the original dimension by dragging it to an appropriate shelf or the new combined group by dragging it to a shelf.

Several options are available to customize the new group:

- To ungroup the just-combined members, select the header of the combined member and click the paper clip again. Or right-click and select Ungroup from the context menu. Although this will return members to their original separate locations, the group will remain in the Data pane and on a worksheet shelf.

- To change the name of the new combined group rather than maintaining the list of original member names, right-click the new member header and choose Edit Alias from the context menu. Type the new name you wish to appear for the combined group.

- To add a combined member to the group, select additional original members as you did previously and use the same paper clip or context menu options as before. An additional combined member will be added.

- To add original members to an existing combined member, select the original members you wish to add, as well as the existing combined member. Use the paper clip or menu options to add.

- To combine one or more already combined members, select the combined members and use paper clip or menu options. They will be combined into yet another new combined member consisting of everything in the original combined members.

In addition to manipulating groups on the worksheet, you may create and modify groups in the Data pane. Begin by selecting the original dimension you wish to group. Then right-click (CONTROL-click on Mac) and choose Create Group from the context menu. The Create Group dialog box appears, displaying the original dimension members for the chosen dimension. Select the existing members you wish to combine with SHIFT- or CTRL-clicks (if the dimension has a large number of members, you may wish to click the Find button and add search criteria to find the members you want to select). Then click the Group button. The selected members will be combined into a new member consisting of the names of the selected members. If you wish to rename the new combined member, simply hold your mouse button down on the name for a second or so, or select it and click the Rename button. Type the desired name for the combined member. You may also change the default name of the group (initially, the name of the dimension the group is based on, followed by the word "group") by selecting the Field Name portion of the dialog box and typing a new name.

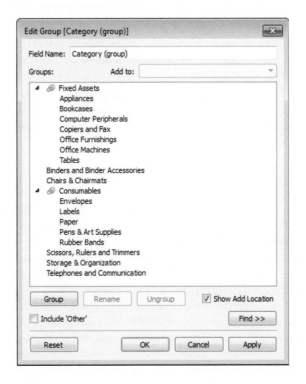

When you've finished customizing the group, click OK. The new group will be added to the dimension list in the Data pane. You may now analyze either the original dimension or the new group by dragging it to a shelf. When you first create a group, or if you select an existing group in the Data pane, right-click and choose Edit Group from the context menu; there are several fine points that can help you maximize use of the group dialog box:

- To expand or contract combined members, click the arrow to the left of the combined member. When expanded, you'll see the original members that have been combined into the new member.

- To ungroup a combined member, select the combined member next to an arrow and click the Ungroup button.

- To create another combined member, select additional original members as you did previously and click the Group button again. A new combined member will be added.

- To add original members to an existing combined member, select the original members you wish to add. Then either drag them inside the existing combined member, or choose the existing combined members you wish to add from the Add To drop-down list at the upper right of the dialog box.

- To combine one or more already combined members, select the new combined group members and click the Group button again. They will be combined into yet another new combined member.

- To create an "Other" combined member that contains all original dimension members that weren't placed in any combined members, click the Include "Other" checkbox. All remaining original members will be combined into one final combined member named Other.

Visual Grouping

There is a variation on grouping (referred to informally as *visual grouping*) that you may prefer for quick visual delineation of group members. As mentioned earlier in this section, when creating groups on the worksheet, you should select the actual member names/ headers, *not* the marks (bars, circles, and so forth). If you do select marks instead of headers (with CTRL/COMMAND- or SHIFT-click, or by dragging over multiple marks), then Tableau behaves somewhat differently.

Once you've selected desired marks, click the group (paper clip) button in the tooltip that appears, click the group (paper clip) toolbar button, or right-click and choose Group from the context menu. As discussed previously, the selected dimension members will be combined into one new member in a new group, which will be placed in the Data pane. However, contrary to earlier steps when headers were selected, the new group *will not* replace the original dimension on a shelf. Instead, the new group will be placed on Color on the Marks card with the originally selected members now showing a different color than the "Other" members (this method of group creation uses the previously discussed Include Others option by default).

As before, the name of the new combined member will be a list of the original member names. You may edit the newly created group in the Data pane to provide a more appropriate name. Or, you may simply select the name in the color legend, right-click, and choose Edit Alias. Type the new name for the combined member.

There are some fine points for using this "visual" method of grouping as well:

- To ungroup the just-combined members, select one or more of the already grouped marks. When the tooltip appears, you'll notice that the previous group paper clip icon now displays a small x, indicating that it now functions as an ungroup button. You may also right-click and select the Ungroup option from the context menu.

- To add a combined member to the group, select additional original members' marks as you did previously and use the same paper clip or context menu options as before. An additional combined member will be added to the group, which will create an additional color.

- To add original members to an existing combined member, select the original marks you wish to add, as well as at least one mark from an existing combined member. Use the paper clip or menu options to add.

- To combine one or more already combined members, select *all* the marks from existing combined members and use paper clip or menu options. They will be combined into yet another new combined member consisting of everything in the original combined members.

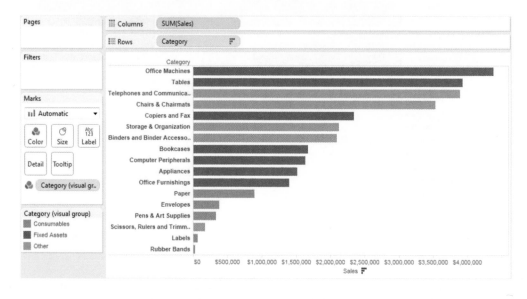

Saving and Reusing Sets

Somewhat like a filter (discussed in Chapter 5), a *set* is a smaller subset of all the data in your underlying data source. For example, a set may consist of just five salespeople who are underperforming. Or, another set could contain all products that have an on-hand quantity at or below a reorder level. Although you may confuse sets with groups, it's important to understand that groups *combine* multiple dimension members into one combined member, whereas sets simply *narrow down* to the selected dimension members—they are not combined. Once sets are defined, they can be used as filters, placed on the Color shelf or other parts of the Marks card, and so forth to help analyze the subsets of data that you've defined. Any custom sets you create are saved with a custom data connection so that they may be reused and shared within your organization (saving data connections is discussed in Chapter 3).

There are two types of sets you can create in Tableau. The first, a *constant set,* contains a specific set of dimension members. An example of this type of set is one that specifies five salespeople who are underperforming. You may use this constant set to analyze, color, filter, and so forth, based on the five specific salespeople you've added to the set. Even if one of the salespeople improves his or her sales dramatically, this person will remain in the set until you manually edit the set and remove him or her. The second type, a *computed set,* uses a conditional formulaic expression to define what the set contains. For example, a set can be defined that determines the top 10 selling products as of the current moment based on a "Top" database query. Any product dimension members that meet that condition will be included in the set. As data changes, different dimension members may be added to or removed from the set automatically based on changing sales.

There are several ways of creating a constant set. If you already have a chart defined in your worksheet, you may select as many marks or headers as you'd like to add to the set via CTRL-/COMMAND- or SHIFT-click, or by dragging to highlight a series of marks (in a scatter plot, for example). From the tooltip, click the Create Set button. Or, right-click and choose Create Set from the resulting context menu.

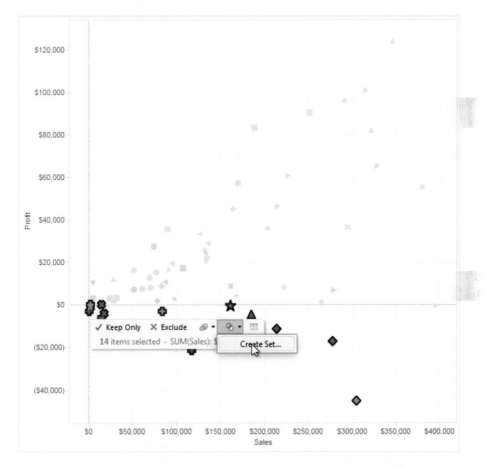

The Create Set dialog box will appear with the dimension members you selected appearing as a list (if your visualization contains multiple dimensions, they will appear in separate columns). If you wish to remove an entire dimension in a multidimension set, hover your mouse over the column heading of the dimension and click the red X. In addition, any dimension members may be removed by hovering over the row and clicking the red X. Give your set a meaningful name by typing it in in the Name area. If you wish to immediately filter your worksheet by the new set, check the Add To Filters shelf. Click OK to create the set. The new set will appear in the Sets area of the Data pane. Like any other field in the Data pane, you may drag the set to a shelf or to a portion of the Marks card to analyze only the data included in the set.

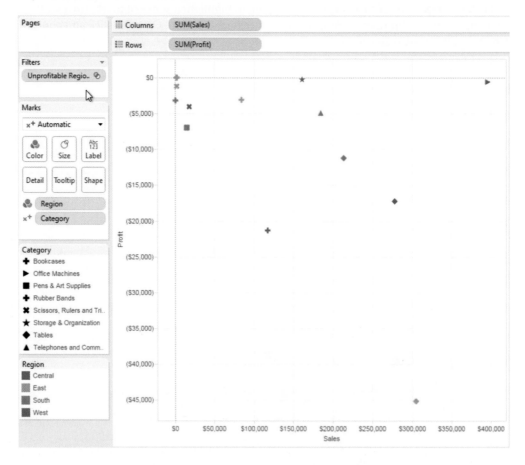

You may also create a set by right-clicking an existing dimension in the Data pane and choosing Create | Set from the context menu. The Create Set dialog box will appear containing three tabs: General, Condition, and Top. The General tab will simply list all the members of the dimension. Just click as many members as you wish to add to the set and click OK. However, if you want to create a computed set, select either the Condition or Top tab and select some sort of condition, based on the dimension itself, or a measure. For example, to create a set containing top 10 selling items, select the Top tab, choose By field, select Top, type **10**, and choose the Sales measure and Sum aggregation.

One feature of sets that you will find handy in overall set analysis is the In/Out feature. Depending on where you use a set (dragging a set to Color on the Marks card is a prime example), your chart will break data down into "in set" and "out of set" delineations. For example, if you create a bar chart that displays sales by category, you may drag a saved filter set (described later) on Color to separately highlight the portion that is "in" the set (placed by U.S. customers) and "out of" the set (place by non-U.S. customers). If you prefer to highlight the actual members that make up the set rather than whether items are in or out of the set, click the context arrow on the set's field indicator on the shelf and choose Show Members In Set.

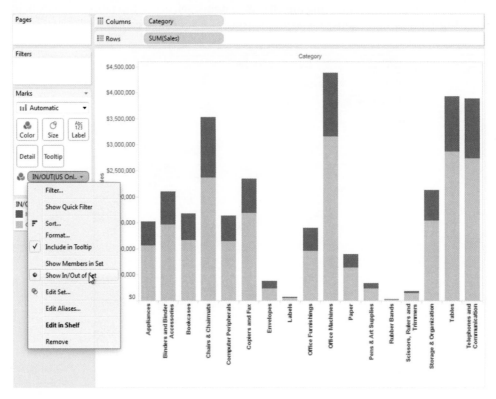

Tip *Because sets are based on dimensions in a particular data connection, they will only appear in the Data pane when their corresponding data connection is selected. If your workbook contains multiple data connections, sets won't appear when other data connections are selected.*

Combined Sets

If you remember math class from your grade school years, you may remember the teacher drawing intersecting circles on the whiteboard while conducting a discussion of sets. That knowledge may come in handy as you work with Tableau, as Tableau allows creation of combined sets. A *combined set* is a set that uses two existing sets to create some combination of members from both sets. Perhaps you wish to analyze category/region combinations that sell at high dollar amounts but still lose money because of low profit. If you have created two distinct sets for each of these categories, you may combine them for more thorough analysis.

To create a combined set, select the two existing sets in the Data pane. Right-click (CONTROL-click on Mac) and choose Create Combined Set from the context menu. The Create Set dialog box will appear, but with a different organization than previously illustrated. Give the combined set a meaningful name, and then choose the intersection of the two original sets that you wish the combined set to return (the four icons will take you back to those school days). Click OK when finished. A new combined set will appear in the Sets area of the Data pane that you may drag and drop onto your visualization.

Saving Filters as Sets

If you have one or more filters that you wish to use frequently, you may choose to save the filters as sets. Then, you may use them again on any worksheet by simply dragging them from the Sets area of the Data pane to the Filters shelf. Simply right-click (CONTROL-click on Mac) an existing filter on the Filters shelf and choose Create Set from the context menu.

The set will be created and placed in the Sets portion of the Data pane. You may replace the initial filter with the set by dragging the set to the Filters shelf directly on top of the original filter. Since the set will be saved with the workbook (as well as any custom data connections that are saved and reused), you may apply the same filter in any worksheet in the workbook by simply dragging the set to the Filters shelf.

Note   *Since sets are similar to filters, Tableau displays the results of filter actions (described in Chapter 5 for worksheets and in Chapter 8 for dashboards) as sets in the Data pane. Tableau Server user filters, discussed in Chapter 9, also appear as sets.*

Creating Binned Fields

Sometimes you'll encounter a requirement to break a numeric measure into static ranges of values. This new field, even though it's derived from a numeric measure, will behave as a dimension, creating different categories for each range of values. Tableau accomplishes this with binned fields. A *binned field* is a measure that is broken into "buckets," or bins, with each bin consisting of a range of values. For example, if your data source contains an Age measure, you may prefer to analyze data for people aged 0–10, 10–20, 20–30, 30–40, and so forth. Each of these age ranges would become a member of a new dimension, allowing you to analyze sales, website hits, or a similar measure for each of the age ranges.

Consider the following bar chart (this type of chart is often referred to as a *histogram*). This chart consists of a large number of dimension members, each consisting of a $50 range of profitability. The dimension members start at the minimum profit in the data source and end at the maximum profit in the data source, with $50 bins appearing in between. The measure being charted is the Sum of Number of Records, indicating the number of line items falling in each profit range. Notice the large concentration of line items near minimal loss or profit. Although there are a few extreme loss and profit line items on each end of the range, the largest concentration is at the little loss/little profit portion of the range. This is not at the center of the range, however, indicating that, overall, more line items are profitable than not profitable.

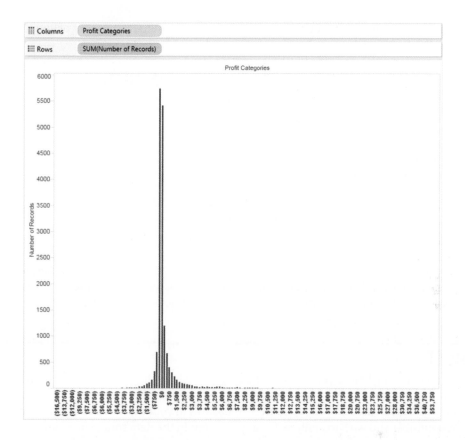

The key to this histogram is the $250 profit "buckets" or bins. Tableau's built-in bin capability makes this very simple. By just right-clicking the Profit measure and choosing Create | Bins from the context menu, a new dimension is created. In this case, the new dimension is given a meaningful name (by default, Tableau will give the dimension the same name as the measure, followed by "bin"), and the bin size is specified. Once created, the new bin field will appear in the Dimensions portion of the Data pane. As with any other dimension, it may be dragged to the desired location on the workspace. In this histogram example, a simple record count becomes the measure to count the number of line items in each profit bin.

Edit Bins [Profit]		
New field name:	Profit Categories	
Size of bins:	250 ▼	
Range of Values:		
Min:		Diff:
Max:		Load
		OK Cancel

Tip *Sometimes situations arise where you need to create bin measures as just described, but require bin sizes that are not evenly distributed. This necessitates creation of a calculated field (described next) to create bin measures according to your variable needs.*

Calculated Fields

It won't be too long before you encounter a situation where the data in your underlying data source or database won't fit your analysis needs exactly. For example, you may need to calculate the result of one or more numeric measures in your data source to determine a desired number you wish to analyze. Or, a dimension in the data source may not be organized precisely in the way you wish to use it.

For these types of situations, Tableau provides calculated fields. A *calculated field* is a custom calculation (often simply referred to as a formula) that can use combinations of existing dimensions and measures from the underlying data source, combined with built-in operators and functions, to create a custom result. The resulting calculated field can be placed on a shelf or card just like a standard dimension or measure.

Tableau 9 introduces an innovative new way to create calculated fields. Although a more traditional calculation editor continues to be available, a new ad hoc calculation capability has been introduced with version 9. Ad hoc calculations may be created quickly directly on shelves and cards. Although not required, they can be added to the Data pane for reuse in other worksheets.

 Video *Creating Calculated Fields*

Ad Hoc Calculations

Ad hoc calculations are quick, "on-the-fly" calculation formulas that may be created with a simple double-click. If a dimension or measure is already on a shelf or card, double-clicking it will place the field into edit mode. You may either replace the contents of the field with a new formula or add components to the existing field name in the formula.

For example, you may have already placed a Quantity measure on the Rows shelf, resulting in a bar chart illustrating sum of Quantity. You now decide that you prefer the bar to represent Total Cost, which is the existing Quantity measure multiplied by another measure, Unit Cost. Double-click the Quantity measure on the Rows shelf. The field will enter an edit mode.

:≡ Rows	SUM([Quantity])

Although there are several ways of creating the desired Total Cost formula, you may choose to backspace to remove the SUM function, as well as the parentheses surrounding the Quantity field, and type a simple multiplication formula. Notice that as you type, Tableau will attempt to auto-complete the formula for you by displaying existing dimensions, measures, parameters, or Tableau formula functions. When the formula element you wish to use (such as Unit Cost) appears in the list, use cursor keys to highlight it and press TAB or ENTER to select it, or click it with your mouse.

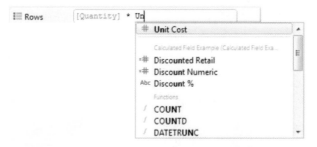

As you type, Tableau will check the *syntax* (correct spelling and organization) of your formula. If Tableau detects an error in the formula text, it will underline the error with a red squiggly. Hover your mouse over the suspect text to display a tooltip expanding on the error. When you're finished adding or editing formula text, press TAB or ENTER. If you want to see the results of the ad hoc calculation while still editing, press CTRL-ENTER (COMMAND-ENTER on a Mac) to display the results of the calculation on the chart but remain in edit mode. You may continue to modify existing formula text or add new text, and then press TAB or ENTER when you're finally ready to end editing and save your formula.

Tip *If you want to use another dimension or measure in your ad hoc calculation, you may also drag it from the Data pane into the ad hoc edit box instead of typing it or selecting it from the auto-completion list.*

You may also create a brand-new ad hoc calculation by double-clicking directly the shelf or card where you want calculation to appear. For example, you may have a bar chart analyzing sales by year of order. You desire to break the single-color bars into two stacked colors, breaking down sales between the first and second halves of the year. Because the formula that breaks dates into the first or second half will appear on Color on the Marks card, double-click at the bottom of the Marks card below any existing fields. Tableau will simply display an empty edit box.

Type a formula that will test the month of Order Date field for the first or second half of the year and return the appropriate "1st Half" or "2nd Half" text string.

```
IIF(Month([Order Date]) < 7,"1st Half","2nd Half")
```

Once the ad hoc calculation displays no errors, press ENTER to save it. Then, click to the left of the ad hoc calculation (which, by default, will now appear on Detail on the Marks card), and select Color.

Although ad hoc calculations are specifically designed for quick, temporary analysis, you may wish to save the calculation for use in other worksheets in the workbook, or perhaps in a saved data source (saving data sources is discussed in Chapter 3). To save an ad hoc calculation for later use, just drag it from its original shelf or card to the Data pane. Tableau will prompt you for the calculated field name. Supply a descriptive name for the calculated field and click OK. Tableau will add the new calculated field to the Data pane.

The Calculation Editor

For more involved calculated fields that include, for example, multiple If/Then/Else constructs, Case statements, and so forth, you'll need to use the more traditional calculation editor (which has been significantly streamlined in Tableau 9). There are several ways to create a calculated field using the calculation editor:

- In the Data pane, right-click an existing dimension or measure that you wish to use in a calculated field and choose Create | Calculated Field from the context menu. The calculation editor will appear with the selected field appearing in the formula.

- Click the drop-down arrow at the top of the Dimensions portion of the Data pane. Choose Create Calculated Field from the context menu. The calculation editor will appear with no fields pre-added.

- Choose Analysis | Create Calculated Field from the drop-down menu. The calculation editor will appear with no fields pre-added.

The calculation editor, illustrated in Figure 6-1, has changed dramatically in Tableau 9 compared with previous versions. It is significantly smaller and simpler, permitting it to be displayed on top of the Tableau workspace. This allows you to try variations on calculated

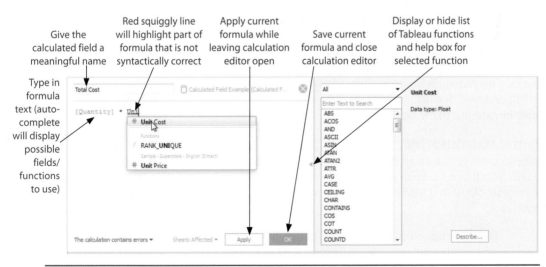

Figure 6-1   The calculation editor

field logic and just click the Apply button, seeing the result appear immediately in the workspace. You may also hide or display the Functions/Help portion of the calculation editor at will with the small arrow.

Tip *You may find that the default size of text in the calculation editor is too small for comfort. You may resize text by holding down the CTRL key (COMMAND key on Mac) and using the scroll wheel on your mouse. Note that the new size will only persist until you close the calculation editor. The next time you display it, text will appear at the default size.*

As with ad hoc calculations, discussed earlier in this section, you may type formula text directly into the calculation editor. As you type, Tableau will attempt to auto-complete the formula for you by displaying existing dimensions, measures, parameters, or Tableau formula functions as you type. When the formula element you wish to use appears in the list, use cursor keys to highlight it and press TAB or ENTER to select it, or click it with your mouse. You may also drag a desired dimension, measure, or parameter from the Data pane directly into the calculation editor where you wish the field to appear.

And, as with ad hoc calculations, Tableau will check formula syntax as you type. If Tableau detects an error in the formula text, it will underline the error with a red squiggly and display a red error indicator at the bottom of the calculation editor. Hover your mouse over the suspect text to display a tooltip expanding on the error. You may also click the small drop-down arrow on the error indicator at the bottom of the calculation editor.

Whereas the calculation editor in previous Tableau versions included lists of fields, parameters, and Tableau formula functions, the new editor will only display functions, and will only display them if you click the small gray arrow to the right of the formula text (remember that you may drag dimensions and measures right into the formula from the Data pane). When you display functions, you may double-click a function to add it to the formula at the current cursor location. You may also get a "quick view" of function syntax by selecting a function from the list. Tableau will display concise background on the function to the right of the editor.

Once you have created your formula, you may click Apply to apply the changes and see the results immediately on the underlying Tableau workspace. This will only work provided the calculated field is in use in the underlying worksheet. Otherwise, click OK to save the calculated field. It will appear in the Data pane, where it may be dragged and dropped to a shelf or card just like a standard database field.

Parts of a Calculated Field

Whether you create an ad hoc calculation or created a calculated field with the calculation editor, you'll need to keep general Tableau formula syntax in mind. Generally speaking, a Tableau calculated field consists of combinations of three items: fields, operators, and functions:

- *Fields* are dimensions, measures, parameters, sets, and other calculated fields that may be dragged into a formula from the Data pane.

- *Operators* include arithmetical operators, such as addition, subtraction, multiplication, and division. Logical operators are also available, such as equals, less than, greater than, and not equal to. These must be typed in directly and cannot be added from the Data pane or chosen from a list in the calculation editor.

- *Functions* provide various capabilities for manipulating and converting data. For example, there are functions to convert string values to all uppercase or all lowercase characters, or to strip off characters from the beginning, end, or middle of a string. Data-type conversion functions exist to, for example, convert numbers to strings or strings to dates. Arithmetic functions exist to return cosine, absolute value, and other standard mathematic results. Aggregating data is possible with functions such as SUM, AVG, and COUNT. And manipulating date or date/time values is possible with functions to extract just the month, day, or year from a date and so forth. Functions are different from operators in that they typically require one or more *arguments*— data source fields, other calculated fields, or specific values that are supplied to determine what the function will use to perform its calculation or manipulation.

There are some general tips and techniques you'll want to keep in mind as you create calculated fields:

- Give the calculated field a meaningful name. The default "Calculation1" won't be helpful when you are evaluating fields in the Data pane to add to your chart.

- If you add fields from the Data pane, or if you let auto-complete add a fieldname, Tableau will always surround them with square brackets. If you type fieldnames in manually, you may leave the square brackets off, provided the fieldname doesn't contain any spaces. If the fieldname does contain spaces, you'll receive a syntax error if you fail to surround the fieldname with square brackets. If the fieldname itself includes square brackets, type two additional matching square brackets before or after the fieldname's bracket to ensure proper syntax.

- Once you've saved a calculated field, it will appear in the Data pane with a small equal sign to the left of the data-type icon. To edit the calculated field, right-click the field in the Data pane and choose Edit from the context menu.

Types of Calculated Fields

You may notice that there's no place in an ad hoc calculation or in the calculation editor to specify the data type of the resulting calculated field. However, just like a database field, a calculated field will take on a specific data type that will be indicated by the small icon to the left of the field in the Data pane. And the resulting data type, along with specific types of functions used in the formula, will determine whether the calculated field is added to the Dimensions or Measures portion of the Data pane.

Numeric Calculations

If your data source contains various numeric measures that you wish to use in a calculated field, add them to the Formula box. Use standard numeric operators, such as * (multiplication), / (division), + (addition), and – (subtraction). For example, you could create a calculated field called Total Cost that multiplies Quantity by Unit Cost.

```
[Quantity] * [Unit Cost]
```

Because this calculated field includes two existing numbers and a numeric operator, the result of the calculated field will be numeric. As such, the calculated field will be placed in the Measures box of the Data pane.

If you wish to use a percentage value in the data source to mark up the Total Cost formula, you may use this:

```
[Total Cost] + [Total Cost] * [Markup %]
```

Two items are of note here. First, a previously created calculated field can be used in another calculated field. Second, the order in which the operations are performed will affect the final result. For this calculated field to return the correct result, multiplication must be done first, which is the second operator in the formula. The result is still correct, however, because the standard *order of precedence* you may remember from math class applies. Multiplication will occur before addition, moving from left to right, in a formula. If you want to change the order of precedence, parentheses may be added where needed.

String Manipulation

Often, you may find a need to modify or expand on the way dimension data is presented. For example, you may have string data that is provided in a separate field that needs to be combined in a single field (often referred to as *concatenation*). Or, you may exhibit an opposite situation, where string data residing in a single field needs to be split apart (or *parsed*).

Concatenation is accomplished by using a plus sign to "add" strings together. String fields, as well as string *literals* (values surrounded by apostrophes or quotation marks), may be concatenated into one combined string. For example, if a customer contact's name is contained in three database fields (first name, last name, and middle initial), you may create one combined name with a calculated field:

```
[Customer First Name] + " " + [Customer Middle Initial] + ". " + [Customer Last Name]
```

The first name field from the database will be followed by a space, followed by the middle initial, followed by a period and space, followed by the last name. Because all portions of this calculated field are strings, the result of the calculated field will be a string. As such, it will be placed in the Dimensions portion of the Data pane.

Caution *Note that a plus sign can be used both for addition with numeric fields and concatenation with string fields. If your calculated field mixes both strings and numbers in the same formula, Tableau won't know whether to add or concatenate. A syntax error will result. In this instance, you'll need to either convert the string to a number (with FLOAT or INT functions) for addition, or convert the number to a string (with the STR function) for concatenation.*

One situation that often confounds analysts when dealing with database systems is inconsistent case within string data. Depending on the data entry application that populates your data source, you may find string data appearing in all caps, in all lowercase, or in a (potentially inconsistent) mixed case. General best practices dictate that you display string data in a case that is easy for your audience to read. For example, if the customer names described in the previous example are entered in the database in inconsistent case, you may want to add functions to a calculated field to convert them to the desired case:

```
UPPER([Customer First Name])
```

This formula text will convert all occurrences of the Customer First Name database field to uppercase, whereas the following will convert all characters of the last name to lowercase:

```
LOWER([Customer Last Name])
```

However, you may wish to use mixed case (sometimes referred to as *proper case*) for inconsistent database fields. This presents more of a challenge, as Tableau doesn't include a built-in function to convert string data to proper case. Performing this in Tableau requires more complex parsing (picking apart) of a string in combination with UPPER and LOWER functions.

To capitalize the first letter of an inconsistent string and display the remainder of the string in lowercase requires both determining the number of characters in the string (using the LEN function) and extracting certain characters from the left (using the LEFT function), right (using the RIGHT function), or middle (using the MID function) of the string. Here's an example of a calculated field named First Name Proper Case:

```
UPPER(LEFT([Customer First Name],1)) +
LOWER(RIGHT([Customer First Name], LEN([Customer First Name])-1))
```

You may find undesirable results if any database field you add to your calculated field contains a *null* (an empty value in the data source, where no data has been added for a particular field in the underlying data source). Depending on the underlying data source, a calculated field that contains any underlying data field that contains a null may itself return a null. For example, if any records in the database don't contain a middle initial for a customer, the entire value returned by the Combined Name calculated field for that customer will return a null, even though the first and last names contain values.

Tableau features built-in functions (ISNULL and IFNULL) to detect null values and change your calculated field accordingly. Once calculated fields to create proper case versions of a customer first name and customer last name field have been created, another calculated field can test for a potential null value for middle initial and return just first and last names in this instance. Here's the formula text for a calculated field named Customer Full Name (IF/THEN/ELSE/END logic is covered later in the chapter under "Logic Constructs"):

```
IF ISNULL([Customer Middle Initial]) THEN
    [Customer Last Name ProperCase] + ", " + [Customer First Name ProperCase]
ELSE
    [Customer Last Name ProperCase] + ", " +
    [Customer First Name ProperCase] + " " +
    UPPER([Customer Middle Initial]) + "."
END
```

Date Calculations

Tableau provides a great deal of analytical power when using date or date/time fields from the underlying data source. Automatic date hierarchy drill-down (year to quarter to month, and so forth), built-in date level flexibility, and discrete versus continuous date treatment are all benefits of using date or date/time fields.

It's possible, however, that the underlying data source contains date or date/time data that's not presented in a true date or date/time data type. In particular, older database systems (perhaps converted from mainframes) or proprietary vendor-based systems may present dates in a number or string field. In some cases, these are presented in "yyyymmdd" format, which facilitates proper date sorting, or in some form of numeric value, whereby a number indicates the number of days since a particular "start" date, such as a Julian date. Until these types of dates are converted to actual date or date/time data types, none of Tableau's rich date capabilities will be available.

Depending on the original data type and layout of these fields, different approaches are required to convert them to date or date/time fields. For example, if an underlying data source contains a numeric field with a date in "yyyymmdd" numeric format, this calculated field will convert it to an actual date field:

```
DATEPARSE("yyyyMMdd",STR([Date]))
```

In this example, the DATEPARSE function uses the first "format" argument to define which parts of the second string argument are used to represent the month ("MM"), day ("dd"), and year ("yyyy"). Because the underlying data source presents the date as a number, the STR function is used to convert it to a string value, which is required for DATEPARSE.

Another common use of date-oriented calculated fields is determining the difference between two dates (in days, weeks, months, or otherwise), as well as adding or subtracting a number of periods (days, weeks, and so forth) to an existing date. If, for example, a shipping goal exists to ship a product within one week of its order date, the following calculated field will return the expected ship date:

```
DATE(DATEADD('week',1,[Purchase Date]))
```

The DATEADD function accepts three arguments: a "period" value, expressed as a string literal, indicating what type of date interval to add to the existing date; the number of intervals to add, expressed as a positive or negative number; and the existing date field/ date calculated field to add the intervals to. Because the DATEADD function returns a date/ time data type, the DATE function is used to strip the time value away from DATEADD and return just the date portion of the field.

Creating Custom Dates Without Calculated Fields

When you initially drag a date field to a shelf, Tableau will display the date at the year level. If you wish to change the date level to quarter, month, or some other level in addition to determining whether the date appears as a discrete or continuous value, you may right-click the date field indicator and make choices from the context menu. If you prefer to always show a particular date at a particular date level, you may consider creating a calculated field. You would then use the DATETRUNC or DATEPART functions to specify the date level to use.

Tip *Any date or date/time field—whether a calculated field or database field— may be immediately set to a specified date level when dropping it onto the workspace. Just right-click and drag (OPTION-drag on Mac) the field to a shelf. You'll immediately see a Drop Field dialog box prompting for the date level you wish to use.*

(continued)

However, Tableau permits you to create a duplicate date field at a desired date level right in the Data pane without needing to create a calculated field. Just right-click the desired date or date/time field in the Data pane and choose Transform | Create Custom Date from the context menu. Give the new custom date a meaningful name, and choose the date level you wish to use from the drop-down list. Finally, click the Date Part radio button to assign the custom date a discrete designation (individual values for only actual occurrences of dates), or click the Date Value radio button to assign the custom date a continuous designation (a range of date values from the first date to the last date). The new custom date will now appear directly in the Data pane where it may be dragged to the workspace.

Logic Constructs

More involved calculated field logic may require you to perform one or more tests on various database values or values returned by other calculated fields. These tests will typically use a logical comparison operator, such as an equal sign, less-than sign, greater-than sign, and so forth. Based on the results of these tests, the calculated field will return a particular result.

The most common type of logical test capability comes in the form of If-Then-Else logic, typically found in most standard software programs. Tableau calculated fields require, at a minimum, use of IF, THEN, and END keywords. ELSE and ELSEIF keywords are only required for multicondition tests. Consider a requirement to create categories based on a numeric measure (another way to do this is discussed earlier in this chapter, in the section "Creating Binned Fields"). A Markup % measure contains percent markup numbers. However, you wish to categorize orders into High, Medium, and Low values, with these three values appearing in a dimension created by a calculated field. This example of IF/THEN/ELSEIF/ELSE/END logic will meet the requirement:

```
If [Markup %] >= .35 Then
    "High"
ElseIf [Markup %] >= .20 Then
    "Medium"
Else
    "Low"
End
```

Tip *You may notice that this formula displays mixed-case text for the IF/THEN/ELSEIF/ ELSE/END keywords, as well as line breaks and tabs between parts of the formula. This is perfectly acceptable. The Tableau formula language is not case sensitive (although string literals within quotation marks or apostrophes, as well as fields from the Data pane, are case sensitive). And pressing* ENTER *to break your formula up into multiple lines, as well as pressing* TAB *to indent parts of the formula, will not affect the outcome of the formula and may make the formula easier to read.*

A modified form of test logic uses the CASE/WHEN/THEN/END construct (the ELSE keyword is only required if a "catch-all" result is desired). Similar to IF/THEN/END logic, CASE logic tests a single field or expression and returns different results for each condition. In some cases, IF/THEN/ELSEIF/END will be required if multiple tests are needed. However, for a single test with many results, CASE logic may be easier to read and modify.

In this example, a combined Product Type-Part Number database field is being tested to determine the type of product the combined field refers to. Using the new Tableau 9 SPLIT function, the calculated field will evaluate the product-type portion of the combined field (which is separated from the part number by a dash) and return one of three descriptive words indicating the type of product. If an unanticipated product-type value is encountered, the calculated field will return "Unknown."

```
CASE SPLIT([Product Type-SKU],"-",1)
    WHEN "SFT" THEN "Software"
    WHEN "HD" THEN "Hardware"
    WHEN "ACC" THEN "Accessory"
    ELSE "Unknown"
END
```

Because the number of characters indicating the product type is variable (in some cases, two characters; in other cases, three), the SPLIT function is used to extract the portion of the source string before the hyphen, which separates the product type from the part number. CASE logic is then used to assign a value to each abbreviated product type. If an unanticipated product type is encountered, the optional ELSE keyword will return the word "Unknown." If ELSE was not used and an unanticipated product type was encountered, the calculated field would return a NULL value.

Aggregation Within Calculated Fields

Tableau, by its nature, makes heavy use of data aggregation. From the simplest of basic charts to more complex visualization requirements, Tableau is typically dealing with "rolled up" rows from the data source that include aggregated numeric measures for each occurrence of a dimension member (by default, using a SUM aggregation). Because of this, you may need to consider aggregation when creating calculated fields in Tableau more than you would in other data analysis products (calculating percentages is a particularly significant example).

(continued)

Consider a simple requirement to determine profitability. In an individual data record, a Profit measure will contain a positive value if the product was sold for more than it cost. If the product was sold at a loss, the Profit measure will contain a negative value. Thus, the following IF/THEN/ELSE calculated field will return a "Yes" or "No" value, depending on whether the record indicates a profit or loss:

```
If [Profit] > 0 Then
     "Yes"
Else
     "No"
End
```

If this calculated field is then placed on Color on the Marks card to indicate profitability of a series of categories, the following will result.

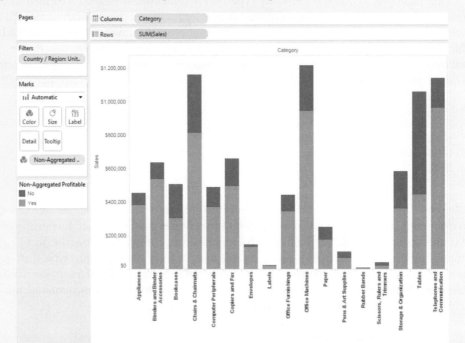

In this instance, the calculated field is evaluated at the underlying data source row level, with each individual row returning a "Yes" or "No" value. Tableau then aggregates the Yes and No values itself, breaking down each bar color based on the count of Yes and No values. The result is a visualization of the portion of each product category that is profitable or not.

But what if you want to analyze the entire category to determine if the category, in its entirety, is profitable or not? Consider the following slight change to the calculated field:

```
If SUM([Profit]) > 0 Then
     "Yes"
Else
     "No"
End
```

Here, the calculated field is making use of a built-in Tableau aggregation function. In this case, the calculated field itself is evaluating the rolled-up aggregate profit value, determining whether the SUM of profit is positive or negative. When this is placed on Color on the Marks card, a different chart results.

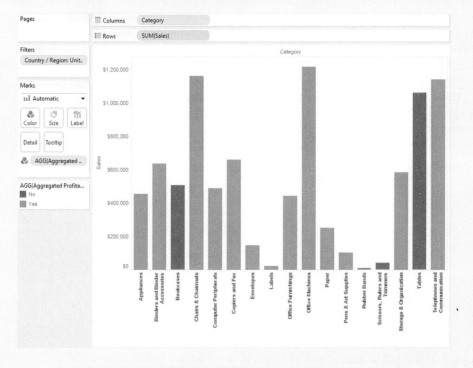

Tip   *If you perform aggregation within a calculated field (by using SUM, MAX, or other aggregation functions), Tableau will always place the calculated field in the Measures portion of the Data pane, even if the calculated field returns a non-numeric result. Also, when placed on a shelf, the calculated field will show an AGG aggregation type. This indicates that the calculated field itself is performing internal aggregation and that Tableau will not attempt to aggregate the field again using a SUM.*

Level of Detail Expressions

One of the most anticipated (and perhaps most misunderstood) features of Tableau 9 is level of detail expressions (sometimes abbreviated as LOD expressions). As with certain chart types, such as Box Plot and Pareto Chart (both covered in Chapter 4), you may not use LOD expressions often. But when you need them, you REALLY need them.

Video *Level of Detail Expressions*

A *level of detail expression* is a calculated field construct that lets you calculate a value using an aggregation that is *different* than the aggregation provided by the dimensions currently in use on a chart. Because Tableau's basic architecture depends heavily on aggregated values being supplied from the underlying data source, LOD expressions allow greater flexibility to analyze aggregated results *within* other aggregated results.

Consider the chart illustrated in Figure 6-2. Here, average sales are being analyzed by category. In this scenario, Tableau is rolling up data in the worksheet to category. The average sales for each category is displayed. Averages are being calculated by the data source for each category and sent to Tableau, which simply displays them as bars.

What if you want to compare these category averages to the overall average for all categories? Traditionally, you might consider a reference line (covered later in this chapter). Figure 6-2 illustrates a reference line set to display the overall average for the

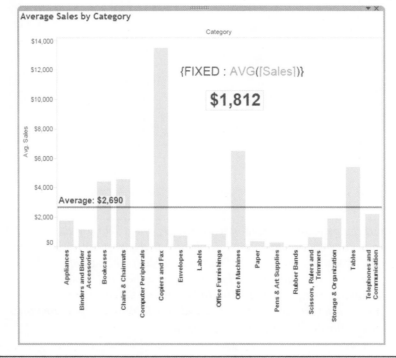

Figure 6-2   What is the overall average?

chart, illustrated as $2,690. But if you look closely at the Reference Line dialog box, you'll notice that the reference line is actually calculating the *average* of the average of Sales.

If you choose to remove this category from the chart, Tableau submits a new data source query aggregating to the overall data source average, not the average by category. Notice the resulting single bar, representing overall average sales. The reference line now matches the bar exactly and indicates an average of $1,812.

Although you may not initially even know this situation exists, it raises an interesting question: What is the actual average sales: $2,690 or $1,812? If the desire is to reference average sales by average of category averages, then the reference line option that you've had in the past is acceptable. However, if the true desire is to compare average sales by category to the *overall* average sales within the data source, regardless of category, you've been limited in your ability prior to LOD expressions. Look back at Figure 6-1. Notice that even with category being used as the chart's aggregation level, the overall average of $1,812 has been derived with the following LOD expression:

```
{FIXED : AVG([Sales])}
```

which is also equivalent to just

```
{AVG([Sales])}
```

Both of these LOD expression examples illustrate the basic syntax requirement of all LOD expressions: curly braces. Both of these variants start and end with curly braces, but one includes a FIXED scope keyword, indicating that the LOD expression will return an aggregated value, regardless of other dimensions used in the current worksheet. And this particular type of LOD expression makes no reference to a dimension, referencing instead only a single aggregated field. This is referred to as a *table-scoped* LOD expression. It returns an overall average value calculated at the data source level, regardless of any and all other dimensions that may be in use on the chart. Hence, no matter what other dimensions may be changing chart aggregation, you can always use this LOD expression to derive overall average, perhaps to compare to individual dimension averages.

```
IF AVG([Sales]) > AVG({FIXED : AVG([Sales])}) THEN
    "Above Overall Average"
ELSE
    "Below Overall Average"
END
```

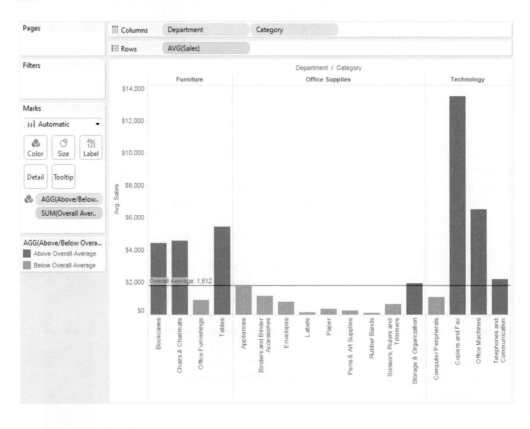

Tip *Although it may initially seem confusing, it's valuable to understand that even though LOD expressions always include an aggregation function, as in {FIXED : AVG([Sales])}, Tableau considers them to be underlying row-level values, just like a traditional measure. If you drag a calculated field using a single LOD expression to a shelf, Tableau will still aggregate the calculation as it does a standard measure. And if you use an LOD expression alongside other dimensions or measures in a calculated field, the same "if you aggregate one part of a calculation, you must aggregate them all" rule applies.*

LOD Expression Scope Keywords

As illustrated previously in the chapter, LOD expressions can include a scope keyword to specify the "aggregation granularity" of the expression. These keywords determine how LOD expressions relate to other dimensions used in the chart. In addition, unless you choose to derive an overall data source aggregation with a table-scoped LOD expression (such as the overall average illustrated earlier in the section), you'll need to supply one or more dimensions to an LOD expression after the scope keyword to determine the dimension or dimensions to roll up to.

Fixed

FIXED LOD expressions aggregate to the specified dimension or dimensions (you may supply more than on dimension, separated with commas), *regardless of any other dimensions in use on the chart.* For example,

```
{FIXED [Customer Name] : YEAR(MIN([Order Date]))}
```

will calculate the year of the first (minimum) order date for each customer name, whether or not customer name is being used on the chart. Depending on their structure, FIXED LOD expressions may be used as dimensions, as is the case with this example. Using this calculated field, the first year a customer made a purchase may be used to color a bar chart, regardless of what dimensions are used in that chart. Here, we see that the vast majority of customers made their first purchase in 2011 across all customer segments.

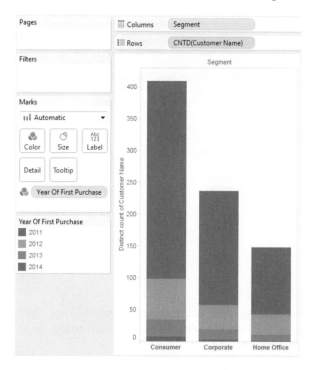

Include

INCLUDE LOD expressions aggregate to a lower level of detail *within* the dimension or dimensions you use on the chart. So even though the lower-level dimension used in the LOD expression doesn't appear on the chart, Tableau will use it to "sub-aggregate" within the existing dimensions. For example:

```
{INCLUDE [Product Name] : MAX([Quantity])}
```

will calculate the highest quantity per product name within other dimensions used on the chart. Because Tableau still treats INCLUDE LOD expressions as disaggregated measures, you may choose how to roll up the resulting calculated field, as you would any traditional measure. In this example, total quantity is used as the chart measure, with bars sorted high to low. The maximum of the LOD expression, which retains the highest quantity within the sub-category, is placed on Color on the Marks card. This analyzes correlation between total quantity by sub-category and the highest order quantity by product within the sub-category. The chart shows that there is general correlation, in that higher-quantity sub-categories consist of orders of 14 of a particular product within the sub-category. Whereas one of the bottom five sub-categories still includes a 14 quantity product, others fall to as low as 9 within the sub-category.

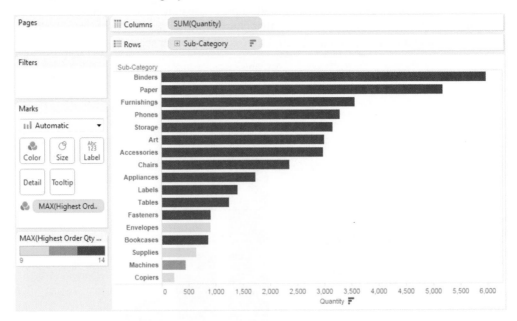

Exclude

EXCLUDE LOD expressions, as their name suggests, remove a specified dimension from a calculation, aggregating to dimensions in use on the chart, *except* the specified dimension or dimensions. For example:

```
{EXCLUDE [Category] : AVG([Sales])}
```

will calculate average sales by any dimension or dimensions currently in use on the chart, excluding category before the average is calculated. So in the first row of this example, the result will be average sales for each year, as the nested category dimension is being excluded from the calculation. Therefore:

```
AVG([Sales]) - AVG({EXCLUDE [Category] : AVG([Sales])})
```

will calculate the difference between the individual category/year average sales and overall average sales for the year. Although it may seem like a fine point, it's important to distinguish this LOD example from a WINDOW_AVG table calculation function (discussed in the next section of the chapter) that could be used to accomplish much the same thing. As discussed at the beginning of this section, the EXCLUDE LOD expression used here will return the average sales for the year, not the average of averages, which is what is returned by a table calculation function.

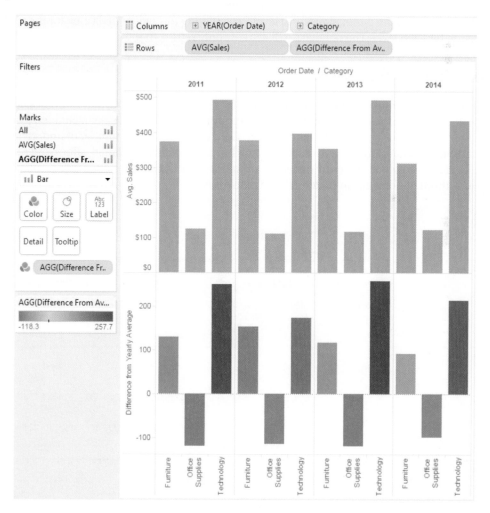

Caution *Because LOD expressions make use of data source sub-queries, they may negatively affect data source performance. For the same reason, a small number of data sources don't support LOD expressions.*

Table Calculations

By design, Tableau takes maximum benefit of your underlying data source or database and requests that *it* perform aggregation, only returning summarized rows to your visualization (the exception to this rule comes into play if you uncheck Aggregate Measures from the Analysis drop-down menu). And with level of detail expressions, even more data source aggregation flexibility is afforded you. For example, even if your underlying database contains many (perhaps billions) of underlying rows and you build a visualization that simply displays one measure for a dimension that exposes only 10 members, the database itself will "roll up" the dimensions to 10 levels, calculating the aggregated value for the measure for each level. The database will actually only return 10 rows to Tableau.

▶ **Video** *Using Table Calculations*

Consider the simple crosstab illustrated in Figure 6-3, which only displays sum of sales by year and region. Notice that both row and column grand totals have been enabled from the Analysis | Totals drop-down menu. In this case, regardless of the number of underlying records in the data source, the data source itself has calculated all summed values and only returned 25 aggregated values to Tableau—all Tableau has done is formatted and displayed them without performing any calculations whatsoever.

Region	2011	2012	2013	2014	Grand Total
Central	$103,838	$102,874	$147,429	$147,098	$501,240
East	$128,680	$156,332	$180,529	$213,239	$678,781
South	$103,846	$71,360	$93,539	$122,977	$391,722
West	$147,883	$139,966	$186,976	$250,633	$725,458
Grand Total	$484,247	$470,533	$608,474	$733,947	$2,297,201

Figure 6-3   Simple crosstab

But what if you want to perform some other kind of analysis on this data instead of, or in addition to, just looking at total sales by year and region? Perhaps, for example, you would like to analyze how much sales has changed from year to year, either in dollars or percent. Or, maybe you would prefer to visualize these numbers as a running total that gets larger and larger as it "runs" across the crosstab by year or down the crosstab by region. In these types of cases, an additional calculation will need to be done once the aggregated values have already been returned by the database.

As a general rule, standard industry databases don't have the capability to carry out these "secondary" calculations, performing multiple "passes" over the data to calculate a secondary result based on the values from a primary result. Well, Tableau provides the ability to perform these additional calculation passes by way of *table calculations,* additional calculations that Tableau performs *after* aggregated values have been returned from the underlying data source.

To create a table calculation, you must first design a visualization using standard dimensions and measures, as discussed previously in this book. Once a measure has been added to the workspace and assigned an aggregation type (Sum, by default), you may then create a table calculation. There are several ways of creating table calculations:

- Select one of the sub-menu options from the Analysis | Percentage Of drop-down menu.

- Right-click (CONTROL-click on Mac) the measure on the workspace and choose one of the sub-menu options from the Quick Table Calculation context menu item.

- Right-click (CONTROL-click on Mac) the measure on the workspace, choose Add Table Calculation from the context menu, and complete the resulting dialog box.

Revisiting the "percent change from year to year" requirement discussed earlier, Figure 6-4 shows the crosstab originally displayed in Figure 6-3 after Percentage Of | Table has been selected from the Analysis drop-down menu.

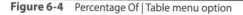

Figure 6-4   Percentage Of | Table menu option

One change is blatantly obvious. Rather than displaying dollar values indicating aggregated sales for each combination of year and region, the crosstab now displays percentages, with each individual year/region value showing as a percentage of overall sales. Row and column dollar totals have also been replaced with percentages of the overall total they are responsible for. And the "grand-grand total" at the lower right indicates that it is, in fact, 100 percent of the total amount. What may not be so obvious is the change to the SUM(Sales) field indicator on the Marks card. Looking closely, you'll notice that a small delta (triangle) icon now appears on the field indicator. This confirms that this measure has been converted to a table calculation.

SUM(Sales)   Δ

If you undo the previous Percentage Of option (or choose Analysis | Percentage Of | None) to return the measure to its original aggregation and then right-click the measure and choose Quick Table Calculation | Percent Of Total from the context menu, you'll see a slightly different result, as illustrated in Figure 6-5. Here, the percentages are still displayed, but are calculated across each region row rather than the entire crosstab.

One of the immediate questions you may ask after creating a table calculation is: How do I see the original measure, as well as the table calculation, to help me analyze further? Especially when you first start working with table calculations, you'll probably want to see the original measure along with the table calculation to begin to understand how table calculations behave. This is a fairly simple process. Just re-add the original measure to the visualization again. In the case of a crosstab, you may drag the original measure to Text on the Marks card, or just double-click the original measure to invoke Measure Names and Measure Values on the crosstab. The original measure won't display the delta icon, but the table calculation will.

			Order Date			
Region		2011	2012	2013	2014	Grand Total
Central	Sales	$103,838	$102,874	$147,429	$147,098	$501,240
	% of Total Sales alo...	20.72%	20.52%	29.41%	29.35%	100.00%
East	Sales	$128,680	$156,332	$180,529	$213,239	$678,781
	% of Total Sales alo...	18.96%	23.03%	26.60%	31.42%	100.00%
South	Sales	$103,846	$71,360	$93,539	$122,977	$391,722
	% of Total Sales alo...	26.51%	18.22%	23.88%	31.39%	100.00%
West	Sales	$147,883	$139,966	$186,976	$250,633	$725,458
	% of Total Sales alo...	20.38%	19.29%	25.77%	34.55%	100.00%
Grand Total	Sales	$484,247	$470,533	$608,474	$733,947	$2,297,201
	% of Total Sales alo...	21.08%	20.48%	26.49%	31.95%	100.00%

Pages		III Columns	⊞ YEAR(Order Date)		
		≡ Rows	Region		

Region	2011	2012	Order Date 2013	2014	Grand Total
Central	20.72%	20.52%	29.41%	29.35%	100.00%
East	18.96%	23.03%	26.60%	31.42%	100.00%
South	26.51%	18.22%	23.88%	31.39%	100.00%
West	20.38%	19.29%	25.77%	34.55%	100.00%
Grand Total	21.08%	20.48%	26.49%	31.95%	100.00%

Filters

Marks

Abc Automatic ▼

Color   Size   Text

Detail   Tooltip

Abc123 SUM(Sales) Δ

Figure 6-5   Quick table calculation – percent of total

Caution   *Using the Percentage Of drop-down menu option prohibits the original measure from being added to the visualization alongside the table calculation. If you wish to display both the original measure and a percentage table calculation, use right-click menu options to create the table calculation instead of the drop-down menus.*

Even though the table calculation illustrated in both Figures 6-4 and 6-5 was created with a percent of total option, you'll notice a difference. When using the pull-down menu Percentage Of | Table option, the table calculation evaluated for the entire table—each combination of year and region was calculated as a percent of the overall total. However, when the Percentage Of Total quick table calculation was used, each region row was calculated individually, with the total for each region row indicating 100 percent and the yearly values for each region contributing to the region total, rather than the overall total for the entire crosstab. You may wish to modify the second table calculation to behave like the first—calculating each year/region combination as a percentage of the overall total. Or, perhaps you prefer to have the percentages calculated down the yearly columns with each region total contributing to a 100 percent yearly total.

What determines the end result is a table calculation's direction and scope. A table calculation's *direction* refers to the order in which individual table "cells" are calculated—left to right (referred to as *across*), top to bottom (referred to as *down*), left to right and then top to bottom (referred to as *across then down*), or top to bottom and then left to right (referred to as *down then across*). A table calculation's *scope* determines when the table calculation will reset to a beginning value.

Sometimes, it's difficult to separate the two properties. For example, the direction used in the table calculation illustrated in Figure 6-3 is "across then down." The scope used is "table," as the percentage never resets within the entire table. Conversely, the direction used in the table calculation illustrated in Figure 6-4 is simply "across," as the percentage is always reset before any "down" calculation takes place. And the scope used is "table (across)," indicating that the table calculation value will be reset when it reaches the end of a row.

Note *Tableau table calculation documentation also refers to the terms "addressing" and "partitioning." Addressing can be considered similar to direction, whereas partitioning can be considered similar to scope.*

Direction and scope choices are set automatically for quick table calculations and for Percentage Of pull-down menu choices. However, you may edit direction and scope after a quick table calculation has been created by right-clicking (CONTROL-clicking on Mac) the table calculation field indicator (it will display a delta icon) and choosing either the Compute Using or Edit Table Calculation context menu option. If you wish to customize direction and scope options when initially creating a table calculation, you may right-click the desired measure and choose Add Table Calculation from the context menu. The Table Calculation dialog box will provide a choice of calculation type (Running Sum, Percent Of Total, Moving Calculation, and so forth), as well as direction and scope options in the Running Along drop-down list. You can even select "Advanced" from the Running Along drop-down list to display another dialog box providing precise options for direction and scope options.

Table Calculation [% of Total Sales]   ⊠

Calculation Type: Percent of Total   ▼

Calculation Definition

Summarize the values from: *Advanced...*   ▼

At the level: ▼

Advanced   ✖

Partitioning: Addressing:

Region   [>   ]
Year of Order Date
                                    [<   ]

                                    [Up   ]

                                    [Down   ]

Sort

◉ Automatic

○ Field:

[Category   ▼] [Count   ▼] ◉ Ascending   ○ Descending

                                              [OK]   [Cancel]

Consider another crosstab that analyzes quantity by year and quarter on columns and category and region on rows. Grand totals are shown to help evaluate table calculation behavior.

					Order Date					
			2013				2014			Grand
Category	Region	Q1	Q2	Q3	Q4	Q1	Q2	Q3	Q4	Total
Furniture	Central	79	105	154	218	91	107	116	187	1,057
	East	116	118	131	227	56	133	209	299	1,289
	South	68	77	82	122	20	130	65	162	726
	West	63	154	193	286	104	158	238	362	1,558
Office Supplies	Central	129	293	451	465	324	410	518	687	3,277
	East	223	496	479	587	230	387	604	768	3,774
	South	152	242	309	284	152	292	290	469	2,190
	West	152	385	512	763	458	501	703	907	4,381
Grand Total		982	1,870	2,311	2,952	1,435	2,118	2,743	3,841	18,252

Now look at various direction and scope behavior when a running sum table calculation is added:

- **Table (Across)** Notice that the value increments across each row, with the last value in the row equaling the row total. The table calculation resets at the beginning of each row.

		Order Date								Grand
		2013				2014				
Category	Region	Q1	Q2	Q3	Q4	Q1	Q2	Q3	Q4	Total
Furniture	Central	79	184	338	556	647	754	870	1,057	1,057
	East	116	234	365	592	648	781	990	1,289	1,289
	South	68	145	227	349	369	499	564	726	726
	West	63	217	410	696	800	958	1,196	1,558	1,558
Office Supplies	Central	129	422	873	1,338	1,662	2,072	2,590	3,277	3,277
	East	223	719	1,198	1,785	2,015	2,402	3,006	3,774	3,774
	South	152	394	703	987	1,139	1,431	1,721	2,190	2,190
	West	152	537	1,049	1,812	2,270	2,771	3,474	4,381	4,381
Grand Total		982	2,852	5,163	8,115	9,550	11,668	14,411	18,252	18,252

- **Table (Down)** Notice that the value increments down each column, with the last value in the column equaling the column total. The table calculation resets at the beginning of each column.

		Order Date								Grand
		2013				2014				
Category	Region	Q1	Q2	Q3	Q4	Q1	Q2	Q3	Q4	Total
Furniture	Central	79	105	154	218	91	107	116	187	1,057
	East	195	223	285	445	147	240	325	486	2,346
	South	263	300	367	567	167	370	390	648	3,072
	West	326	454	560	853	271	528	628	1,010	4,630
Office Supplies	Central	455	747	1,011	1,318	595	938	1,146	1,697	7,907
	East	678	1,243	1,490	1,905	825	1,325	1,750	2,465	11,681
	South	830	1,485	1,799	2,189	977	1,617	2,040	2,934	13,871
	West	982	1,870	2,311	2,952	1,435	2,118	2,743	3,841	18,252
Grand Total		982	1,870	2,311	2,952	1,435	2,118	2,743	3,841	18,252

- **Table (Across then Down)**   Notice that the value increments across each row, with the last value in the row equaling the accumulated value as of that row. The table calculation then continues to increment starting at the next row. The value is never reset and accumulates all the way across, then down, until reaching the overall grand total at the lower right.

			Order Date							
		2013				2014				Grand
Category	Region	Q1	Q2	Q3	Q4	Q1	Q2	Q3	Q4	Total
Furniture	Central	79	184	338	556	647	754	870	1,057	1,057
	East	1,173	1,291	1,422	1,649	1,705	1,838	2,047	2,346	2,346
	South	2,414	2,491	2,573	2,695	2,715	2,845	2,910	3,072	3,072
	West	3,135	3,289	3,482	3,768	3,872	4,030	4,268	4,630	4,630
Office Supplies	Central	4,759	5,052	5,503	5,968	6,292	6,702	7,220	7,907	7,907
	East	8,130	8,626	9,105	9,692	9,922	10,309	10,913	11,681	11,681
	South	11,833	12,075	12,384	12,668	12,820	13,112	13,402	13,871	13,871
	West	14,023	14,408	14,920	15,683	16,141	16,642	17,345	18,252	18,252
Grand Total		982	2,852	5,163	8,115	9,550	11,668	14,411	18,252	18,252

- **Pane (Across)**   Notice that the value increments across each row until it reaches the last quarter in a year (the partition for each year is referred to as a *pane*). It then resets at the beginning of the next year pane. The row grand total consists of the pane accumulated totals.

			Order Date							
		2013				2014				Grand
Category	Region	Q1	Q2	Q3	Q4	Q1	Q2	Q3	Q4	Total
Furniture	Central	79	184	338	556	91	198	314	501	1,057
	East	116	234	365	592	56	189	398	697	1,289
	South	68	145	227	349	20	150	215	377	726
	West	63	217	410	696	104	262	500	862	1,558
Office Supplies	Central	129	422	873	1,338	324	734	1,252	1,939	3,277
	East	223	719	1,198	1,785	230	617	1,221	1,989	3,774
	South	152	394	703	987	152	444	734	1,203	2,190
	West	152	537	1,049	1,812	458	959	1,662	2,569	4,381
Grand Total		982	2,852	5,163	8,115	1,435	3,553	6,296	10,137	18,252

- **Pane (Down)**   Notice that the value increments down each column until it reaches the last region in a department (the partition for each department is referred to as a *pane*). It then resets at the beginning of the next department pane. The column grand total consists of the pane accumulated totals.

		Order Date								
		2013				2014				Grand
Category	Region	Q1	Q2	Q3	Q4	Q1	Q2	Q3	Q4	Total
Furniture	Central	79	105	154	218	91	107	116	187	1,057
	East	195	223	285	445	147	240	325	486	2,346
	South	263	300	367	567	167	370	390	648	3,072
	West	326	454	560	853	271	528	628	1,010	4,630
Office Supplies	Central	129	293	451	465	324	410	518	687	3,277
	East	352	789	930	1,052	554	797	1,122	1,455	7,051
	South	504	1,031	1,239	1,336	706	1,089	1,412	1,924	9,241
	West	656	1,416	1,751	2,099	1,164	1,590	2,115	2,831	13,622
Grand Total		982	1,870	2,311	2,952	1,435	2,118	2,743	3,841	18,252

Although this is not a complete overview of all possible direction and scope options, you should now have a good idea of the general approach to using table calculations. You'll want to experiment with various table calculation options—you may always "undo" or make another choice—until you arrive at the correct result.

Tip *Although their name may imply that table calculations are only appropriate for "tables," such as text tables or crosstabs, they perform equal functions with any chart type. As with text tables, simpler single dimension/single measure charts will provide fewer scope and direction options than charts that use multiple dimensions/measures on rows and columns.*

Using Table Calculation Functions in Calculated Fields

When creating a new table calculation with the Add Table Calculation option or editing an existing table calculation, there are many choices in the dialog box, such as the type of calculation (Running Sum, Difference From, and so forth), the type of aggregation to use in the calculation (Sum, Average, and others), and direction and scope options. Although this dialog box makes specifying table calculations straightforward, there are yet more ways to customize a table calculation. For every table calculation you create with the dialog box, an option to view and customize becomes available, which will result in a new calculated field in the Data pane.

Consider this table calculation, created to act as the right axis line chart value of a Pareto chart.

Table Calculation [% of Total Running Sum of Sales]		⊠
Calculation Type:	Running Total ▼	
Calculation Definition		
Summarize values using:	Sum ▼	
Running along:	**Table (Across)** ▼	
Restarting every:	▼	
☑ Perform a secondary calculation on the result		
Secondary Type:	Percent of Total ▼	
Secondary Calculation Definition		
Summarize the values from:	**Table (Across)** ▼	
At the level:	▼	
☐ Compute total across all pages		
	OK Cancel Apply	

This particular table calculation actually performs two calculations (this is sometimes referred to as a *two-pass* table calculation). The first is a running sum to accumulate sales totals across the bars that make up the left axis of the Pareto chart. Then, a second calculation is selected (again, calculating across the "table," or bars of the left axis) to determine the percent of total based on the running sum first. The ultimate purpose of this table calculation is to determine when 80 percent of product sales have occurred.

Tableau actually considers table calculations placed on a shelf to be an ad hoc calculated field (as discussed earlier in this chapter). As such, you may drag the table calculation from the shelf to the Data pane, give it a meaningful name, and reuse it in other worksheets. Or, you may double-click the table calculation or choose Edit In Shelf from the table calculation's context menu to expose the underlying table calculation logic. You may then modify the original table calculation logic, as with an ad hoc calculation or copy the table calculation logic to the Clipboard for use in a different calculated field.

☰ Rows	SUM(Sales)	RUNNING_SUM(SUM([Sales])) / TOTAL(SUM([Sales]))

In this example, the table calculation logic is copied to the Clipboard and then pasted into a new calculated field with IF/THE/ELSE logic to determine if the 80 percent

(continued)

value from the original two-pass table calculation has been achieved. When this calculated field is placed on Color on the Marks card for the left axis bar chart, the same logic used to calculate the percent of total running sum will color bars based on the 80 percent "Pareto Principle."

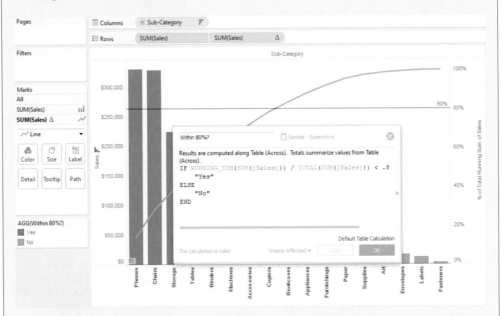

Once you become more familiar with table calculation logic, you may even choose to create calculated fields directly (as ad hoc calculations on a shelf or using the calculation editor) that include table calculation functions and logic. If you expand the functions list in the calculation editor and narrow the list of functions to table calculation functions only, you'll notice some of the same logic that appears when you expose pre-created table calculations. Using these in a calculated field, you may create very advanced chart logic that makes full use of Tableau table calculation features.

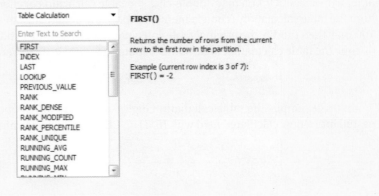

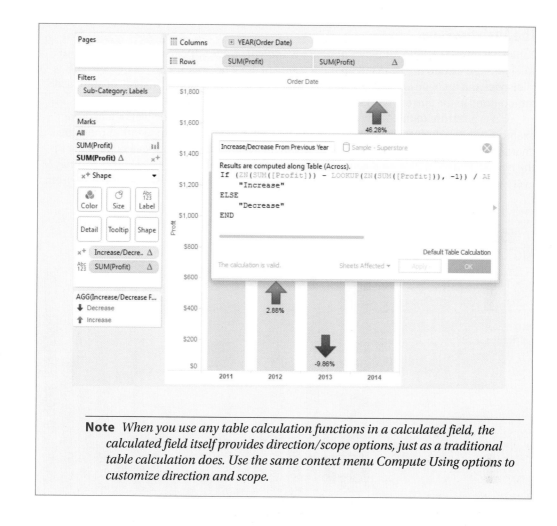

> **Note** *When you use any table calculation functions in a calculated field, the calculated field itself provides direction/scope options, just as a traditional table calculation does. Use the same context menu Compute Using options to customize direction and scope.*

Statistical Analysis

Whereas calculated fields and table calculations permit you to create custom dimensions or measures to add to your chart, other Tableau features provide associated visual annotations and statistical indicators, such as reference lines and bands, trend lines, and forecast lines. There are two ways to use these features: using the new Analytics pane, or from pull-down menus or right-click context menus.

 Video *Statistical Analysis*

The Analytics Pane

Tableau 9 introduces the Analytics pane. The *Analytics pane* appears when you click the Analytics tab next to the Data tab on the left side of the workspace. The resulting list of statistical and analytic options provides a streamlined way of adding analytic or statistical annotations to the current worksheet with simple drag-and-drop functionality.

To use a feature of the Analytics pane, drag the desired item to the worksheet. For example, to display an average reference line for each category pane in a multidimension chart, drag Average Line to the chart. A selection of destinations will appear, depending on the type of analytic annotation you are adding. In this example, since the desire is to analyze average sales for each category (the first nested dimension), the Pane destination is chosen.

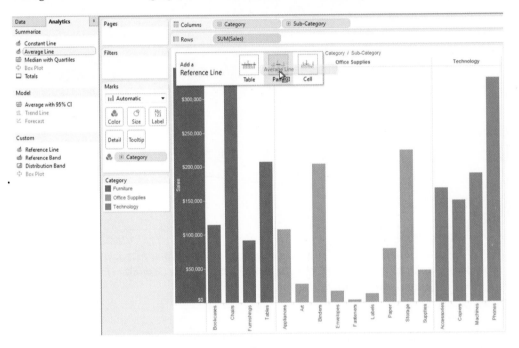

If you drag any of the Custom items to the worksheet, Tableau will add the item with a basic set of default options and then display a dialog box (the same dialog box discussed in more detail later in this section), where you may make more detailed choices. And since the Analytics pane creates traditional analytic and statistical annotations, such as reference lines, trend lines, and forecasts, you may edit specific properties of the annotation by right-clicking (CONTROL-clicking on Mac) in the appropriate place (such as right-clicking a reference band or right-clicking the chart to view a trend model). More detail on specific Analytics pane options follows in this section.

Note *Analytics pane options may be dimmed, depending on the type of chart currently being edited. For example, because forecasting is only available on charts using certain types of date or date-time dimensions, the Forecast option will be dimmed if an appropriate chart is not being edited.*

Instant Analytics

Tableau 9 introduces *Instant Analytics,* the ability to display two sets of analytic annotations (reference lines, forecast lines, and so forth) at the same time: one for the entire chart, and a second for a series of one or more marks that you specifically select. This helpful new feature allows you to do quick trend, forecast, or reference comparisons for overall values versus specifically selected values.

Regardless of whether analytic annotations have been added with the Analytics pane or traditional options (discussed next), simply select one or more chart marks via an elastic box selection or control-click (COMMAND-click on Mac) options. An additional analytic annotation will immediately appear for just the selected marks, and the overall annotation will be dimmed.

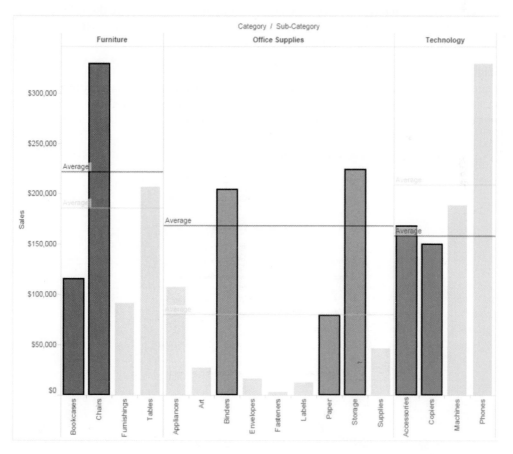

Tip *If you wish to disable Instant Analytics for an existing reference line, trend line, or forecast line on a chart, simply edit the annotation from the right-click menu. Uncheck the Show Recalculated Line For Highlighted Or Selected Data Points option.*

Reference Lines, Bands, and Distribution

Although not strictly tied to statistical analysis, reference lines are often helpful in highlighting a desired portion of a visual chart. A *reference line,* as the name implies, is a line that is drawn across the numeric axis of a chart denoting a particular desired value, such as the average, maximum, median, or some other constant value (such as a sales goal). Variations of reference lines include a *reference band,* a shaded portion of a numeric axis beginning and ending at specified values. Another variation, a *reference distribution,* results in several gradient shaded bands at various intervals across the numeric axis. And finally, a *box plot* is a specific type of reference distribution/line combination set aside for a box plot chart type (box/whisker plots are covered in detail in Chapter 4).

No matter which option you prefer, begin by right-clicking (CONTROL-clicking on Mac) in the numeric axis on your chart and selecting Add Reference Line from the context menu. If reference lines already exist on your chart, you may also edit or remove them via context menu choices. You may also select an existing reference line on the chart itself, right-click, and choose appropriate options from the context menu.

Single Reference Line

A single reference line denotes one particular point on the numeric axis. It may be based on a variety of calculations, using existing measures in your chart. You may also base the value on a constant number that you "hard code" into the dialog box, or the value of a parameter.

In this case, one line will appear across each "pane" (outer dimension in a multidimension row or column). The average of the sales measure is being displayed by the reference line. A custom label has been specified, which enables a freeform text box where literal text and a combination of existing values from the chart may be used to label the reference line. The line has been formatted as a bold red line with no fill options.

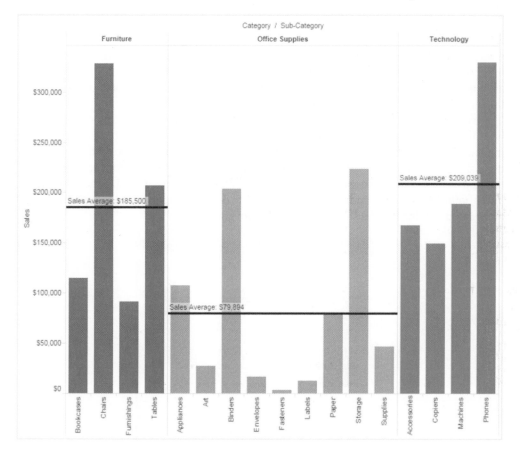

Tip *A measure must be "in use" somewhere on your chart in order to base a reference line on it. If you want to base a reference line on a measure other than the one actually being displayed on the chart, drag the desired measure to Detail on the Marks card. Then, when you create or edit a reference line, the additional measure will be available in the Reference Line dialog box.*

Reference Band

A reference band highlights a range on the numeric axis. The beginning and ending values may be based on a variety of calculations, using existing measures in your chart. You may also base the beginning and ending values on a constant number that you hard code into the dialog box, or the value of a parameter.

In this case, a separate band will appear for the "table" (the overall chart, regardless of how many nested dimensions are used). The lower portion of the band is based on the median of the sales measure, with the upper band based on the maximum of the same measure. Custom labels have been specified, which enables a freeform text box where literal text and a combination of existing values from the chart may be used to label the upper and lower boundaries of the band. No line is specified to denote the upper and lower boundaries of the band, but the band is shaded with a medium gray color.

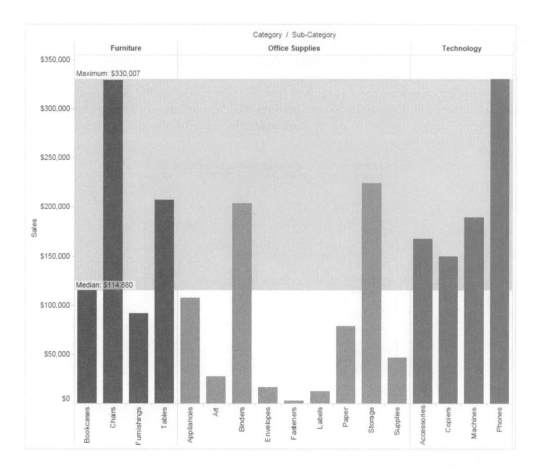

Reference Distribution

Like a reference band, a reference distribution shades a defined area on the numeric axis. However, rather than just specifying a beginning and ending point for a distribution, you may specify several points, which are shaded with various gradients. Variations may be based on a number of statistical values, including confidence interval, percentages, percentiles, quantiles (four quartiles, five quintiles, and so forth), or standard deviation. Reference bands are particularly helpful for certain chart types, such as bullet charts and box plots (both are covered in Chapter 4).

In this case, a separate band will appear "per pane" (outer dimension in a multidimension row or column). The distribution is based on three standard deviations above and below. No label or line is being specified. A gray light fill is specified, as is the option to fill above and below the distribution.

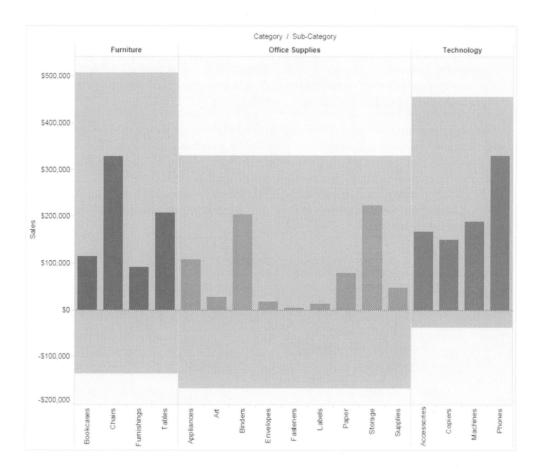

Trend Lines

As the name indicates, a *trend line* is a line (or series of lines) that appears on a chart indicating the general trend the underlying marks on the chart are exhibiting. A trend line uses various built-in statistical models (which are selectable) to determine appearance and behavior. To create a trend line, choose Analysis | Trend Lines | Show Trend Lines from the drop-down menus, or right-click the chart (not an axis or header) and select Trend Lines | Show Trend Lines from the context menu.

Tip *Trend lines are available when both the Column and Row shelves contain a numeric measure (typically, this results in a scatter plot, covered in Chapter 4). A trend line is also permitted if a chart is based on a date or date/time dimension (unless they are set to month/day/year or month/year date levels) and a measure. If you attempt to display trend lines otherwise, an error message will result.*

A default trend line will appear. You may immediately hover your mouse over a trend line, or select it, to display a tooltip. The tooltip will display basic statistical information about the makeup of the trend line. If you wish to examine or modify the statistical model that creates the trend line, right-click (CTRL-click on Mac) a selected trend line or the chart itself. From the context menu, choose Edit Trend Lines. Or, select Analysis | Trend Lines | Edit Trend Lines from the drop-down menus. A dialog box will appear, permitting you to change trend line behavior.

A more detailed discussion of the statistical model making up the trend line may be displayed by choosing Describe Trend Model from the same right-click menu or by choosing the Analysis | Trend Line drop-down menu.

Forecasting

Tableau provides *forecasting*, the ability to examine data and trends in existing date- or date/time-based data and forecast what trend may occur in the future. The first requirement when forecasting is to create a chart based on a date or date/time dimension. If you choose to change the default discrete Year date level of the dimension, you must choose a continuous date level—discrete date levels other than Year won't permit forecasting.

Once your initial chart is displayed, you can forecast by using the Analytics pane (described earlier in the chapter) or the Analysis | Forecast | Show Forecast drop-down menu option. Or you can just right-click (CONTROL-click on Mac) the visualization and choose Forecast | Show Forecast from the context menu. Tableau will look at the existing time-based data and forecast future trends based on it. The chart will be extended to show the forecast data, and a forecast icon (a slanted up arrow) will be added to the forecast measure on the workspace shelf. Also, a forecast indicator will be placed on Color on the Marks card to distinguish existing data from forecast data.

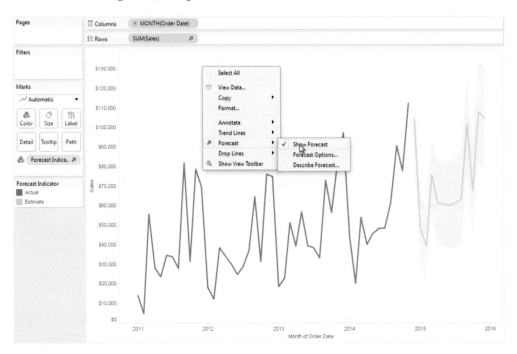

You can also use two other options from the Analysis | Forecast drop-down or Forecast right-click menus to customize or document the forecast. Forecast Options will display the Forecast Options dialog box, where you can change the duration of the forecast, change the date-level granularity used for aggregation, choose to ignore a specified number of periods at the end of the actual data range, elect whether or not to fill missing values with zeroes, choose from a variety of forecasting models, and select prediction interval options.

Describe Forecast will display a dialog box exposing details about the way the forecast was calculated via both Summary and Models tabs.

Note *Although line and area charts are typically used to trend data over time, forecasting will work equally well with other chart types based on date or date/time dimensions, such as a bar chart showing sales by year.*

Tableau Maps

If you've used other Business Intelligence or Data Discovery tools, you may have yearned for a comprehensive solution for analyzing geographic data via maps. Although many "legacy" toolsets fall far short in this area, Tableau provides a rich mapping capability. By using a combination of geocoded data (data that Tableau interprets as containing a geographic location) and Internet-supplied background maps, you may perform detailed analysis geographically.

Consider this dimension portion of the Data pane from the Sample - Superstore data source that's included with Tableau. In particular, note the Location hierarchy and the four dimensions within it. Although the underlying field type in the data source for these fields is String, they do not appear with the standard Abc icon that appears on other string fields. Instead, they are denoted with a small globe icon. And if you glance at the Measures portion of the Data pane, you'll notice two "generated" fields that you may not have seen before: Latitude and Longitude.

Double-clicking one of the geographic dimension fields (a field preceded by a globe icon) will create a map displaying a blue circle on each occurrence of the underlying geographic field you double-clicked. This very quick default map gives you a basic idea of the power of Tableau mapping. Note that the actual geographic field has not been placed on the Rows or Columns shelf, but instead appears on the Marks card without any of the standard Marks card icons next to it. This denotes that the geographic field is on the Detail portion of the Marks card, which simply ensures that the members of the geographic dimension are included on the worksheet (but they are not used to denote color, size, shape, or any other mark property). The Rows and Columns shelves, instead, have been populated with the generated Latitude and Longitude measures.

Data	Analytics	
Sample - Superstore		

Dimensions

- ▲ Customer
  - Abc Customer Name
  - Abc Segment
- ▲ Order
  - Order Date
  - Abc Order ID
  - Ship Date
  - Abc Ship Mode
- ▲ Location
  - ⊕ Country
  - ⊕ State
  - ⊕ City
  - ⊕ Postal Code
- ▲ Product
  - Abc Category
  - Abc Sub-Category
  - Manufacturer

Measures

- # Discount
- # Profit
- # Profit Ratio
- # Quantity
- # Sales
- ⊕ Latitude (generated)
- ⊕ Longitude (generated)
- # Number of Records
- # Measure Values

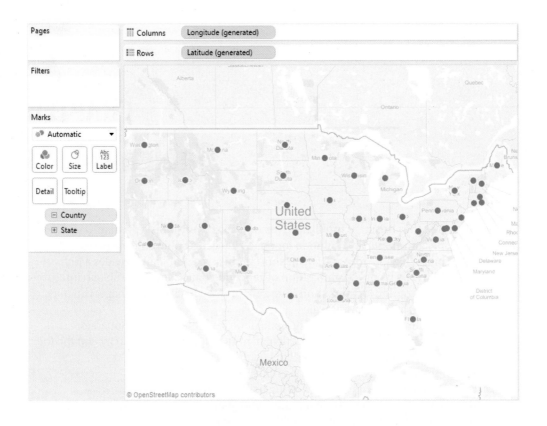

Tip *You may also create maps by selecting at least one geocoded field (with a globe icon) and clicking either of two map options in Show Me.*

There are some basic concepts of mapping that this chapter will expand on:

- Tableau must evaluate a dimension as geographic to use it for maps. The globe icon indicates a geographic field.
- Tableau actually plots generated latitude and longitude derived from the geocoded dimension members as X and Y coordinates.
- Tableau displays a background map (by default, downloaded from the Internet) behind the X/Y coordinate map marks.

In particular, you will get an idea of basic Tableau mapping functionality from comparing the just-illustrated United States map and the following, which is the exact same map with "None" chosen from the Map | Background Maps drop-down menu. With no background map set, the chart looks like a standard scatter plot (discussed in Chapter 4), simply showing X and Y coordinates of the two numeric measures. A quick glance at the scatter plot, however, will still give you the general outline of U.S. geography.

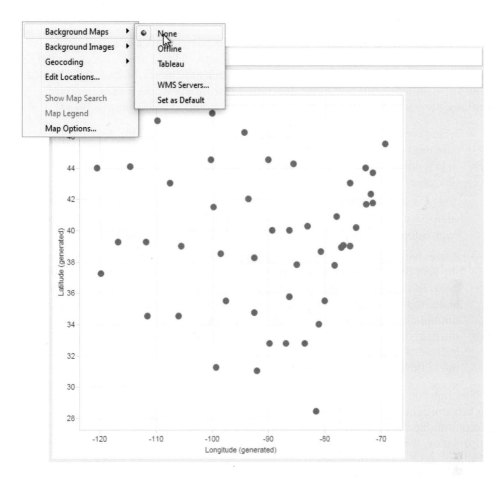

Download *At www.tableaubook.com, download* Chapter 7 - Tableau Maps.twbx *file to see examples that relate to this chapter.*

Geocoded Fields

Video *Using Geocoded Fields*

The first requirement to use mapping is a proper dimension field or fields. *Geocoded fields* are fields that Tableau interprets as containing geographic data. Tableau automatically converts the string values of these fields to latitude and longitude that can be used as X/Y coordinates on the Rows and Columns shelves. These fields appear with a small globe icon instead of another data-type icon—when they are double-clicked, a map will result. Tableau automatically assumes a field is geographic and will add the globe icon to it if its name includes some type of geographic keyword, such as Country, State, City, ZIP Code, and so forth. Although this automatic geocoding assignment works well in standard situations, there are some situations where misinterpretation will occur:

- A field contains a name that Tableau interprets as a geographic field, but the field contains nongeographic data. A globe icon appears next to the field, but when the field is double-clicked, a map will result with no marks and a message indicating "x unknown" at the bottom right.

- A field contains geographic data, but the field name is not recognized by Tableau as such. No global icon will appear. If the field is double-clicked, a standard text table containing a row for each dimension member will appear instead of a map.

- A field will be interpreted as a geographic field based on field name. Although the field does contain geographic data, Tableau will misinterpret the *type* of geographic data contained in the field. For example, a field named "Location State" may actually contain country data rather than state data. When the field is double-clicked, Tableau will create a map, but will be unable to interpret any of the fields as state fields. No marks will appear on the map, and a message indicating "x unknown" will appear at the bottom right.

Although you may be tempted to return to your original data source to modify field names to accommodate Tableau's field-naming interpretation, there's a simple context menu that allows you to assign or unassign a geographic identification. Right-click (CONTROL-click on Mac) the misinterpreted field in the Data pane, choose Geographic Role from the context menu, and make the desired choice from the sub-menu. If a field has not been assigned a geographic role because of its field name, choose the role you wish to assign to the field. If a field has been mistakenly assigned a geographic role because of its field name but it doesn't contain geographic data, select None. If a field has been assigned the wrong role (for example, the field name contains the word "State," but actually contains country data), select the correct role.

"Out of the box," Tableau includes geocoding interpretation for the following types of geographic data (some of these roles have been expanded in Tableau 9):

- **Area Code**   Standard U.S. three-digit telephone area codes. Other North American area codes, such as those in Canada, are not properly interpreted.

- **CBSA/MSA**   United States Core Based Statistical Area/Metropolitan Statistical Area. This will interpret both standard strings, such as "Denver-Aurora-Lakewood, CO" and many three-character codes (such as 216, which refers to Denver-Aurora-Lakewood, CO).

- **City**   Worldwide city names. In some cases, smaller towns may not be recognized. Note that because there can be more than one occurrence of a city name in the world, it may be beneficial to include country and state/province fields in the data source to narrow down to a unique country/state-province/city hierarchy (geographic hierarchies are discussed later in the chapter).

- **Congressional District**   U.S. congressional districts. This geographic role interprets variations of numbers, such as 1st, 4, 6th District, and 23rd. Note that because there can be more than one occurrence of a district in the United States, it may be beneficial to add a state field to Detail on the Marks card to narrow down to a unique state/district hierarchy (geographic hierarchies are discussed later in the chapter).

- **Country/Region**   International country and region names. This geographic role will interpret full spellings of countries/regions, as well as Federal Information Processing Standard (FIPS) 10-4 and International Organization for Standardization (ISO) two- and three-character abbreviations.

- **County**   U.S. county names and equivalent second-level administrative divisions for certain countries, such as France and Germany. Note that because there can be more than one occurrence of a county name in a country, it may be beneficial to add a state or country field to Detail on the Marks card to narrow down to a unique state-country/county hierarchy (geographic hierarchies are discussed later in the chapter).

- **State/Province**   States and provinces, interpreted worldwide. Both spelled-out and abbreviated values may be supplied. Note that because there can be more than one occurrence of a state/province name in the world, it may be beneficial to add a country field to Detail on the Marks card to narrow down to a unique country/state-province hierarchy (geographic hierarchies are discussed later in the chapter).

- **ZIP Code/Postal Code**   Standard U.S. ZIP codes. Postal codes are also interpreted from Canada, the United Kingdom, Australia, New Zealand, France, Germany, and New Zealand. Note that because there can be more than one occurrence of a ZIP/postal code in the recognized countries, it may be beneficial to include a country field in the data source to narrow down to a unique country/postal code (geographic hierarchies are discussed later in the chapter).

Dealing with Geocode Mismatches

Although Tableau properly interprets and geocodes a fairly wide variety of standard geographic data, you may encounter situations where Tableau doesn't fully understand some (or all) of your geographic values. This may be due to data entry errors or variations on city or state names that Tableau doesn't understand. When Tableau doesn't find a latitude/longitude match in its internal geocoding tables for a value in a geographic field, a message will appear on the lower right of your map indicating how many values Tableau failed to resolve.

In these cases, you'll probably want to choose some way to deal with the mismatched values (although you may choose to simply hide the message by right-clicking it and choosing Hide Indicator). Several choices exist when you left-click the message. A dialog box will appear providing three options:

- **Edit Locations**   Displays a dialog box that allows you to match the misinterpreted geographic values to a value that Tableau understands. The mismatched values will appear at the top of the list. On the Matching Location columns to the right, click to display a drop-down list of locations. Select the location you want Tableau to use for the misinterpreted location. Selecting the Map | Edit Locations drop-down menu option will also display this dialog box.

Edit Locations

Geographic roles

Country/Region: Country

State/Province: **State**   ⚠ 3 issues

Match values to locations

⚠ State/Province | Country/Region

Your Data	Matching Location
Massachussetts	
Misissippi	Martinique
Tennesee	Mārupe
Alabama	Mary
Arizona	Maryland
Arkansas	Masaka
California	Masalli
Colorado	Masaya
Connecticut	Mascara
	Maseru
	Mashonaland Central
	Mashonaland East
	Mashonaland West
	Masindi
	Masovian
	Massachusetts
	Masvingo
	Matabeleland North
	Matabeleland South
	Matagalpa
	Matam
	Matanzas
	Mato Grosso
	Mato Grosso do Sul
	Matruh
	Maule
	Mavrovo and Rostusa
	Mayabeque
	Mayaguana
	Mayaro/Rio Claro
	Mayo

☐ Show only unmatched location in drop down list

Reset Matches

- **Filter Data**   Filters out the mismatched values. The Latitude and Longitude fields will be added to the Filters shelf, set to exclude null values. If you later want to read the mismatched values and edit locations, you may remove Latitude and Longitude from the Filters shelf.

- **Show Data at Default Position**   This option will display a mark on the map for the mismatched values at the intersection of the equator and prime meridian (latitude/longitude 0, 0). Unless your mismatched geographic fields, in fact, *do* refer to the Gulf of Guinea in the Atlantic Ocean, this probably is the least desirable of these options.

Geographic Hierarchies and Ambiguity

Consider Tableau's challenge of determining an exact latitude and longitude for a city if there is more than one city with the same name in your country, much less in the entire world. In order for Tableau to properly narrow down ambiguous geographic locations, it employs a geographic hierarchy. This *geographic hierarchy* relies on a series of geographic dependencies to narrow down an ambiguous geographic location until it becomes unique. For example, Tableau employs a Country/Region-to-State/Province-to-City hierarchy to determine the correct latitude and longitude for a particular city. Similar hierarchies are provided for Country/Region-to-State/Province, Country/Region-to-State/Province-to-County, Country/Region-to-ZIP/Postal Code, Country/Region-to-Area Code, and Country/Region-to-CBSA (Core Based Statistical Area).

If your data source contains a combination of these fields that Tableau interprets as containing geographic data (as mentioned previously, Tableau determines this based on field name), Tableau will automatically show the hierarchy in the Data pane. The advantage of the pre-defined hierarchy comes when you use one of the lower-level geographic fields as the primary dimension for your map. For example, if your data source contains Country, State, and City fields, and you double-click City to generate a map for cities in your data source, Tableau will automatically add the hierarchical fields above city to Detail on the Marks card. This ensures that "city uniqueness" is employed to avoid ambiguous city names.

However, even if the set of geographic fields in your data source includes fields that would result in a hierarchy, a hierarchy *won't* appear if another geographic field that would break the hierarchy also exists in the data source. Consider a data source that contains Country, State, City, and ZIP Code. This would appear to present the opportunity for a geographic hierarchy. However, Tableau's built-in hierarchies start at the Country/Region level, end at the City level, and don't include ZIP Code; or they start at Country/Region and end at ZIP Code, but don't include City. As such, a data source that includes all four fields won't result in an automatic hierarchy. If you use a lower-level field that may be ambiguous, such as City, higher-level fields that would resolve the ambiguity are not automatically added to the Marks card. Results may be mixed, with some cities plotting properly but others being placed in

the wrong country and/or state, or an "unknown" message appearing at the lower right of the map.

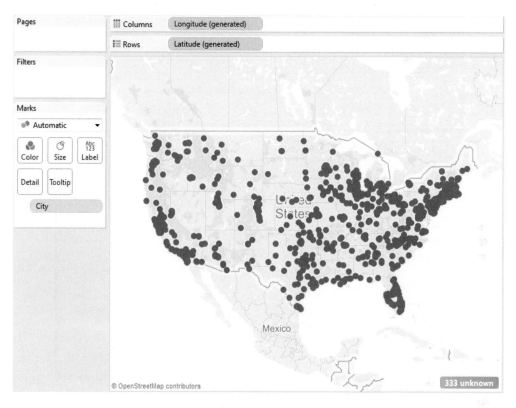

Several options exist to resolve this ambiguity:

- Before creating a map, manually create the necessary hierarchy by dragging and dropping geographic fields in the Data pane (a discussion on how to create hierarchies in the Data pane for all fields—not just geographic fields—appears in Chapter 3). Then, when you use a lower-level field to create a map, Tableau will automatically add higher-level fields to Detail.

- Drag higher-level geographic fields that will resolve the ambiguity on the Marks card. If you simply drag to the white area at the bottom of the Marks card (not on Color, Shape, and so forth), those fields will be placed on Detail. In particular, ensure that you drag these fields *above* the existing field in order of priority so that Tableau will understand the proper hierarchy to follow.

- If the set of geographic data in your data source is limited to certain countries or states/provinces, click the Unknown indicator at the lower right of the map and choose Edit Locations from the Special Values dialog box, or choose Map | Edit Locations from the drop-down menus. The Edit Locations dialog box will appear. Choose the desired dimensions at proper hierarchical levels to eliminate the ambiguity.

Custom Geocoding

Although Tableau has a fairly extensive built-in set of geographic roles (as discussed earlier in the chapter), you may find more customized geographic roles are necessary for your particular needs. For example, you may need to map locations of smaller towns that aren't automatically included in Tableau's built-in geocoding. Or, you may have custom roles (such as airport codes or your own sales divisions/regions) that you wish to use for mapping. Tableau enables you to both extend its existing geographic roles by adding data (such as additional smaller cities) and add your own custom geographic roles and hierarchies.

Consider a data source that refers to a set of small towns in the author's home state of Wyoming. Although the file contains the proper series of Country-State-City fields to adhere to Tableau's geographic hierarchy, double-clicking the City field only plots two cities in the state of Wyoming with relatively large populations. The remaining smaller towns are unrecognized, as indicated by the Unknown indicator at the lower right of the map. This is an opportunity to add to Tableau's existing Country/Region-to-State/Province-to-City geographic hierarchy.

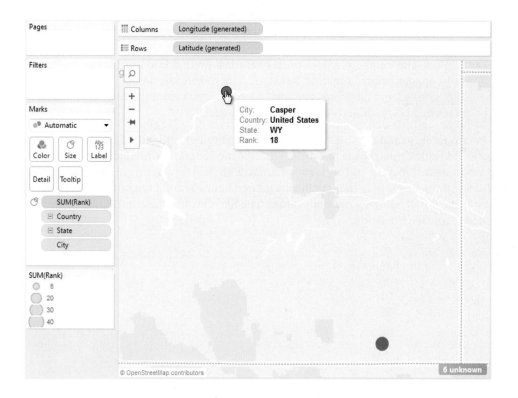

Regardless of whether you wish to extend existing Tableau geographic roles or add your own custom roles, there are some basic requirements:

- You must create comma-separated value (.csv) text files. You may create these with Microsoft Excel, a text editor, or some other toolset that creates a CSV file. The file must be saved with a .csv file extension.

- If the file will extend an already existing Tableau geographic role, it must contain all fields that match a Tableau geographic field. Further, if the field you wish to add is part of a standard Tableau geographic hierarchy (existing hierarchies are discussed earlier in this chapter), a matching field for each member of the hierarchy must be included in the .csv file. For example, if you wish to add new cities to the existing Tableau City role, you must also include a Country (Name) field and a Province/State field for each new city to ensure that Tableau won't confuse cities you're adding with other cities of the same name in other states or countries. Fields must be named the same as the geographic role already defined in Tableau (right-click a field in the Data pane and choose Geographic Role to see the sub-menu of existing geographic roles—fields must be named exactly the same in your .csv file).

Caution *Despite Tableau's display of Country/Region in the Data pane's geographic role list, you must use a column labeled Country (Name) in the .csv file to properly import custom geographic roles.*

- Latitude and longitude values must be the last two fields in the .csv file. Latitude must appear before longitude, fields must be specifically named "Latitude" and "Longitude," and they must contain "real" numeric values (at least one decimal place must be included—they cannot be integers).

For example, to add the small Wyoming cities exhibited earlier to Tableau's existing set of geocoded cities, this .csv file may be used. Note the geographic hierarchy of Country/Region-to-State/Province-to-City is maintained, with fields appearing in that specific order. Following these fields, note the specifically named Latitude and Longitude fields (again, in that specific order), with real number values. The file is given a descriptive name and contains a .csv file extension.

Furthermore, you may wish to add your own custom geocoded values, such as Sales Divisions, Plant Locations, and so forth. These can be independent of any existing Tableau geographic hierarchies, can depend on existing fields (such as Country/Region or State/Province), or can establish their own hierarchies separate from any existing Tableau hierarchies. As with the previous example, field names in the .csv file need to be specific. In particular, any existing Tableau hierarchies must be accounted for with matching field names. New geographic fields should be properly named. And Latitude and Longitude fields should be the last two fields in the .csv file and should contain real number values. The file is given a descriptive name and contains a .csv file extension.

In this example, custom sales division locations need to be added to Tableau's geocoding. Because there are duplicate division names, they must be added to Tableau's existing Country/Region hierarchy.

Once you have created one or more .csv files containing your custom geocoding, you may import them. Choose Map | Geocoding | Import Custom Geocoding from the pull-down menus. Because Tableau does not give you the opportunity to import individual .csv files, but imports all .csv files in a folder path, you'll be prompted to choose a folder. Choose the folder (or sub-folders) that contains the .csv files you wish to import. Click OK. Tableau will merge your custom geocoding with its existing geocoding (a large number of row counts will result, even if you are only importing a small number of new values).

Once the import is complete, your custom geocoding values will be available to use for your own maps. After importing the small cities in Wyoming, as discussed previously, a map will now properly interpret the small town names in a data source.

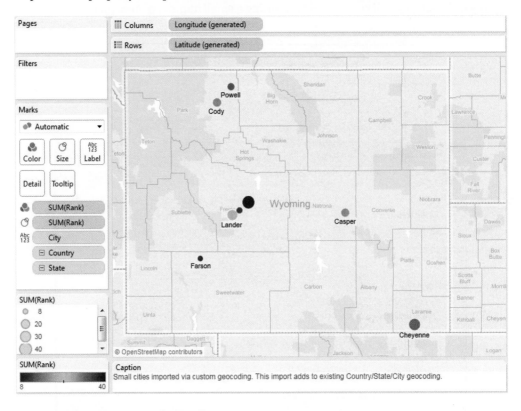

If you import your own custom role, it will now be available on the Geographic Role context menu when you right-click a field. Assign the custom role to a geographic field from your data source. Then, the new custom geocode will properly map your custom latitude and longitude values.

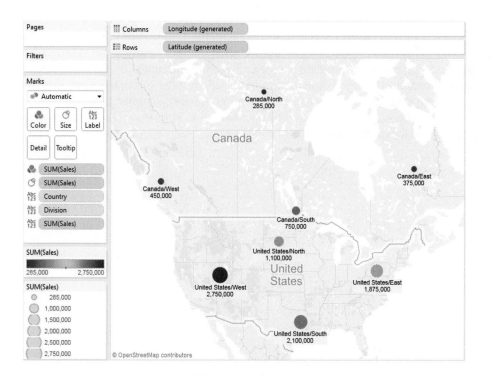

Note *To remove previously imported custom geocoding, select Map | Geocoding | Remove Custom Geocoding. Also, if you open a Tableau Packaged Workbook (a .twbx file), such as sample workbooks downloaded from TableauBook.com, any custom geocoding saved in the workbook will be retained for that workbook. You can even import custom geocoding saved with a workbook into your local repository to use for other workbooks. Just choose Maps | Custom Geocoding | Import Custom Geocoding, and select the Import From Current Workbook radio button.*

Mapping Latitude and Longitude Directly

Custom geocoding allows you to add custom latitude/longitude values to your own geographic dimensions. This is helpful when you need to create various maps on a regular basis using these custom values. However, if you happen to possess latitudes and longitudes as part of your regular data source, you may map directly using the latitude and longitude values. Custom geocoding (or any geocoding, for that matter) will not be required.

Although not absolutely necessary, it's helpful if the latitude and longitude values in your data source are specifically named "Latitude" and "Longitude" and are numeric values. If so, Tableau will automatically assign them geographic roles (globe icons will precede them) and place them in the Measures portion of the Data pane. If Latitude/Longitude fields are named differently and Tableau doesn't automatically recognize them, simply right-click the fields and choose Geographic Role | Latitude Or Geographic Role | Longitude from the context menu. Tableau will then place the globe icon on the fields and treat them as latitude and longitude values. If latitude and longitude are stored in your data source as non-numeric values, or if you need to create customized latitudes and longitudes based on some sort of business rule, you may create calculated fields (covered in Chapter 6). The calculated fields should return "real" numeric values with at least one decimal place. They may then be assigned the latitude and longitude geographic role.

Drag Longitude onto the Columns shelf and Latitude onto the Rows shelf. Tableau will automatically plot these fields to their geographic locations and display an appropriate background map. Depending on how your data is organized, you may only see a single point on the map consisting of the aggregated latitude and longitude values for all records in your underlying data source. In this eventuality, you may place a field that provides a breakdown of individual locations (a location, name, or customer field and so forth) on Detail or Label on the Marks card. You may also choose to disaggregate your data so that Tableau plots each individual record in the data

(*continued*)

source rather than aggregating to a higher-level dimension. Uncheck Analysis |
Aggregate Measures from the drop-down menus to do this.

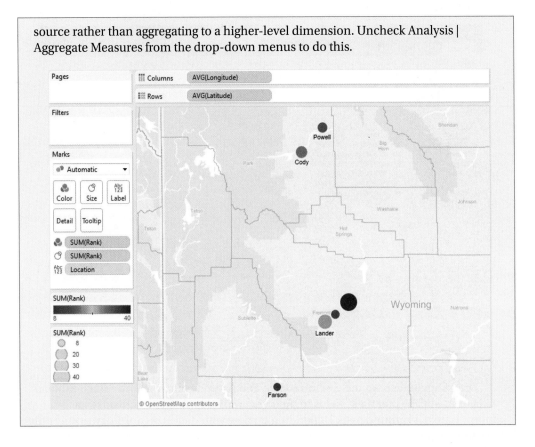

Background Maps and Layers

As has been discussed previously in this chapter, double-clicking a geographic field, using
the map options in Show Me, or adding Latitude and Longitude fields to shelves will draw a
Tableau map. Although the end result is placement of marks at particular latitudes and
longitudes, the other major necessity for mapping in Tableau is the image of the map itself
(as demonstrated earlier in the chapter, if a background map image is turned off in Tableau,
a map simply becomes a scatter plot).

Based on the extreme upper-left, lower-left, upper-right, and lower-right marks placed
on the map, Tableau determines the portion of a background map to display. For example,
if your map plots a mark in Seattle, Los Angeles, Miami, and Boston, Tableau will display a
map of the United States, as it must show the entire country to plot the four marks in the
four corners of the country. However, if the data your map encompasses only includes
cities within a certain Canadian province, only that province will appear on the map. By
default, Tableau uses *online maps,* which are downloaded via the Internet as needed. If you

don't happen to have an Internet connection at the time of map generation, you'll receive an error indicating that the online map can't be loaded.

Video   *Background Maps and Map Options*

If your Internet connectivity is sporadic, or nonexistent (for example, you're working on an airplane or similar location), you may choose to use *offline maps,* which are built into Tableau and are available regardless of Internet connectivity. However, they offer limited flexibility and features when compared with online maps. To use offline maps, choose Map | Background Maps | Offline from the drop-down menus.

Navigating Maps and Selecting Marks

No matter the map source, you will soon find a need to navigate around a map by zooming in and out, panning the map view, or selecting one or more marks on the map for include/ exclude filters, and so forth. By default, when you hold your mouse down while on top of a map, pan mode will be selected. The mouse cursor will change to a four-arrow cursor, and the map will move as you drag. To return to the original position where the map was displayed, click the pushpin button on the view toolbar (discussed next) or the Tableau toolbar.

Additional options are available with the view toolbar, which has been redesigned in Tableau 9. By default, the view toolbar appears in the upper left when you hover your mouse over a map. If you prefer not to see the view toolbar, or if you prefer to see it on other charts that make use of zoom/pan/selection options (such as scatter plots), you may make choices from the Worksheet | Show View Toolbar menu.

- **Zoom In**   Click the plus sign control to zoom in on the map. If the view toolbar is hidden, double-click the map to zoom in. If you are using offline maps, you may be presented with a message indicating that additional map detail is only available with online maps.

- **Zoom Out**   Click the minus sign control to zoom out on the map. If the zoom controls are hidden, SHIFT–double-click the map to zoom out.

- **Reset**   Click the pushpin control to return the map to the default zoom level that appeared when the map was first created. This button is also duplicated on the Tableau toolbar.

Additional options appear when you hover your mouse over the arrow control. If you wish to "lock" these additional options, press SHIFT before clicking the desired control. The selected control will remain active until you select another control within the arrow sub-set.

- **Area Zoom**   Click the magnifying glass/box control to turn on area zoom mode. The mouse cursor will change to a magnifying glass with plus sign. Hold down the mouse button and draw an elastic box around the portion of the map you wish to zoom into. If the zoom controls are hidden, CTRL-SHIFT (SHIFT-COMMAND on Mac) will display the magnifying glass with plus sign for area zoom.

- **Rectangular Selection**   Click the dashed box control to turn on rectangular selection mode. Hold down the mouse button and draw an elastic box around marks on the map you wish to select. Once the desired marks are selected, right click (CONTROL-click on Mac) and choose options from the context menu. If the zoom controls are hidden, pressing the A key will turn on rectangular selection mode.

- **Radial Selection**   Click the dashed circle control to turn on radial selection mode. Point your mouse to the center of a circular area you wish to select. Hold down the mouse button and draw a circle extending outward around marks on the map you wish to select. Once the desired marks are selected, right-click (CONTROL-click on Mac) and choose options from the context menu. If the zoom controls are hidden, pressing the s key will turn on radial selection mode.

- **Lasso Selection**   Click the lasso control to turn on lasso selection mode. Point your mouse near the first mark you want to select. Hold down the mouse button and draw a freeform shape around marks on the map you wish to select (you'll need to experiment to determine the fine points of lasso selection). Once the desired marks are selected, right-click (CONTROL-click on Mac) and choose options from the context menu. If the zoom controls are hidden, pressing the D key will turn on radial selection mode.

Map Search

Tableau 9 adds the ability to perform a text search for locations on a map. When you hover your mouse over a map, the magnifying glass search icon appears in the upper left (if you wish, you may disable map search by unchecking Map | Show Map Search). When you click the control, a search text box appears. Type in a geographic location you wish to search for (map search will search for continent, country, state or province, county, city, or postal code). As you type, Tableau will use a combination of data from the workbook's data source and a larger selection of geographic map data to display five possible matching geographic locations.

When the desired location appears in the list, click it with your mouse or use cursor keys to highlight it and press ENTER. Tableau will zoom to that selected geographic location (and, if the location happens to be far away from the currently displayed map, Tableau will display the searched location regardless of the initial map display). To return to the original map location and zoom level, click the pushpin button.

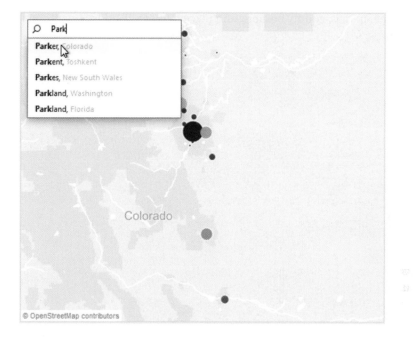

Map Options

Tableau online maps are very flexible, offering views based on worldwide geographic data. You may modify various visual characteristics, such as background style and washout level. Also, background maps have varying levels of detail known as map layers and data layers. *Map layers* are a variety of graphic overlays that can be turned on or off at will. For example, Tableau maps offer country name and boundary, state name and boundary, streets and highways, ZIP and area code boundaries and names, and similar overlays that will appear individually or in combination with each other on top of the initial map detail (some map layers are limited by the country being shown on the map). *Data layers* are colored shades that may be enabled on maps based on U.S. demographic data. Tableau map data layers include such various data breakdowns as population, occupation, housing, and so forth.

Set map and data layer options by selecting Map | Map Options from the drop-down menus. The Data pane will be replaced by the Map Options pane. Here, you may change the map style (which changes the color and intensity of the map background), washout level (which changes the contrast of the map background), and the Repeat Background option, which will replace white space with repeated portions of the map, depending on screen size or zoom level.

Map layers may be checked on and off on this pane. Note that some layers may be dimmed, based on the current zoom level of the map. Zooming in farther on the map will eventually enable these choices. Check layer options you wish to view. For example, checking street names, county borders, and place names will add elements on top of the existing map.

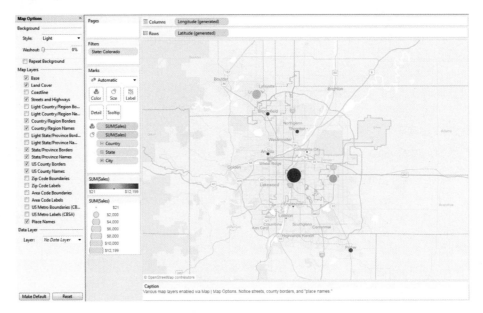

Data layers (which are only available on U.S. maps) may be enabled by clicking the drop-down menu in the Data Layer section of map options. Select the data layer you wish to display. You may also choose the geographic area (such as state, county, or ZIP code) that you wish to highlight for the chosen data layer, as well as the color palette you wish to use. The map will be shaded to match your choices, and a color legend will appear denoting the data layer.

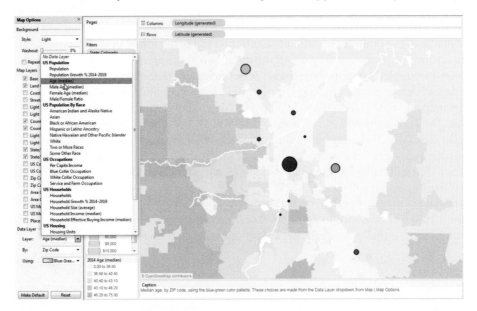

Web Map Services

Although Tableau's built-in background maps are very flexible and provide a wide array of map and data layer options, you still may find occasion to use more customized or industry-specific map backgrounds. To expand these capabilities, Tableau supports external WMS servers. *Web Map Services* (WMS) is a web-based standard that connects Tableau to a different set of custom background maps via the Internet. Various paid and open-source WMS servers exist (web searches will reveal a plethora of options) that may be added to Tableau for custom requirements.

To add a WMS server to Tableau, choose Map | Background Maps | WMS Servers from the drop-down menus. The WMS Server Connections dialog box will appear, showing any existing WMS servers that have already been added (if any). Click the Add button to specify a new WMS server to add. Type or paste the URL for the WMS server. If the selected WMS server supports tiled maps, checking the Use Tiled Maps option may improve performance. You may add as many WMS servers as you prefer—each will create an additional entry in the WMS Server Connections dialog box.

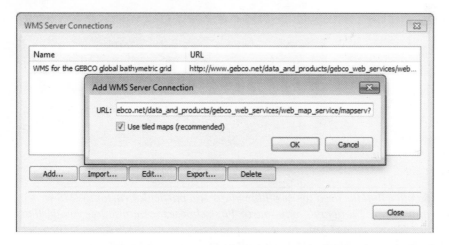

If you wish to edit or delete existing WMS servers in the WMS Server Connections dialog box, select the desired entry and select Edit or Delete. WMS servers will be available to all worksheets in the workbook. If you wish to share the WMS server URL with other Tableau users, you may select an entry in the dialog box and click Export. Tableau will display a Save As dialog box, prompting you for a filename. The file will contain a .tms (Tableau Map Source) extension. This file may be shared with other Tableau users, who can then add the WMS server to their copy of Tableau by clicking the Import button in the WMS Server Connections dialog box (all a .tms file contains is the URL—you may find that simply e-mailing the URL or providing it via some other interoffice communication method is preferable to creating a .tms file).

Once you have added one or more WMS servers and Tableau has validated their capabilities, a list of additional background map options (beyond None, Online, and Offline) will appear on the Map | Background Maps sub-menu. Choose the desired WMS-supplied map that you wish to use. In this example, a WMS is providing a custom background map displaying "bathymetry," the underwater counterpart to topography. Note that a separate set of map and data layers will exist in the Map Options dialog box, based on the particular WMS server's capabilities.

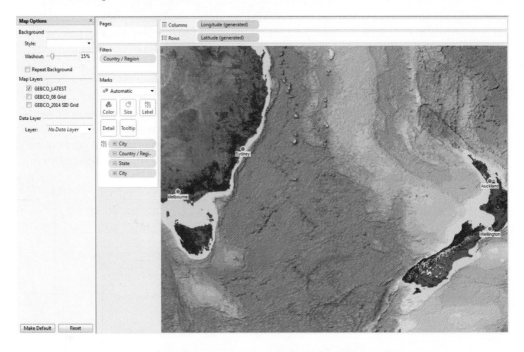

Tip *If you often find the need to use offline maps or a particular custom WMS server, you may change the default map source. First, choose the map source you wish to use (Online Maps, Offline Maps, None, or a previously added WMS server). Then, select Map | Background Maps | Set As Default from the drop-down menus.*

Mapping and Mark Types

When you first create a map via Show Me or by double-clicking a geocoded dimension (a globe icon will denote these), Tableau initially creates a map containing a mark for each occurrence of the field you used when creating the map. As discussed previously in the chapter, more fields may be added to the Marks card (Detail, in particular) to increase granularity of the map.

By default, Tableau suggests visualization best practices when creating a map by automatically choosing a blue circle as the mark type. However, you are free to choose a different mark type, as well as using all options at your disposal on the Marks card, as you would with any other chart type. For example, you may prefer to denote geographic areas on your map with a square instead of a circle. This is as simple as choosing Square from the Mark Type drop-down on the Marks card. The Shape mark type may even prove more appropriate, allowing you to not only choose a single shape from a variety of shapes and shape palettes, but to use variable shapes on the map based on another dimension (just drop the desired dimension on Shape on the Marks card). Color and Size on the Marks card may also be used either to change default size and color choices or to control with other dimensions or measures. And don't forget Label on the Marks card. By dropping various dimensions or measures here, marks on the map may be appropriately annotated.

Tip *Although you may think you need geocoded fields to take full advantage of Tableau mapping, you may use other nongeocoded fields to enhance your map. For example, by simply color-coding a map based on another nongeocoded dimension (such as region), your map exhibits various colors based on related geographic areas.*

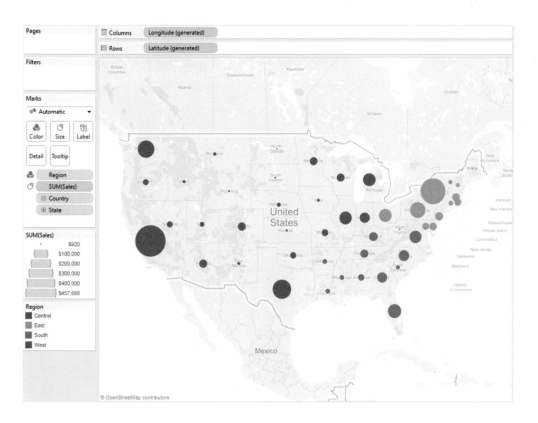

Two mark types have particular possibilities with maps. The first, Filled Map, is used automatically if you choose the Filled Map option in Show Me when first creating the map. However, if you initially created a map by just double-clicking a dimension, you may change the mark type on the Marks card to Filled Map to replace the default circle mark with a filled map. Filled maps benefit in particular from another dimension or measure added to Color.

The second mark type that may not initially come to mind for map usage is Pie. Used judiciously, this mark can provide extra value to maps by breaking down geographic data by another dimension and measure. Once a map has been created, change the default mark type to Pie. Drop the dimension you wish to subdivide the pies by on Color (each dimension member will create a pie wedge)—but be careful, as any dimension with more than four or five members will probably create too many wedges to be of use. Then, drop the measure you wish to determine the size of pie wedges on Angle. Although you may find it diminishes the value of the map if overused, you may even consider dropping another dimension or measure on Size to vary the size of each pie.

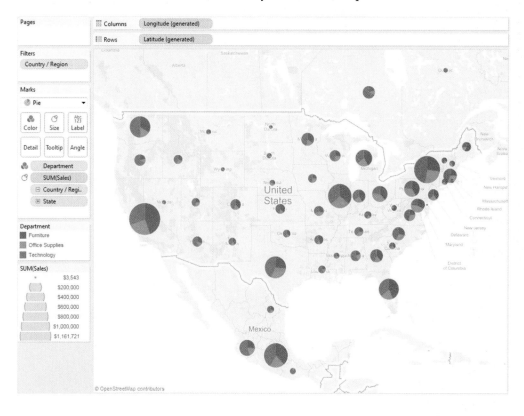

Custom Background Images

Video *Custom Background Images*

With all the possibilities discussed earlier in this chapter, you may still find uses for geospatial data representation in Tableau that built-in geocoding, Tableau background maps, or custom WMS servers can't satisfy. Well, Tableau provides yet another way to plot data on your own custom background images. The possibilities are as rich as are the availability of pictures or drawings.

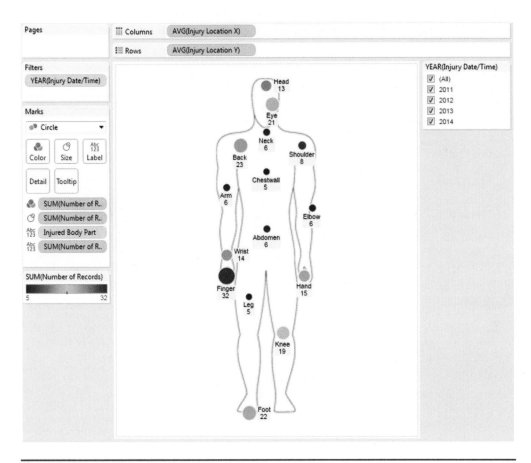

Figure 7-1   Custom background image

Consider the image illustrated in Figure 7-1. This type of visualization could be invaluable to an orthopedic surgical practice that is analyzing its case mix. Or a company that evaluates employee injuries on a regular basis might find this of immense benefit.

Much as with the two main components of Tableau mapping (geocoding data to derive latitude and longitude, and background maps), Figure 7-1 depends on two main components: (1) a consistent X/Y coordinate system to plot marks, and (2) a custom background image.

Generating Your Own Coordinate System

The first requirement for using a nonmap background image is to establish your own representation of X and Y coordinates, as opposed to latitude and longitude. As with a map, the underlying chart type for this equates to a scatter plot (scatter plots are discussed in Chapter 4). An individual mark is placed on the chart based on a combination of X and Y values. Measures or dimensions representing these X and Y values are placed on the Row and Columns shelves, which determine the specific location on the visualization where a particular mark will appear.

Determining the proper placement and relationship of these X/Y coordinates (the "coordinate system") will be dependent upon the background image the marks will appear on top of. Referring again to Figure 7-1, if the background image is 99 "units" wide and 325 "units" tall and the mark to indicate "Head" needs to appear at the top center of the image, the X coordinate should be 50 (halfway across the image) and the Y coordinate should be 318 (close to the maximum height of the image).

Determining the number of "units" wide and high will be the first decision you'll need to make. Although the width and height of the background image in pixels is one way to achieve this (and the example in Figure 7-1 has been specified this way), this is not required. In fact, you may specify any beginning and ending X and Y values you wish when you add the background image. So, theoretically, the beginning X and Y values could be set to 0, with the ending X and Y values set to 1. Your coordinate system would then assume that all X and Y values used to plot marks would be fractional numbers between 0 and 1. The specified beginning and ending values could be 0 and 100, between –100 and 100, and so forth—you may set the minimum and maximum values to anything you choose, as long as the actual X and Y values that will be used to place marks on the visualization will fall between the minimum and maximum. In fact, you may often have to change the initial minimum and maximum values you assign to a background image to achieve proper placement of marks—a fair amount of experimentation may be required to get desired results.

Prior to adding a custom background image, you'll need to identify the X and Y fields you wish to use to place marks on the image. They can be existing dimensions or measures in your data source, or they can be calculated fields you create (calculated fields are covered in Chapter 6). In the example illustrated in Figure 7-1, the X and Y coordinates are created in calculated fields that assign specific values based on the type of injury being plotted.

```
Injury Location X                    Sample Injury Data Extract          ⊗

CASE [Injured Body Part]
    WHEN "Abdomen" Then 50
    WHEN "Arm" Then 10
    WHEN "Back" Then 24
    WHEN "Chestwall" Then 50
    WHEN "Elbow" Then 95
    WHEN "Eye" Then 56
    WHEN "Finger" Then 10
    WHEN "Foot" Then 32                                    ▶
    WHEN "Hand" Then 87
    WHEN "Head" Then 50
    WHEN "Knee" Then 66
    WHEN "Leg" Then 32
    WHEN "Neck" Then 50
    WHEN "shoulder" Then 85
    WHEN "wrist" Then 10
End

The calculation is valid.          Sheets Affected ▼      Apply         OK
```

```
Injury Location Y                    ⬚ Sample Injury Data Extract              ⊗

CASE [Injured Body Part]
    WHEN "Abdomen" Then 180
    WHEN "Arm" Then 220
    WHEN "Back" Then 260
    WHEN "Chestwall" Then 235
    WHEN "Elbow" Then 200
    WHEN "Eye" Then 300
    WHEN "Finger" Then 135
    WHEN "Foot" Then 3
    WHEN "Hand" Then 135                                                   ▶
    WHEN "Head" Then 318
    WHEN "Knee" Then 80
    WHEN "Leg" Then 115
    WHEN "Neck" Then 273
    WHEN "shoulder" Then 260
    WHEN "wrist" Then 155
End

The calculation is valid.        Sheets Affected ▾    Apply        OK
```

Adding a Custom Background Image

After establishing which fields you'll use for X and Y values, choose Maps | Background Images from the drop-down menus. You'll be presented with a list of data sources used in the workbook. Because a custom background image is matched to specific X/Y fields in a particular data source, you must initially choose the data source that will be used with your image. The Background Images dialog box will appear, showing any existing images that may have been added to the data source previously.

Click the Add Image button to add a new image. The Background Images dialog box will appear:

- Provide a descriptive name for the image. This name will appear in the list of images presented by the Background Images dialog box.

- Specify a filename or URL that points to the image. Tableau supports most standard image formats, such as JPG, BMP, TIF, PNG, and so forth. Once you specify a filename, a thumbnail of the image will appear on the dialog box. Slide the Washout slider to change the contrast of the image.

- From the drop-down field list, specify the field in the data source to act as the X field. Only numeric fields will appear in the drop-down. Make the same field choice for the Y field.

- Specify left, right, bottom, and top values to establish the boundaries of your coordinate system. For example, the background image illustrated in Figure 7-1 is 99 "units" (in this case, pixels) wide by 325 "units" (in this case, pixels) tall, and the X and Y calculated fields have been designed to provide integer values between these limits. As such, left and right values are set to 0 and 99, with bottom and top values set to 0 and 325.

- On the Options tab, check Lock Aspect Ratio if you wish Tableau to maintain the same width-to-height ratio of the image as marks or zoom levels change. Otherwise, the image may be stretched horizontally or vertically when the worksheet resizes.

- On the Options tab, check Always Show Entire Image if you want Tableau to not zoom in past the edges of the image.

- On the Options tab, click the Add button if you wish to add filter conditions to determine when to show the images. For example, you may wish to choose from a variety of background images, depending on a Male/Female filter or a Child/Adult parameter.

Once the image has been added, any time you drag the specified X and Y fields to the Rows and Columns shelves, the background image will automatically display behind the marks. Note that you won't want Tableau to aggregate the X and Y values when placing them on the worksheet, or the positions won't match to the desired values. For example, if the X/Y value for a particular dimension member should be 10-20, but there are five records in the underlying data source for that dimension member, Tableau will sum the X/Y values and place the mark on the chart at position 50-100. This may not display the background image at all, or may display it as a very small picture. In any event, marks won't be plotted at proper positions in front of the image.

To avoid this issue, either change the aggregation type for the X and Y values to something that returns the actual underlying value (such as Average, Minimum, or Maximum) or convert the numeric values to dimensions. Both of these approaches may be accomplished by right-clicking the field indicators on the Rows and Columns shelves and making the desired choice from the context menu.

Tip *Charts displaying custom background images may still show an axis for the X and Y values. You may hide these by right-clicking on the axis and unchecking Show Header. You still may see unwanted lines next to the image. These "zero" lines are desirable when charts and axes are denoting numeric values, but are probably a distraction when displaying a custom background image. Set them to None with the Lines formatting option.*

Creating Dashboards and Stories

I n many cases, the finished product in a business intelligence project consists of one or more dashboards. A Google search on "dashboard" probably will return more computer-related definitions than descriptions of the portion of a car that displays the speedometer, fuel gauge, and other key performance indicators. Still, a business intelligence (BI) *dashboard* serves a similar purpose: to combine in one viewable space more than one key performance indicator, chart, or diagram to present a unified view to your audience.

Although you can use dashboards with actions to create a "guided analytic," Tableau features a built-in option specifically for this purpose. By combining multiple worksheets and/or dashboards into a Tableau story, an organized, guided "move forward or move backward view by view" chart series is simple to create.

Depending on how the workbook is finally distributed or viewed (in a copy of Tableau Desktop or Tableau Reader, exported to a PDF file, or posted to Tableau Server or Tableau Public), the end user may view the combined dashboard, individual sheets, stories, or everything.

Download   At *www.tableaubook.com, download* Chapter 8 - Dashboards.twbx *to see examples that relate to this chapter.*

Creating a Simple Dashboard

As mentioned previously, Tableau's basic dashboard paradigm revolves around existing worksheets. As such, you'll want to think about your ultimate dashboard requirement as you create individual worksheets. Probably the most basic, but sometimes ignored, consideration is the names given to worksheets. Not only will meaningful worksheet names help you keep track of desired views when designing the dashboard, but worksheet names will automatically appear on the dashboard as individual titles.

Other dashboard considerations include additional visual elements in each worksheet beyond the basic visualization. For example, visible color legends, size legends, and quick filters will be included on the dashboard when you initially add the worksheet. Although you can move or remove any extra element that you don't want on a dashboard, you may choose to hide any extraneous legends or quick filters on the worksheet itself before you even begin dashboard design.

Video *Creating a Dashboard*

When you're ready to create a dashboard in an existing workbook, right-click (CONTROL-click on Mac) on the tab list, filmstrip, or sheet sorter view and choose New Dashboard from the context menu; click the New Dashboard tab along the bottom of the workspace; or choose Dashboard | New Dashboard from the drop-down menus. A blank dashboard will appear with the Data pane replaced by the Dashboard window. This contains four sections: a list of existing worksheets in the workbook, a selection of additional dashboard elements (covered in the next section of this chapter), a layout section containing the organization of items added to the dashboard, and a sizing section for customizing dashboard element sizes.

Setting Dashboard Size

The first choice to make is dashboard size. Make choices from the bottom-left portion of the Dashboard window. By default, Tableau initially sets the dashboard to a pre-defined "Desktop" size of 1,000 pixels wide by 800 pixels high. If you wish to choose other fixed sizes more appropriate for devices that you plan to target with the final dashboard, choose from a variety of pre-defined device sizes from the drop-down list, or select the Fixed option and specify your own height and width.

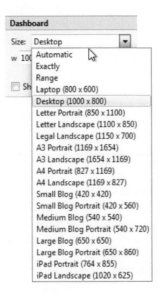

Although a fixed dashboard size lets you plan for specific device screen sizes, there are tradeoffs. The first issue you may encounter with a fixed dashboard size is introduction of scroll bars. Depending on how many sheets you add and how you size individual sheets, horizontal/vertical scroll bars may appear. This may require inconvenient sizing or placement requirements of some dashboard elements. The other tradeoff is compromises for devices with other screen sizes that may use your dashboard. Whereas a dashboard sized to the specific iPad pre-set may be sized perfectly on an iPad, a full computer screen will suffer from the small overall dashboard size.

There are two alternatives that may better serve a wider array of devices or a varied set of dashboard objects. Automatic size eliminates scroll bars and resizes objects within the dashboard automatically as viewers resize their screens. The Range option provides a potential "happy medium" between a restrictive fixed dashboard size and an unpredictable, fully automatic dashboard size. Here, you may specify upper and lower width and height limits, which will permit automatic sizing as long as the dashboard stays within the specified limits. If the end user sizes their screen beyond the limits, the dashboard will size to the specified limit and scroll bars or white space will appear. You may wish to experiment with an initial dashboard size setting (perhaps automatic) and later modify to a range or fixed size based on behavior of specific devices and feedback from viewers.

Adding Sheets

Next, you can begin adding worksheets to the dashboard. One immediate choice to make is whether to add worksheets in tiled or floating mode. There are two buttons midway down the Dashboard window that permit this selection, which applies to any worksheets you add to the dashboard moving forward. If the default tiled setting is retained, worksheets will be placed on the dashboard in a logical side-by-side, top-and-bottom fashion, with no worksheet, legend, title, caption, or quick filter permitted to overlap any other dashboard element. If floating is chosen, any worksheet added to the dashboard from that point forward (even if there are already tiled worksheet elements on the dashboard) can be freely placed in any location.

New objects:
| Tiled | Floating |

Best Practice   *You may be immediately tempted to add all dashboard elements with the floating option for maximum flexibility. You'll soon discover, however, that perfectly aligning dashboard elements may prove difficult. It may be preferable to use the tiled option to facilitate good element alignment. You can then select individual dashboard elements that you want to move freely (such as legends), and choose the floating option for them only, as discussed later in the chapter under "Floating Placement."*

Tiled Placement

This default setting places worksheets and their associated elements (captions, quick filters, and so forth) in a strict "no-overlap" order on the dashboard. The most basic way to use tiled placement is to simply double-click worksheet names in the order you want to add them to the dashboard. Tableau will add each worksheet to the dashboard in a side-by-side, then top-and-bottom order.

For example, if you double-click two worksheets, the second will be placed to the right of the first, with the dashboard divided in half vertically. If you double-click a third sheet, the dashboard will split vertically on the left, with the third worksheet appearing below the first. A fourth double-click will divide the dashboard into four even quarters, with one worksheet being placed in each. All related worksheet elements (such as quick filters and legends) will be placed on the right side of the dashboard. Figure 8-1 illustrates a simple dashboard containing four worksheets that were double-clicked in order of appearance in the worksheet list.

You can also drag and drop worksheets from the worksheet list onto the dashboard. Although the resulting placement of new views can seem confusing if you're just getting

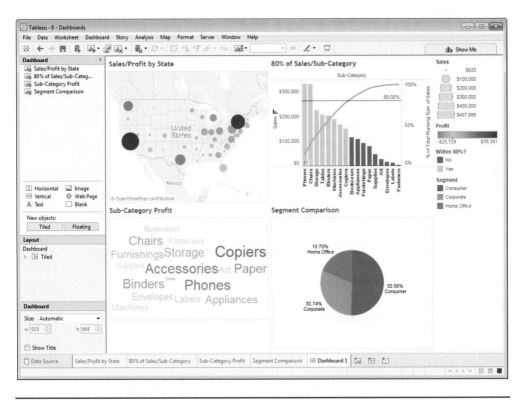

Figure 8-1   Basic tiled dashboard created using double-click

used to dragging and dropping sheets, there are a few tips that will help you master exactly where the sheet you are dragging will appear in relation to existing sheets:

- A large gray box indicates that the sheet will split the dashboard in half vertically or horizontally.

- A thin gray box (typically at the very edge of the dashboard, but also between legends and worksheets) indicates that the sheet will take up that entire portion of the dashboard, resizing all other dashboard elements to accommodate it.

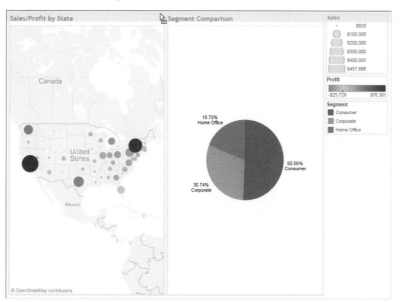

- A medium gray box indicates that the sheet will be placed in between the two elements on either side, resizing the other two elements to accommodate it.

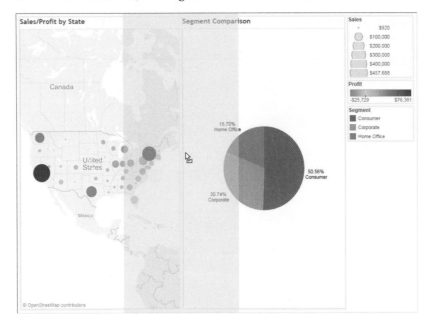

Once you've placed a worksheet on the dashboard, you can move it to a different location. When you select the desired sheet on the dashboard, you'll notice the small series of white dots at the top of the title bar (known as a "move handle"). Hold your mouse down on the move handle and drag the sheet to the desired location, keeping in mind the tips just discussed.

You can also resize a worksheet or legend once it has been placed on the dashboard. Point to the top, bottom, left, or right edge of the element you want to resize until you see a double-arrow cursor. Drag to resize the selected element, and resize adjoining elements accordingly. Tableau makes experimenting easy. If you don't like the result of a worksheet placement or resize, simply click the undo button in the toolbar or press CTRL-Z (COMMAND-Z on Mac) and try again.

Tip *After you add a worksheet to the dashboard, you may find that the visualization in the worksheet is not properly sized. There may be scroll bars that you don't want to see, or an object may be too small or too large for the space it's been allotted on the dashboard. Similar to the fit option available in the toolbar when you're creating a worksheet, you can size the object separately within the dashboard. Select the desired sheet on the dashboard and click the context arrow in the upper right of the title bar. Make the desired choice from the Fit option on the context menu.*

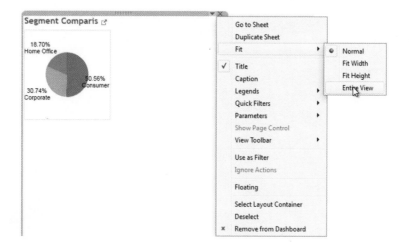

Floating Placement

Although tiled dashboards guarantee perfect alignment, they also present a degree of rigidity that may eliminate flexibility with certain dashboard layout requirements. *Floating placement* permits worksheets and associated dashboard elements to be placed freely anywhere on a dashboard.

After clicking the Floating button under Add New Sheets And Objects As, worksheets can be freely placed anywhere on the dashboard. If the worksheet includes legends, quick filters, or a caption, these items will also be placed on the dashboard as freeform elements. Once they have been dropped, worksheets and their associated elements can be freely moved and resized without limitation. An immediate benefit of floating placement is the ability to move legends on top of existing worksheets that may have blank areas, such as maps. Figure 8-2 illustrates this.

Tip *You may alternate between floating and tiled behavior of individual worksheets when you move them on the dashboard. If you hold down SHIFT and drag a floating sheet, it will become tiled. Conversely, a tiled worksheet will float with SHIFT-drag.*

If you already have existing tiled worksheets on the dashboard, floating worksheets will always appear on top of them. If you have multiple floating worksheets, you can choose the floating order, placing one object on top of or behind other floating objects. Select the desired floating sheet on the dashboard, click the context arrow in the upper right of the title bar on the object, and make the desired floating-order choice from the context menu. You may accomplish the same task by dragging and dropping floating objects into a different order within the Layout section in the left of the Dashboard window.

Object transparency becomes important with objects as well. Although text you add from the Dashboard window, worksheet legends, and transparent images (such as transparent PNG files) will permit the underlying worksheet image to show through, other worksheets and some associated elements (such as quick filters and parameters) aren't transparent and won't reveal the underlying worksheet image.

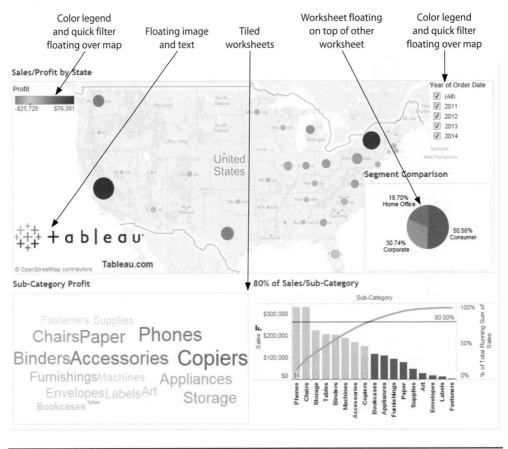

Figure 8-2   Floating worksheets and legends

You may find that a combination of tiled and floating dashboard elements, such as that exhibited in Figure 8-2, gives you the best of both worlds. For example, you may prefer the perfect alignment of several tiled worksheets. However, you then may want to place map legends over unused areas of a map (such as open water). Simply select the legend you want to float, click the context arrow in the title bar, and check Floating from the context menu. The legend can then be moved to any place on the dashboard.

Associated Worksheet Elements

Any visible legends, titles, quick filters, and parameters originally belonging to a worksheet will appear on the dashboard when you add the worksheet. If you add a worksheet in tiled mode, the associated elements will be tiled. If you use floating mode, associated elements will be free-floating on the dashboard. If the worksheets that make up your dashboard contain even a moderate number of these associated elements, the dashboard can quickly become cluttered with multiple legends, quick filters, and parameters.

Consider removing extraneous elements that don't add to overall dashboard effectiveness. For example, if a worksheet mark is size encoded and the actual values of the size aren't necessary for effective use of the dashboard, a size legend may unnecessarily take up valuable dashboard space. The same consideration may apply to a color legend if general color encoding can be deduced by simply looking at the worksheet, or if you've labeled the marks with the same information. In these cases, simply select the legend and click the small × in the upper-right corner to remove the legend. If you later want to redisplay a dashboard element, just select the associated sheet on the dashboard. Then make the desired choice from the Analysis drop-down menu or context menu (displayed by clicking the context arrow in the title bar).

You can also move elements away from their default location (the right side of the dashboard for tiled worksheets and next to the associated worksheet in floating mode). For example, a tiled legend on the right side of the dashboard may be more effective if it appears next to its associated worksheet that may have been placed in the lower left of the dashboard. Don't forget the option to float legends, even if the associated worksheet is tiled, permitting the legend to be placed partially or fully on top of the associated worksheet.

Best Practice *If you have several worksheets that use the same quick filter, consider one of several approaches to eliminate duplicate quick filters appearing on a dashboard. Look for choices to apply the quick filter to all worksheets using the data source, or one or more sheets on the dashboard. You may also consider using a parameter instead of a quick filter (for example, if you want a single prompt to apply to worksheets not based on the same data source). The parameter can be applied flexibly to more than one worksheet, but need only be displayed on the dashboard once. Quick filters and parameters are covered in detail in Chapter 5.*

Supplementary Dashboard Features

So far, this chapter has discussed adding worksheets and their associated elements to a dashboard. Tableau includes additional elements you can add from the left side of the Dashboard window. These additional elements permit text and images to be placed on the dashboard, as well as additional items to support web pages within dashboards, blank objects for spacing, and containers to help further refine the way a dashboard is organized. In addition, the Layout and Size sections provide various ways of laying out your dashboard.

Layout Container

A *layout container* is an outline or box that contains other objects, such as worksheets, legends, and quick filters. The main benefit of a layout container is automatic resizing of objects within it. If, for example, a quick filter changes the size of a worksheet in a container (perhaps a crosstab shows fewer rows), the other objects in the container will automatically resize to accommodate the smaller worksheet.

With tiled worksheets, layout containers are an integral part of a dashboard. In fact, even though you don't explicitly choose them, layout containers are added in quantity when you add worksheets in tiled mode. Consider the dashboard illustrated in Figure 8-3, which was created by simply dragging three worksheets to a new dashboard with tiled mode selected. Because one worksheet includes two legends and a quick filter and each of the other worksheets includes a legend, several layout containers are automatically created to accommodate the combination of worksheets and associated dashboard elements.

There are two general ways to familiarize yourself with automatic layout container creation:

- From a worksheet's context menu (click the context arrow in a worksheet's title bar), choose Select Layout Container. This will highlight the layout container that the worksheet is contained within.

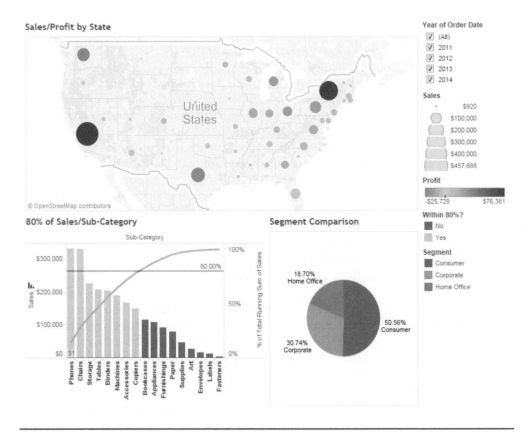

Figure 8-3   Layout containers automatically added to a dashboard

- Examine the Layout section of the Dashboard window on the left side of the screen. This section outlines the layout container hierarchy of the dashboard, indicating how many layout containers there are, whether they are horizontal or vertical, and what dashboard elements are contained within them.

Based on the Layout section, you can determine that Figure 8-3 includes an overall container that the entire dashboard is enclosed in (the Tiled/Horizontal container directly underneath the dashboard). Within this container are two others: another Tiled container that encompasses the three charts (you'll notice the three chart names within the Tiled container), and a Vertical container that encompasses the legends and quick filter (legend/quick filter names appear within it).

You can add your own layout containers to your dashboard by dragging them from the left side of the screen to the dashboard. Choose a horizontal or vertical container, depending on whether you want worksheet widths or heights to automatically resize, respectively. Then drag worksheets into the just-added containers. Look carefully—a thin blue outline around an existing container indicates that a worksheet will be dropped in that container.

As with worksheets, you may add layout containers to the dashboard in either tiled or floating mode. If you add a floating layout container, it will prompt you to hold down the SHIFT key to drag floating worksheets or other dashboard objects into the floating layout container. Interestingly enough, objects you add to the floating container will be tiled *within the container,* even though the container itself is floating.

You can add a border and background shading to layout containers with the Format option. Select the desired layout container and click the context arrow in the title bar, choosing Format from the context menu. You can also right-click the container name in Layout and choose Format Container. The Dashboard window will be replaced by a Format Container pane. Choose the type of border you would like the container to display, as well as the color and intensity of shading to fill the container with.

Blank

Another dashboard element that's primarily intended for tiled dashboards is the *blank.* When dragged to a dashboard and sized to a desired width or height, this element simply inserts white space that can be used to separate dashboard elements from each other.

Text

In addition to individual worksheet titles (which appear automatically when a worksheet is added to a dashboard), as well as an overall dashboard title that can be displayed by way of the Dashboard | Show Title drop-down menu item, you can add text by dragging this item from the left side of the Dashboard window. When you drop the text element, an Edit Text dialog box will appear, allowing you to type and format text, including adding pre-defined dashboard fields from the Insert drop-down menu. Text can be added in either tiled or floating mode. In tiled mode, text will exhibit the same "gray box" behavior as other dashboard elements when being placed or moved on the dashboard.

Image

Also usable in tiled or floating mode, a bitmap graphic can be added to your dashboard by dragging Image from the left of the Dashboard window. Once dropped on the dashboard, a dialog box will appear prompting for the choice of an image file from a local or network drive. Navigate to the desired folder and select an image file. You can also type in a full URL to an image on a web server. Once an image has been added, you can change the image file, add a URL to permit the image to act as a web page hyperlink, center the image, or scale the image to fit by right-clicking the image on the dashboard or right-clicking on the image item in Layout.

Note *Tableau 9 on the Mac takes special advantage of a high-resolution Retina display for maps (covered in Chapter 7) and high-resolution image files on dashboards. By default, Tableau will reduce the resolution of dashboard images to maintain similar image size on standard resolution and high-resolution displays. If you wish to retain the high resolution of the original image, place the characters "@2x" at the end of the image filename before the file extension (such as* HighRes Logo@2x.png*). Tableau will add the image to the dashboard in full resolution.*

Best Practice *Many a dashboard includes a large company logo, often in the upper left of the dashboard. Reconsider this approach. As the human eye generally processes information from left to right and top to bottom, the upper left of a dashboard is often the first thing seen. A key metric is probably better suited for upper-left placement in a dashboard.*

Web Page

A web page can be embedded in a dashboard by dragging Web Page from the left side of the screen. A URL prompt accepts any standard web page address. All typical web page interactivity, such as hyperlinks, is available on the web page in the dashboard. Although this allows you to include a static web page in your dashboard, exceptional flexibility to customize web page interactivity exists with dashboard actions, which are discussed later in the chapter.

Setting Dashboard and Element Sizes

As a general rule, placing worksheets on dashboards is a simple drag-and-drop process. And sizing elements once they appear on a dashboard is simple—just point to the element and resize when the sizing handles appear. However, Tableau provides the Size section in the lower left of the Dashboard window, which provides precise control over the position and size of individual dashboard elements (provided they are in floating mode). Either on the dashboard itself or in the Layout section above the Size section, select the worksheet, legend, or other element that you want to change. Then make desired entries in the Size section. Sizing the overall dashboard is also accomplished here, as discussed earlier in this chapter.

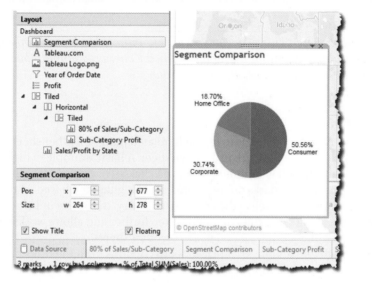

Dashboard Actions

Tableau provides flexible interactivity in your dashboards beyond the default tooltips that appear when you hover your mouse over worksheet marks. This interactivity is supplied via *dashboard actions,* interactive settings that allow you to highlight, filter, and navigate from any mark on any worksheet on your dashboard.

Note *Some of the interactivity discussed in this section also applies to individual worksheets. When editing a worksheet, choose Worksheet | Actions from the drop-down menus to create and edit actions.*

Video *Using Dashboard Actions*

There are three types of dashboard actions:

- **Highlight**   Highlight matching marks on one or more sheets in the dashboard.
- **Filter**   Filter one or more sheets on the dashboard based on a chosen mark, or navigate to another sheet or dashboard in the workbook.
- **URL**   Navigate to a web page. Optionally, pass selected information from the worksheet to the URL to personalize it.

Furthermore, there are three ways that the viewer can initiate a dashboard action:

- **Hover**   Simply hover your mouse over a mark.
- **Select**   Click on a mark.
- **Menu**   Choose the option from the tooltip or right-click context menu.

Caution *Be judicious with use of dashboard actions initiated by hovers. Typically, only highlight actions are appropriate for this method. Otherwise, simple mouse movement may initiate time-intensive or undesired actions.*

Highlight Action

The purpose of a highlight action is to highlight related marks on other sheets in your dashboard based on a chosen mark in a source sheet. A basic example of highlighting that Tableau provides by default is exhibited when you click an individual entry in a color legend. You'll typically see marks on the related sheet highlighted based on the legend entry you click. When you deselect the color legend entry, marks are unhighlighted on the sheet. A highlight action takes this capability a step further and allows worksheet marks (not legends) to highlight other related marks on other sheets.

To create a highlight action, select Dashboard | Actions from the drop-down menu. The Actions dialog box will appear. Click the Add Action button and choose Highlight from the Edit Highlight Action dialog box, select the method of initiating the action (hover, select, or menu). In the Source Sheets section of the dialog box, choose one or more worksheets that you want the action to occur on. In the Target Sheets section, choose one or more worksheets that you want to be highlighted based on the selected mark in the source sheet or sheets. There should be a common dimension in source and target sheets, or highlighting won't have the desired effect.

In this example, when the mouse is hovered over a section of a Region Profit Comparison pie chart, corresponding regions will be highlighted in the Profit by State sheet.

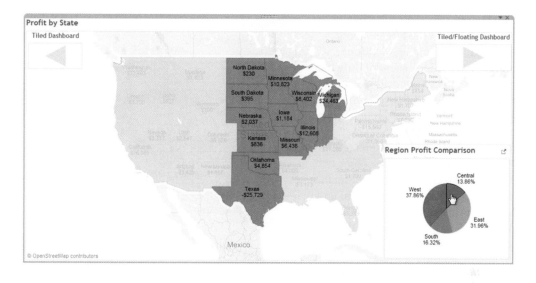

Filter Action

Although quick filters and parameters are options for filtering interactivity on a dashboard, a filter action permits additional interactivity, where one or more worksheets on the dashboard are filtered based on a chosen mark on the source sheet. For example, when a certain mark is clicked on one sheet, other sheets will refresh, only showing marks that match the item that was clicked on the source sheet.

Filter actions can be created directly from a worksheet's context menu or from the Dashboard | Actions dialog box discussed earlier. Decide which sheet you want to act as the filter source. Select the context menu in the title bar (or right-click the desired sheet in Layout) and check Use As Filter from the context menu. Thereafter, when you click any mark in the source sheet, all other sheets on the dashboard will be filtered to only show values matching what you clicked on the source sheet. Choose the same context menu and uncheck Use As Filter if you want to turn this option off.

When you use the context menu option, a "generated" filter action will appear in the Dashboard | Actions dialog box. If you want to remove or customize the generated filter action, make choices from the Actions dialog box. You can also create new filter actions directly from this dialog box. After creating a new filter action, select the method of initiating the action (Select and Menu are probably the best two choices). In the Source Sheets section of the dialog box, choose one or more worksheets that you want the action to be executed from. In the Target Sheets section, choose one or more worksheets that you want to be filtered based on the selected mark in the source sheet or sheets.

By default, you can multiselect marks on the source sheets with CTRL-click (COMMAND-click on Mac) to filter on more than one mark. If, however, you only want to allow a single mark to be highlighted to filter, check Run On Single Select Only. The three options under Clearing The Selection Will allow you to specify behavior when a filter action is cleared (for example, if the viewer clicks the same mark that was initially filtered, or clicks on a blank area of the source sheet). Leave The Filter will leave the filter active on other sheets. Show All Values will return all values to target sheets as though no filter was applied.

And Exclude All Values will display no data at all on the target sheets. Although the Exclude All Values option may initially seem of little use, it comes in handy for drill-down types of actions, where you only want target sheets to appear when a filter has been selected and to display nothing when no filter is selected. Finally, the Target Filters section allows you to choose a limited set of fields to apply the filter action to and to map source and target fields if different sheets are not using the same field names.

In this example, clicking a mark in the Profit by State sheet will filter the Customer Detail crosstab on the dashboard. When the filter is cleared on the source sheet, the crosstab will show no data.

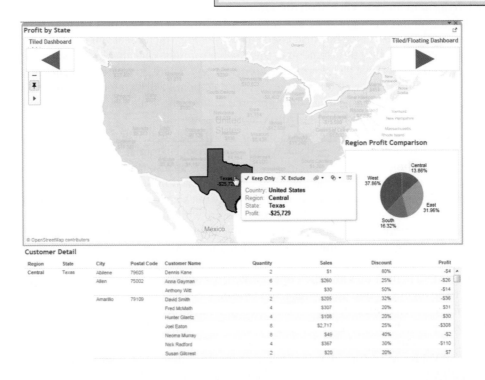

Another capability of a filter action that may not be initially obvious is the ability to navigate to another sheet or dashboard in your workbook. In this case, a standard filter action is created as described previously, but a dashboard or worksheet other than the current dashboard is selected in the Target Sheets area. In this example, an "arrow" visualization has been placed on the dashboard to appear as a navigation button. A filter action is initiated when it's clicked. Notice, however, that the Target Sheets section displays a completely different dashboard than the Source Sheets section.

URL Action

A URL action allows a web page to be launched from within your dashboard. Furthermore, any field in use on the source worksheet can be used to customize the URL. This permits Tableau to display custom web pages from the Internet or to integrate with other web-based systems in your organization.

After creating a new URL action, select the method of initiating the action (Select and Menu are probably the best two choices). In the Source Sheets section of the dialog box, choose one or more worksheets that you want the action to occur on. Then type or paste the desired URL into the URL box. To customize the URL depending on which mark is selected to initiate the action, click the small right arrow at the end of the URL to display fields that are used in the source sheets. When you select one of the fields, a placeholder will be added to the current cursor position in the URL. When the URL is executed, the current value from that field will be placed in the URL.

URL options at the bottom of the dialog box allow you to URL-encode custom field values added to the URL (for example, to replace spaces or other special characters with % encoded characters). You can permit multiple marks to be selected when the URL action is initiated with the appropriate checkbox. You can then specify the item and escape delimiter to separate the multiple values and end-of-the-value list in the URL.

In this example, if a user clicks a measure or right-clicks a dimension in the Customer Detail sheet, he or she will be presented with a hyperlink option to Google the currently highlighted customer. When this is clicked, a URL action will display the Google web page with the current customer name added to the URL at an appropriate point (as a value to a "q=" parameter).

Note *If your dashboard contains a Web Page element added from the dashboard menu, it will be updated in place when a URL action takes place. If there is no such element in your dashboard, Tableau will launch a separate web browser window as the target for the URL action.*

Creating Stories

Generally speaking, a *guided analytic* is a series of charts/worksheets or dashboards that are navigated through in an orderly, or "guided," fashion from one to the next. A viewer can progress through the views step by step to see the progression of charts in order. Although you can use Tableau dashboards to create a guided analytic, Tableau *stories* are specifically designed for this purpose. Although similar to creating dashboards, the concept of combining existing worksheets together in a single screen isn't applicable to a story. Instead, *story points* are added one at a time, each consisting of a single existing worksheet or single existing dashboard (if you want more than one worksheet to appear on the same screen in a story, you must create a dashboard combining the worksheets first and then add the dashboard to the story).

 Video *Creating Stories*

When you're ready to create a story in an existing workbook, right-click (CONTROL-click on Mac) on the tab list, filmstrip, or sheet sorter view and choose New Story from the context menu. Click the New Story tab along the bottom of the workspace, or choose Story | New Story from the drop-down menus. A blank story will appear with the Data pane replaced by the Story pane. This contains three sections: a list of existing worksheets and dashboards in the workbook, the Navigator section where you choose whether or not to show back/forward buttons, and a sizing section for sizing the story.

Setting Story Size

As with a dashboard, the first choice to make is story size. Make choices from the bottom-left portion of the Story pane. By default, Tableau initially sets the story to a pre-defined "Story" size of 1,016 pixels wide by 964 pixels high. If you wish to choose other fixed sizes more appropriate for devices that you plan to target with the final dashboard, choose from a variety of pre-defined device sizes from the drop-down list, or select the Fixed option and specify your own height and width.

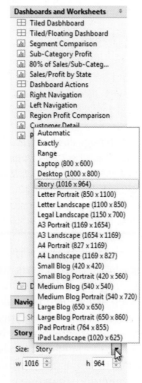

As with dashboards, there are pluses and minuses to using fixed story sizes as opposed to automatically sized stories (see "Setting Dashboard Size" earlier in the chapter). And, as with dashboards, you may want to start by setting your story to an Automatic or Range size and then modify it later, based on user feedback.

Adding Sheets and Dashboards

Next, drag the initial worksheet or dashboard you want to appear as your first story point (a story consists of multiple *story points* that the viewer will move through one at a time forward or backward). All related worksheet or dashboard elements, such as legends, quick filters, parameters, and so forth, will appear on the story point. If you prefer that the current story point reflect a specific worksheet or dashboard "state" (certain marks selected, specific parameter or quick filter values chosen, and so forth), make those choices. When the story point is saved, this state will be preserved.

Edit the caption for the current story point by double-clicking it and typing in descriptive text. If the current size of a caption is insufficient to show all text, you may make the caption taller by dragging on the bottom of the caption. All captions will resize accordingly. If a caption isn't tall enough to expose all text, a scroll bar will appear.

You may also add one or more descriptions to the story point by dragging from the Story pane on the left. A description will float over the worksheet or dashboard, and you may resize and position the description wherever you like. Initially, a description will appear with a shaded background, which won't fully permit the underlying visual element it floats over to show through. You may right-click (COMMAND-click on Mac) the description and choose Format from the context menu and choose a smaller shading value to add more transparency to the description.

Once you are satisfied with the current story point, you have two immediate options to create the next point. Click Duplicate to duplicate the current story point as the next point in the story. Or click New Blank Point to add a story point with no included worksheet or dashboard. If you duplicate a story point, all visual elements from the original point are duplicated, with the exception of the caption. You may now change the state of the story point, such as choosing different quick filter or parameter options, or selecting different marks on the story point. Click Update above the caption to save the updated caption and story point state. The undo icon (left circle arrow) will undo any state changes you made and revert to the original story point state.

Adding a new blank story point permits dragging a different worksheet or dashboard from the Story pane, as you did for the first point in the story. And, as with other story points, you may add descriptions, type in the caption, set quick filter or parameter values, and select marks before saving the story point.

Tip *Reordering story points is simple. Just drag the caption of the desired story point to the new position you wish it to hold. If you wish to add a new point to the middle of an existing story, create the new point at the end of the story and then just drag the caption to the desired position.*

Formatting Stories

There are several approaches to formatting different parts of a story. To format individual descriptions on a story point, right-click (COMMAND-click on Mac) the description and choose Format. You may also select Story | Format from the drop-down menus. The Story pane will be replaced with a format dialog box. Make various formatting choices for the story background, title formatting, caption navigation options, and description formatting.

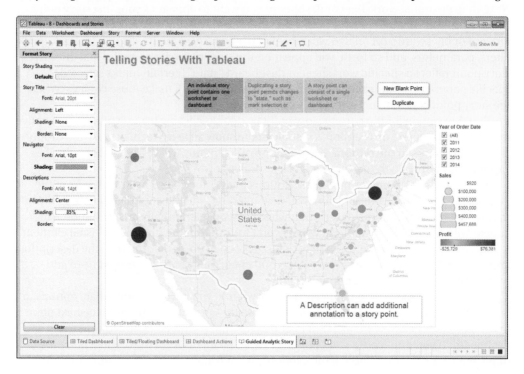

Working with Tableau Server

S o far, this book has presented a great deal of information on how you, as a visualization designer, can use Tableau Desktop to its fullest. But what happens when you want to share the results of your work with others? The fullest capabilities that provide complete interactivity in a web browser or tablet, including the ability to modify existing workbooks or create new workbooks, are provided by Tableau Server. Most of this chapter covers this flexible, web-based tool. However, your organization may not have access to an in-house Tableau Server. Tableau provides options to connect to a hosted version in the "cloud" via Tableau Public and Tableau Online. Or, you may just choose to export the underlying data from one or more of your worksheets for use in Microsoft Excel, Microsoft Access, or other data tools. Or, you may want to include the chart or graph from one or more worksheets in a presentation or word-processing document.

Although most of this chapter discusses the myriad ways of publishing, interacting with, and managing Tableau Server, Tableau Desktop has options for sharing both the visual and data elements of individual worksheets and dashboards, or entire workbooks, with other applications.

Exporting Worksheets and Dashboards

Tableau Desktop facilitates exporting information from individual worksheets in your workbooks, as well as combined dashboards, in a variety of ways:

- Create a .pdf version of one or more worksheets or dashboards.
- Export the data that makes up individual worksheet charts or graphs. You may copy data to the Clipboard for pasting into another application, pass data to an Excel worksheet (Windows)/save to Excel format (Mac), or export the data to Microsoft Access format (Windows)/.csv format (Mac).

- Export an individual worksheet image, either from the worksheet tab itself, or when an individual worksheet is selected in a dashboard. You may copy it to the Clipboard for pasting into other documents, or export it to a variety of standard graphic file formats.

Printing to PDF Format

With Tableau Desktop on Windows, it's easy to create a Portable Document Format (PDF) version of one or more worksheets or dashboards in your workbook. Choose File | Print To PDF from the drop-down menus. The Print To PDF dialog box will appear. If you wish to print a separate page in the PDF file for every sheet and dashboard in your workbook, click the Entire Workbook radio button. Active Sheet will print just the currently selected sheet or dashboard. If you are displaying your worksheets in Filmstrip View and you have CTRL-clicked more than one worksheet or dashboard in the filmstrip, each will appear in a separate page in the PDF. Select the desired paper size and orientation. If you check Show Selections, any selected marks in a worksheet will be highlighted in the resulting PDF as they are on the worksheet. Otherwise, all marks will appear unselected in the resulting PDF. Click OK.

A standard Windows dialog will appear, prompting for a filename. Specify the desired file and click OK to save the .pdf file. If you checked the View PDF File After Printing checkbox, the .pdf file will appear in Adobe Acrobat or Adobe Reader for your review.

Note *On Mac, just choose File | Print. Then, choose PDF options from the standard print dialog box, as you can with any Mac application.*

Exporting Worksheet Data

With the exception of text tables (also known as crosstabs), Tableau worksheets are typically graphical in nature. However, the data that's used to make up bar charts, maps, and other visual elements in your worksheets may be helpful when shared with other applications or shared with colleagues. There are several ways of exporting the data that makes up a chart or graph:

- **Copy as Crosstab**   Copies the underlying data that makes up your worksheet to the Clipboard as a row/column matrix of data. This may be pasted into a spreadsheet, word processor, or other application. Right-click (CONTROL-click on Mac) in a blank area of the worksheet and select Copy | Crosstab, or choose the Worksheet drop-down menu and select Copy | Crosstab.

- **Copy Data**   Similar to Copy as Crosstab, but may not organize in the same row/column format, depending on the data that the worksheet is based on. Right-click (CONTROL-click on Mac) in a blank area of the worksheet and select Copy | Data, or choose the Worksheet drop-down menu and select Copy | Data.

- **Export Crosstab to Microsoft Excel/Save .xlsx File**   Organizes the underlying data that makes up your worksheet as a row/column matrix of data and places it in a new Microsoft Excel worksheet (on Windows). The worksheet may be modified as you prefer and then saved as an Excel file. On Mac, this option saves a Microsoft Excel .xlsx file to a location you choose. From the Worksheet drop-down menu, choose Export | Crosstab To Excel.

- **Export Data to Microsoft Access .mdb File/.csv File**   From the Worksheet drop-down menu, choose Export | Data. On Windows, this will create a Microsoft Access .mdb database file containing one table that includes the data that makes up the selected worksheet. A standard Windows file dialog will appear. Specify the location and name of the file you wish to create and click Save. The Export Data To Access dialog box will appear. Specify the name of the table you wish Tableau to create in the database. If you wish to immediately have Tableau create a data connection to the resulting table so that it may be used in another worksheet, check Connect After Export and specify the connection name. If you had selected a set of marks prior to choosing the menu option, you'll have the choice of exporting data from the entire worksheet or just the selected items. Click OK. An Access database will be created containing the table. On Mac, this option will simply prompt for a file location and name. The result will be a comma-separated values (.csv) file.

Exporting Worksheet Images

The visualization in each worksheet or dashboard can also be exported for use in other applications, such as PowerPoint presentations, word-processing documents, or graphics programs. Select the worksheet or dashboard you wish to export and then choose one of two options:

- **Copy to Clipboard**   Right-click (COMMAND-click on Mac) in a blank area of the worksheet or dashboard, or click the Worksheet drop-down menu, and select Copy | Image. The Copy Image dialog box will appear. Depending on the related items appearing in the selected worksheet (legends and so forth), various checkboxes will be enabled, allowing you to choose what to include in the copied image. Also, you have several choices of where to place legends. Make the desired choices and click Copy. The image will be copied to the Clipboard. You may now paste it into another application.

- **Export to Image File**   From the Worksheet drop-down menu, choose Export | Image. The same dialog box described for copying an image to the Clipboard will display. Choose which portions of the visualization to include, as well as preferred legend placement, and click Save. A standard Save dialog box will appear prompting for a file location and name. You may choose a JPEG, PNG, or BMP format (EMF file format is also available in Windows only). Click Save to export the image to the specified filename and format.

Exporting Dashboard Images

If you have combined worksheets into one or more dashboards, you may export the entire dashboard as a single image. Select the dashboard you wish to export and choose either Dashboard | Copy Image or Dashboard | Export Image from the drop-down menus.

If you choose Copy Image, the entire dashboard will be copied to the Clipboard. Navigate to an alternative application and paste the copied image in the appropriate location. If you choose Export Image, a standard Save dialog box will appear prompting for a file location and name. You may choose a JPEG, PNG, or BMP format (EMF file format is also available in Windows only). Click Save to export the dashboard image to the specified filename and format.

Tip *If you have a dashboard selected, only the selected view in the dashboard will be exported with the Worksheet drop-down menu options. Use the Dashboard drop-down menu options to export the entire dashboard image.*

Using Tableau Reader

A read-only version of Tableau Desktop, *Tableau Reader,* is available as a free download from the Tableau Software website. Tableau Reader is a "fat client" product, requiring installation on your Windows or Mac computer. Once installed, Tableau Reader will open Tableau Packaged Workbooks (.twbx files).

In Tableau Desktop, you may save a workbook for distribution to Tableau Reader by saving your workbook in .twbx format. Simply choose the .twbx format within the Save dialog box when saving your workbook. The resulting .twbx file may be distributed to Tableau Reader users to open and interact with.

Tableau Reader requires that all data sources be embedded in the .twbx file, as it is unable to connect to server-based data sources, such as standard SQL databases or cloud-based data sources. Desktop data sources (Excel, Access, Tableau Data Extracts, and so forth) will automatically be included in the packaged workbook. However, if your workbook makes use of some external data source, such as a standard corporate SQL server, Tableau Reader won't be able to connect to the data source and the user will receive an error message. If this occurs, open the original workbook in Tableau Desktop, extract these data sources (extracts are covered in Chapter 3), resave the .twbx file, and redistribute it to Tableau Reader users.

Tableau Public and Online

Although Tableau Reader is an economical method for distributing finished workbooks to your audience, it requires that every user maintain a "fat client" installation on their Windows or Mac computer. Users of Linux or other operating systems, as well as smartphone and tablet users, will be unable to use Tableau Reader. Also, as previously discussed, Tableau Reader cannot make real-time connections to corporate databases, which reduces the ability to analyze with the latest data available. To solve these issues, Tableau workbooks can be published to a number of web-based server systems for distribution to any user with a standard web browser.

In addition to your own internal Tableau Server (discussed later in the chapter), there are two options for web-based publication:

- **Tableau Public**   A free hosted version of Tableau Server, permitting workbooks based on Tableau Data Extracts to be posted on the Web. There are limitations on the amount of data that may be included, no connection to internal corporate SQL databases is supported, and all data and worksheets posted are fully viewable by the public—there is no security available.

- **Tableau Online**   A paid hosted version of Tableau Server, permitting workbooks based on Tableau Data Extracts to be posted on the Web. There are limited capabilities to update extracts with fresh data. Workbooks posted are not publicly viewable. And there is a limited user/group security system permitting granular viewing capabilities and rights assignments.

Tableau Public

Once you have created a Tableau Public account (visit the Tableau Software website to create an account), make sure your workbook meets Tableau Public requirements before attempting to save it to the Tableau Public server:

- Data sources must be Tableau Data Extracts.
- Data sources cannot contain more than 10,000,000 rows of data.
- Total storage space for all workbooks/data cannot exceed 10GB.

Choose Server | Tableau Public | Save To Web. The first time you interact with Tableau Public after starting Tableau Desktop, you'll be prompted for your user ID and password. Specify a name for the workbook on the server and click OK. A confirmation dialog will display illustrating the workbook you just saved. You may now share or view the workbook on the Web via your Tableau Public account.

From the confirmation screen, click the Edit Details link to specify a few fine points for your just-uploaded workbook. In particular, you may choose to disable the ability for viewers to download the workbook with embedded data. By Tableau Public's nature, everything is viewable to everyone on the Internet. By default, anyone will also be able to download your workbook and, if they have Tableau Desktop, make use of the embedded data. Make sure to disable this option if you wish to only permit the viewing of your workbook.

Other options on the Server | Tableau Public menu are helpful for managing content and settings on Tableau Public:

- **Open From Tableau Public**   Download an existing workbook from Tableau Public to Tableau Desktop for editing or analysis.
- **Save to Tableau Public As**   Saves the current workbook to Tableau Public. If the existing workbook was initially opened from Tableau Public, it permits saving the workbook to a different Tableau Public location.
- **Manage My Profile**   Launches a web browser displaying settings for your Tableau Public account.

Note   *Tableau provides a free version of Tableau Desktop just for use with Tableau Public. You'll find options to download this version from the Tableau Public website. Although the techniques discussed earlier in this book generally apply to Tableau Public Desktop, the list of data sources available is limited, as is the ability to save to any output location other than the Tableau Public site.*

Tableau Online

As with Tableau Public, Tableau Online is hosted by Tableau Software "in the cloud," negating the need for your organization to dedicate space on an internal network or provide administrative or management resources. However, because of the hosted nature of Tableau Public, connection to live SQL data sources in your network may be limited or unavailable (although a limited set of "cloud" data sources, such as Amazon Redshift and Google Big Query, as well as cloud-hosted SQL Server, MySQL, and PostgreSQL, are available). And you won't have the ability to integrate with any internal authentication systems, such as Windows Active Directory. However, unlike Tableau Public, Tableau Online is user segmented, allowing individual users to post content and limit the ability of other users to see the content. Also, a limited set of permissions is supported to permit selected users to access specific features.

Tip   *Publishing workbooks to Tableau Online is mostly identical to publishing to an internally hosted Tableau Server. Steps related to publishing and viewing Tableau Server content later in this chapter generally apply. Tableau Online management tasks mirror those of a full version of Tableau Server, although to a limited extent. As such, some examples that follow in the full Tableau Server section will be available to you in Tableau Online and others won't.*

Using Your Data With Tableau Online

One of the first considerations with Tableau Online is how you'll include source data for your workbooks. Because Tableau Online is hosted in the cloud and cannot penetrate a firewall to connect to your internal data sources, your Tableau workbooks will need to be based on one of three types of data sources:

- **Tableau Data Extracts (.tde files)**   As discussed in Chapter 3, various data sources in use in your organization can be imported into this Tableau-proprietary data format. When your workbook is uploaded to Tableau Online, the associated TDE file is uploaded with it and stored on the Tableau Online server. If you attempt to save a workbook to Tableau Online that doesn't use a .tde file (even if it's a Tableau Packaged Workbook with embedded desktop data sources, such as .xls or text files), you'll be prompted to create a Tableau Data Extract first.

- **Certain Cloud-Based Data Sources**   Other cloud-based systems, such as Google BigQuery, Google Analytics, Amazon Redshift, and Salesforce.com, can be connected directly to with Tableau Desktop using the OAuth data connection standard. When associated workbooks are published to Tableau Online, these live connections are maintained.

- **Limited Cloud-Hosted Traditional SQL Databases**   If you maintain Microsoft SQL Server, PostgreSQL, or MySQL databases hosted by a cloud provider (such as Amazon Relational Database Service [RDS] or Microsoft Azure), you may maintain live connections in Tableau Online. These data sources need not be converted to Tableau Data Extracts before workbooks are published to Tableau Online.

Note   *In order to fully support cloud-based SQL databases as just discussed, you must check Allow Live Data Source Connections in Tableau Online Settings. In addition, you must add a Tableau Online IP address block to the database server's "whitelist" in order to ensure that the database will accept queries from Tableau Online (this may be a requirement for other online data sources as well, such as Google and Salesforce.com). The set of Tableau Online IP addresses may be found in the current version of Tableau Online help from Tableau.com.*

Refreshing Tableau Online Data From Within Your Network

Posting Tableau workbooks based on data sources within your corporate network that are behind your corporate firewall to hosted Tableau Online may seem impractical. Although a full version of Tableau Server needs to be installed within your network to provide direct, live connection to these databases, you can still publish these workbooks to Tableau Online as long as you create a Data Extract first (a full discussion of Data Extracts appears in Chapter 3 and later in this chapter). You may then refresh the Data Extracts manually (this is the only option if you're using Tableau for Mac), with a Tableau Online schedule using the Tableau Sync Client, or by running an extract refresh from the Windows command prompt.

Manual Extract Refresh   Before you publish your workbook to Tableau Online, extract data from your corporate database to a local .tde file on your computer. You may choose to set either an incremental refresh field or full refresh. If you only want to use this data connection with the currently connected workbook, just publish your workbook to Tableau Online. Tableau Online will store the extract as an "embedded" data source. That is, the extract file will be uploaded to Tableau Online, but only will be accessible to the single workbook you extracted it from.

If you wish to use the data source for multiple workbooks on Tableau Online, then *after you create the initial extract*, "publish" the data source to Tableau Online from the data source context menu. This will save the extract file as a stand-alone data source on Tableau Online, permitting other workbooks to use it. Then, when you manually refresh the published extract, all other connected workbooks will immediately reflect the updated data extract.

When you are ready to manually update the extract with new data, using either a full or incremental refresh, just open the original workbook you extracted from and choose the desired option from the data source context menu (the same menu you originally used to create and publish the extract). The published data source on Tableau Online will be updated manually. Repeat the process the next time you wish to update the Tableau Online data source.

Caution *As discussed in Chapter 3, make sure to save the original workbook you used to create the initial Data Extract. This is the only workbook that "ties" the original database and extract together. This is required for manual incremental and full refreshes, modifications to the extract, and so forth. Although you can publish an extract to Tableau Server and then use it with other workbooks, you'll be unable to do an incremental or full refresh if you're not using the original workbook you extracted with.*

The Tableau Online Sync Client   The first minor update to Tableau 9, Tableau 9.0.1, adds the *Tableau Online Sync Client*. This utility, available with the 64-bit version of Tableau Desktop for Windows (32-bit Windows and Mac versions don't include the utility), allows connection of the Tableau Online cloud servers to your local computer. With this feature, automatic scheduled updates of Tableau Online data sources from databases behind your corporate firewall can happen behind the scenes without intervention as long as your computer is turned on when the refreshes are scheduled.

Begin by extracting from the original corporate database to a .tde file on your local computer. Specify the appropriate incremental refresh field if you wish to schedule both full and incremental refreshes with the Sync Client. Then, publish the Data Extract to Tableau Online as discussed in the previous section, Chapter 3, and later in this chapter (just saving a workbook with an embedded Data Extract is insufficient—you'll need to publish the extract as a Tableau Online stand-alone data source). When you publish, there's no need to embed source database credentials, even though you may be prompted to do so. Also, choosing incremental or full refresh schedule options from the publish dialog won't be of benefit, as any pre-defined schedules you choose will be deleted when you tie the data connection to the Sync Client later.

Even though you may be tempted to now display Tableau Online in your web browser and attempt to schedule an extract refresh on the just-published data source, any scheduled refresh will fail, as Tableau Online won't be able to resolve the location of the original database that was used—it's behind your firewall!

Make sure you are using the 64-bit Windows Tableau Desktop version 9.0.1 or later (About from the Help menu will display your current Tableau version and bit level). Choose Help | Settings and Performance | Start Tableau Online Sync Client from the pull-down menus. The client will display as an icon in the Windows system tray, and if this is the first time you've started it, you'll be prompted to log in to Tableau Online. If you have previously logged in to Tableau Online, you won't be prompted again—just double-click the icon in the system tray to access the Sync Client.

Most options in the Sync Client will simply redirect you to Tableau Online in a browser. For example, if you select the View All Data Sources option, a browser will open, navigating directly to the list of published data sources in Tableau Online. Select the data source you just published that you wish to refresh automatically with the Sync Client. You'll notice that the Refresh Schedules option within Tableau Online displays a small "0" character, indicating that no extract refreshes are scheduled. Click the link to confirm this.

On the refresh list screen, click Select Where To Run Refreshes in the upper right. A pop-up screen will appear, providing the option to refresh from Tableau Online or a computer on your local network. The Tableau Online option is only appropriate for other cloud-hosted data sources, such as Google BigQuery or SQL Server hosted in a Microsoft Azure cloud. Because you need to access the original database behind your firewall for this data source, select A Computer On My Network and select the computer running the Sync Client (the current computer you opened the Sync Client on will be populated by default).

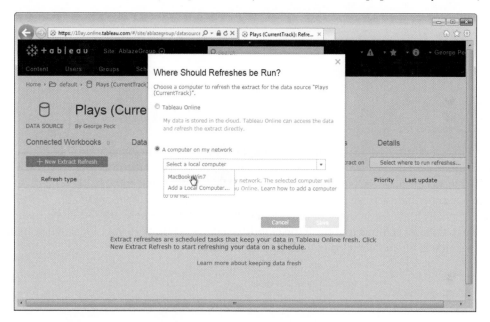

Once you have specified the local computer to use, click the orange New Extract Refresh button on the Tableau Online screen. A pop-up screen will prompt for the refresh schedule. You may choose a combination of full or incremental refresh and refresh time/day options. Click OK to create the scheduled refresh. You may add refresh schedules if you choose (perhaps you want to perform a full refresh one day a week and an incremental refresh every weekday).

Finally, return to the Sync Client on your local computer. If necessary, double-click the icon in the system tray. Notice that any Tableau Online data connections that you assigned to the local computer will now appear within the Sync Client. Select the data connection you just scheduled refresh options for in Tableau Online, and click the small edit "pencil" icon. Specify login credentials for the original database on your network. Otherwise, when Tableau Online attempts to refresh the cloud-based extract through your local Sync Client, the client will be unable to log in to the local database.

As long as your computer is on and the Sync Client icon appears in the system tray (you may close Tableau after you have started the Sync Client), extract refreshes will be launched from Tableau Online according to the schedule you created. Tableau Online will find your local computer, connect to the Sync Client, and instruct the Sync Client to log in to the database on your network. The Sync Client will query for a full or incremental set of data and send it to Tableau Public, which will update the cloud-based Data Extract.

Windows Command Prompt   Prior to release of the Tableau Online Sync Client, the only way to refresh Tableau Online extracts from your local database was through a local copy of Tableau Desktop. Although a manual refresh is a straightforward process (as outlined earlier in this section), performing incremental or full refreshes on a schedule was potentially cumbersome. The Tableau Sync Client has streamlined this process; however, you may still choose to perform an extract refresh by launching your copy of Tableau Desktop through the Windows command prompt.

This feature, available for any Windows version of Tableau (but not Tableau for Mac), may be used on an as-needed basis to refresh extracts manually. It also may be used to add data to a Tableau Online extract from a file (which the Sync Client doesn't support). In addition, by creating batch files that contain various sets of command-line options, you may automatically run command-line–based extracts with Windows Task Scheduler. This is helpful if you wish to perform extracts on a schedule different from that provided by Tableau Online and the Sync Client (for example, monthly).

Open a Windows command prompt and change the directory to the location of the Tableau 9 executable (this will be different, depending on whether you're using 32-bit or 64-bit Tableau Desktop). Once you have navigated to the proper directory, build a command using options documented in Tableau Online help or documented with the commands:

```
tableau refreshextract --help
tableau addfiletoextract --help
```

Best Practice   *Options discussed in this section permit you to expose data from databases in your network to cloud-based systems. Ensure that you adhere to your organization's data governance and data security policies as you publish to Tableau Online. Although Tableau Online is hosted in a secure environment, it is an Internet-based system. You should consider the possible consequences of an unanticipated data compromise.*

Using Tableau Server

So far, this chapter has discussed hosted versions of Tableau Server. However, a full version of Tableau Server can be installed inside your organization's network (or via private hosting services, such as those provided by Amazon and Microsoft), permitting workbooks based on any data source (including live connections to internal or external standard corporate SQL databases) to be shared. Based on your firewall configuration, viewers may be inside or outside your organization. Although not required, data extracts published to your local Tableau Server may be automatically updated from their original data sources on a regular schedule. Tableau Server features a robust security system, permitting various users and groups to be defined for granular viewing and access rights, as well as user-based filtering to provide different views of the same workbook, based on Tableau Server security settings. Tableau Server includes its own user ID/password management system, or it can interface with Windows Active Directory to permit centralized user management. Several approaches to single sign-on capabilities, such as Kerberos and Security Assertion Markup Language (SAML) authentication, are available. Tableau Server also allows (with proper permissions) web-based modification of existing worksheets or creation of new simple worksheets, all in a web browser, tablet, or smartphone.

Viewing Content

If you are primarily concerned with interacting with Tableau Server after workbooks have been published by other designers, or when you're ready to validate that your workbooks have been properly published, you'll need to sign on to and navigate the general Tableau Server interface. Tableau Server 9 has improved this user interface to make navigating and interacting with server content easier.

Launch a web browser and navigate to Tableau Server via the uniform resource locator (URL) that your administrator has provided you (by default, it's simply the name or IP address of the system where Tableau Server is installed). If you don't have a single sign-on method in place, you'll be prompted to sign on with a user ID and password. Use the proper credentials (if Active Directory has been configured, you'll use your standard Windows ID and password). If your server and user ID are configured with multiple sites (creating sites is discussed later in this chapter), you'll be prompted to choose one. Once you successfully sign in, you'll be presented with the main Tableau Server screen. Although you are initially presented with Projects view, you or an administrator may change the default view to one of the other available object views: Workbooks, Views, or Data Sources.

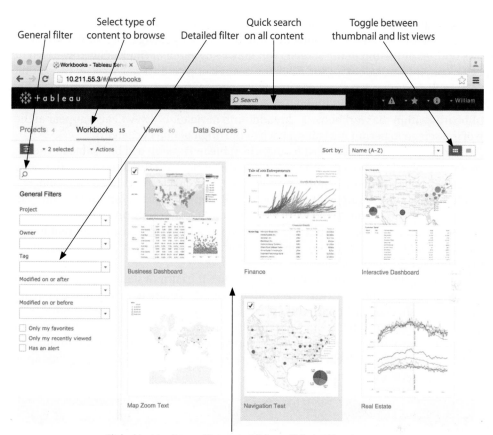

Click object to view and interact with it, or click checkbox in upper left of object and choose options from Actions menu

- **Projects**   Somewhat like folders, projects organize content into related categories. Given the appropriate right, you may create additional projects when you publish workbooks to Tableau Server from Tableau Desktop.

- **Workbooks**   Workbooks published to Tableau Server. When you select a workbook, all nonhidden content within the workbook (worksheets, dashboards, and stories) will be available to view.

- **Views**   Individual worksheets, dashboards, and stories from all workbooks.

- **Data Sources**   Shared data sources stored on Tableau Server. If you have appropriate rights, you may analyze data in your browser or tablet using techniques similar to those available in Tableau Desktop (see "Creating New Content" later in the chapter).

To view and interact with Tableau worksheets, dashboards, or stories published from Tableau Desktop, find the workbook or individual view by navigating the Workbooks or Views options at the top of the screen. You may also search or filter to narrow down to specific content you're looking for. Click the desired object to view it, or select one or more objects with the upper-left checkbox and make choices from the Actions drop-down link. If you click a workbook, an additional Tableau Server screen will show worksheets and dashboards within the workbook. A "breadcrumb navigation" list will also appear at the top of the screen to permit navigation back to the original object category.

When you view an object, most features in Tableau Desktop will be usable in your browser or tablet. Dashboards and worksheets will appear as tabs at the top of the view. Tooltips will appear when you hover over marks. If you click a mark, Keep Only and Exclude action buttons from within the tooltip will appear. Quick filters and parameters will appear and can be interacted with. Sort icons will be available on chart axes and headers. You may zoom in and out on maps, pan maps, and select using different tools. Dashboard and worksheet actions will permit complete interactivity among worksheets and dashboards in the workbook.

If you make filter or parameter choices to change the current state of the worksheet or dashboard, you may choose to save the modified view for future use. You may also wish to share the worksheet or dashboard URL in an e-mail or embed the view into another web page. Or, perhaps you wish to export the current view to a variety of file formats, revert to the original state of the view when it was first opened, pause Tableau Server's automatic updating of the view, or refresh the view against the data source. A series of buttons appear at the top of the view to permit these options.

Note *Some of the features just described may not be available, depending on how the workbook was initially designed or the permissions that may be granted you by the worksheet designer or Tableau Server administrator.*

Subscriptions

In addition to viewing Tableau content interactively in a browser or on a tablet or smartphone, you may elect to receive e-mails of periodic snapshots of Tableau content via *subscriptions*. To subscribe to a workbook or individual worksheet or dashboard, look for the small envelope at the upper right of the screen (if it's not there, expand your browser to make sure it's not hidden or check with your Tableau administrator to make sure subscriptions are enabled).

If an e-mail address isn't already associated with your Tableau Server account, you'll be prompted to add it. Then, specify the subject line of the subscription e-mail and the frequency you'd like the e-mail to be sent (subscription schedules are specified in a Tableau Server administrative screen discussed later in this chapter). You'll also be able to choose whether to include just the current worksheet or all worksheets in the workbook in the subscription e-mail.

Once you've subscribed, Tableau Server will send an e-mail based on the frequency you selected. The worksheet or worksheets you selected will appear in the e-mail as embedded images. If you click an image, a web browser will launch and navigate to the source workbook you initially chose within Tableau Server (you may be prompted to log in to Tableau Server before the workbook will appear in the browser). You may then fully interact with the workbook within the browser.

To modify or delete existing subscriptions, click the Manage My Subscription Settings link within the subscription e-mail, or log in to Tableau Server, click the drop-down arrow next to your user name in the upper right, and choose My Account Settings. Then click the Subscriptions link at the top of the page. A list of existing workbook subscriptions will appear. Check the subscription or subscriptions you wish to modify or delete, and make the desired choice from the Actions link.

Using Tableau with iPad, Android, and Other Smartphones and Tablets

Not only can Tableau web-based options (Tableau Public, Tableau Online, and Tableau Server) provide complete interactivity in a web browser; they can support various mobile devices as well. If your audience will want to interact with a worksheet, dashboard, or story on their smartphone or tablet, several options are available.

Tableau App for iPad and Android

If you search the Apple App Store or Google Play for "Tableau," you'll find the Tableau Mobile app. This free app (for tablets only) will connect to a Tableau Server and present a highly interactive interface to workbooks and dashboards on the server. Full interactivity is available when displaying worksheets or dashboards in the app.

The app also features the ability to modify existing worksheets, including interacting with the Data pane, using Show Me, dragging and dropping dimensions and measures to shelves, manipulating the Marks card, and modifying and creating calculated fields. This powerful feature opens an entirely new set of possibilities by allowing rich design capabilities on an iPad.

Web Access via HTML5 Mobile Browsers

Whereas the Tableau Mobile app only works with iPad and Android tablets, other mobile devices are fully capable of interacting with Tableau Server. If your mobile device includes a web browser that supports HTML5 (most Windows mobile, Apple, and Android devices do), then complete interactivity with Tableau Server is available as well. Just connect to a Tableau Server via the mobile device browser as you would on a desktop computer. Tableau Server will automatically detect the mobile browser and present an appropriately sized presentation of dashboards and worksheets. As with the dedicated app described previously, mobile gestures are accommodated for filters, parameters, tooltips, and other standard Tableau features.

(continued)

And, as with the app, the ability to edit existing worksheets right in the mobile browser is supported. Dimensions and measures can be dragged to and from shelves, options can be set from the Marks card, and Show Me can be used. An additional benefit of connecting via a mobile browser instead of the app is the ability to analyze directly from a Tableau Server–stored data connection (just tap Data Sources from the top navigation area). Tap the checkbox for the desired data source and then choose New Workbook from the Actions drop-down link at the top of the list. A Tableau Desktop–like screen will display dimensions, measures, Rows and Columns shelves, the Marks card, and so forth. Drag and drop as you normally would to analyze data. Show Me may be used, and you can even tap measures or dimensions and choose options from a context menu, including the ability to create and edit calculated fields. You may even double-tap in appropriate places to create an ad hoc calculation!

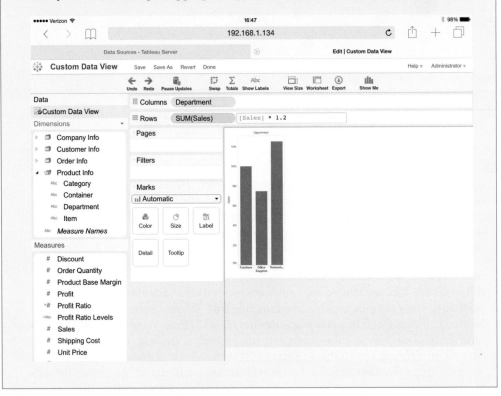

Publishing Content

Before workbooks can be viewed on Tableau Server, they must be published from a copy of Tableau Desktop. Although the process of publishing workbooks to either Tableau Server or Tableau Online is basically the same, Tableau Server will permit publication of workbooks connecting to any data source, including those within your network (just make sure the same data source drivers have been installed on the Tableau Server computer).

Open the workbook you wish to publish in Tableau Desktop and select Server | Publish Workbook from the pull-down menus. If you have not already logged in to a server, you'll be prompted for the server name. If you have a single sign-on method enabled, you will be automatically logged in after you specify a server name. Otherwise, supply a user ID and password. If your server and user ID are configured for multiple sites (Tableau Server sites are discussed later in this chapter), select the desired site. Then, the Publish Workbook To Tableau Server dialog box will appear. Supply the name of the workbook. If you wish to replace an existing workbook on the server, click the drop-down arrow next to the name and choose an existing workbook. In addition, there are other options to complete on this dialog box:

- **Project**   Like a folder, a *project* is a category that you may assign your workbook to. Then, when looking for available workbooks on Tableau Server, you may select a specific project to narrow down your search. Choose an existing project from the drop-down list (projects are created using administration tools on Tableau Server).

- **Description**   Optional free-form description to annotate details about the workbook.

- **Add Tags**   Add one or more optional keyword *tags,* separated by spaces or commas (if the tag itself contains a space, surround it with quotation marks). Tags may be used to search for workbooks on the server.

- **Views to Share**   Select the worksheets/dashboards/stories (generally, Tableau Server refers to an individual worksheet, dashboard, or story as a *view*) you want to be visible within the workbook. You may prefer to only include dashboards or stories in this list, unchecking the worksheets that make them up. This will prevent viewers from navigating to the individual worksheets that make up the dashboard or story (these worksheets, however, will be available if a user downloads the workbook from the server).

- **View Permissions**   By default, all users will be given a set of default permissions (determined by the All Users group), whereas you, as the owner, will have full permissions to the workbook. If you wish to set more granular permissions for your workbook, click the Add button below the View Permissions list. The Add/Edit Permissions dialog box will appear.

Select a user or group on the left side of the dialog box, and set permissions for the user or group on the right. You may choose from a pre-defined set of rights by choosing an entry in the Role drop-down list, or select individual rights with radio buttons. When finished, click OK. The users and groups you added rights for will appear in the View Permissions list.

- **Show Sheets as Tabs**   Much as in Tableau Desktop, checking this option will show tabs for worksheets in the view on Tableau Server. Although you initially choose one view, the other views will be available as tabs at the top of the screen. If you turn this option off, you'll only be able to choose individual views from the main navigation area of Tableau Server (no tabs will appear within a worksheet or dashboard).

Caution   *If you are using filter actions in your worksheets or dashboards (covered in Chapter 8) to navigate from one dashboard or worksheet to another, you must select this option to enable navigation on the server.*

- **Show Selections**   If you've pre-selected any marks on a worksheet, these marks will be pre-selected on your server workbook when initially viewed on the Web.
- **Include External Files**   Upload any desktop data sources (Excel, Access, Tableau Data Extracts, and so forth), images added to dashboards, and background images to the server with the workbook. This will provide the server data sources (perhaps on your local hard disk) that were used to create the workbook. If you don't select this option, ensure that your data sources are accessible by the server, either via standard corporate SQL database connection methods or via a Universal Naming Convention (UNC) name used to connect to network-based desktop data sources.

If your workbook contains a combination of data sources that have been extracted to a Tableau Data Extract (.tde) file or connections to standard corporate SQL databases that require permission to access, an additional Authentication, Scheduling, or Scheduling & Authentication button will appear.

You may choose to automatically refresh Data Extracts that will be published to the server with your workbook via the drop-down list. Schedules such as "End of Month," "Saturday Night," and "Weekday Early Mornings" are configured on the server in advance (as discussed later in the chapter under "Schedules") and will be available for you to choose for automatic extract refresh. If incremental refresh fields are specified for any Data Extracts within the workbook, you'll be able to specify separate schedules for both incremental and full refreshes.

External databases (such as standard corporate SQL databases) may require authentication when processing queries from your on-premise version of Tableau Server. Select any such databases in the Authentication list, and choose how you wish to supply a user ID and password to the database when the workbook is displayed (various options appear, depending on your Tableau Server authentication method and database being used). Click OK to return to the Publish Workbook dialog box.

When all options have been selected, click Publish to publish the workbook to the server. After the workbook and any associated data files are published, a confirmation dialog box will appear. You may interact with the workbook in the confirmation dialog box, click Open In Browser Window to open the workbook in your browser, or just close the confirmation dialog box.

Creating Tableau Server User Filters

One of the benefits of using Tableau Server is its built-in security system. Not only does this determine various rights and privileges granted or denied to users, it can also be used to provide a different view of data to the viewer based on their user ID. This is accomplished with *user filters*: a series of filter settings that are applied based on a Tableau Server user ID. User filters are initially created in Tableau Desktop. Then, when the workbook is published to Tableau Server, the filters will limit data included in views based on Tableau Server credentials.

In Tableau Desktop, open the workbook you would like to customize by user. Using the drop-down menus, choose Server | Create User Filter, and then select the dimension you wish to filter based on user ID. If you're not already logged on to a Tableau Server, you'll be prompted for logon credentials. The User Filter dialog box will appear, displaying a list of Tableau Server users and groups on the left and the members of the selected dimension on the right. Select each user or group on the left, and then check the members of the dimension that the selected user or group should be able to see in the worksheet.

The All and None buttons under the Members list will select all or no members as a starting point. If you have many users and you wish to copy settings from one user to another, click the Copy From button and select an existing user to copy to the currently selected user. When finished setting user/member combinations, click OK to save the filter. It will initially appear in the Data window in the Sets category (with a slightly different icon than traditional sets). The user filter will not take effect until dragged to the Filters shelf.

You may now test the application of the user filter by selecting a user from the pop-up user list at the bottom of the Tableau screen (initially showing the user ID you logged in with). When you select a user from the list, the filter will be applied and will

(continued)

limit the worksheet accordingly. If you need to modify the filter (perhaps you have narrowed the filter too far and some users, such as yourself, cannot see any data), right-click the user filter in the Sets portion of the Data window and choose Edit from the context menu.

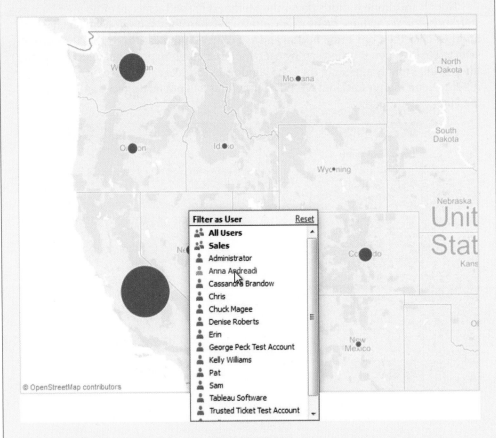

Another way to filter based on a Tableau Server user ID is available if a data source used in your worksheet contains (or can derive) matching user IDs. Because the currently logged-on Tableau user ID is available in a Tableau calculated field, you can create a calculated field that compares a user name from a data source (or other calculated field) to the currently logged-on Tableau Server user. The filter will return only data that matches the currently logged-in user. In this example, the Administrator account will return all data, whereas another user will only return data that matches their user ID. As with other filters, place the calculated field on the Filters shelf and choose the True value.

As with user filters described previously in this section, the filter may be tested by selecting different users from the pop-up list at the bottom right of the Tableau screen.

Editing Content

Once you add a workbook to Tableau Server from Tableau Desktop, you'll almost certainly want to make changes to it at some point in the future. This is straightforward. Choose Server | Open Workbook from the Tableau Desktop drop-down menus. If necessary, log in to the server. Then, navigate to the project and file you wish to modify to open it in Tableau Desktop. Once you've made the desired changes, simply resave to Tableau Server from the Server menu as you originally did (or save to a different project and/or with a different filename).

But, what if you're just using Tableau Server in a browser and don't have a copy of Tableau Desktop? If you have proper permission, a small hyperlink is available, although it may not be immediately obvious. And the power behind it may not immediately come to mind either. If you are viewing a worksheet or dashboard (the option won't be available with a story), look for the Edit hyperlink. Or, if you are displaying the Views page, select a worksheet or dashboard and choose Edit View from the Actions drop-down menu.

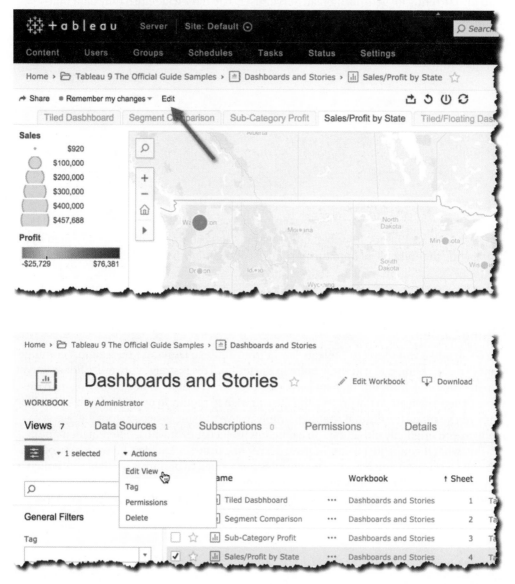

When you choose these options, a separate tab will appear in your browser with the worksheet you were viewing or selected, or the first worksheet in the dashboard you were viewing or selected, appearing in *web edit mode*. Web edit mode looks very much like

Tableau Desktop, permitting you to use many of the techniques discussed in the earlier sections of this book to edit worksheets right in your browser. You'll see the Data and Analytics panes, dimensions and measures, shelves, cards, and a toolbar. You may double-click a dimension or measure to add it to a default location on the worksheet. Drag and drop measures and dimensions to shelves and cards. Right-click (CONTROL-click on Mac), or click the small drop-down arrow, on dimension or measure field indicators or cards to choose options. Click Show Me to select from pre-defined chart types (for example, this will permit you to create shared axis charts because you can't drag a second measure on an existing axis in web edit mode). And you can create or modify both ad hoc and standard calculated fields.

Tabs for all worksheets in the workbook (even those that you didn't explicitly select in the Views To Share list when you originally published the workbook) will appear in your browser. Just click the desired sheet to edit it (dashboards and stories are exceptions and won't be available in web edit mode). A new worksheet tab is also available to create new worksheets within the existing workbook.

Some options behave differently in web edit mode than they do in the full version of Tableau Desktop. Filters are an example. If you drag a dimension or measure to the Filters shelf, web edit mode will immediately treat it like quick filters, displaying an interactive filter on the right side of the worksheet. If you don't want the quick filter to be visible, select the value you wish the "hard-coded" filter to have on the quick filter on the right side of the worksheet. Then right-click the filter on the Filters shelf and uncheck Show Filter. Also, there are options not available in web edit mode at all. For example, even though you may see existing parameters in the Data pane, you can't display them on a new worksheet or make any modifications to them. Although web edit mode is a very flexible way to provide introductory-to-intermediate real-time analysis capabilities in a browser, you may still need to employ the full version of Tableau Desktop to realize complete design capabilities.

Once you've made changes to an existing view, you may revert to the original version, replace the existing workbook with the modified version, or save the modified version to a different project or with a different name. Use the Save, Save As, and Revert options at the top of the screen. Clicking Done will close web edit mode and return to the updated view or the Views page.

Note   *The ability to use most features covered in this section, such as editing existing workbooks, replacing existing workbooks with the Save option, saving to different locations, or creating new workbooks, are all controlled by Tableau Server permissions. Permissions are discussed later in this chapter. If these options don't appear when you log in, you may not be granted the proper permission. Check with a Tableau Server administrator (or change the permissions yourself if you are granted that permission).*

 Video *Editing and Creating Content on the Web*

Creating New Content

Although editing existing workbooks right in a web browser or creating new worksheets in an existing workbook are flexible features, you might also want to create a brand-new workbook from scratch. Tableau Desktop can connect to a variety of data sources for new workbooks, but consider that you will only be creating a new workbook in a web browser or perhaps on a mobile device. The "analyze from a connected data source" paradigm provided by a personal computer won't apply.

However, Tableau Server provides the ability to create a brand-new workbook in your web browser by selecting a *published data source.* A published data source, although originally created on Tableau Desktop, is published to Tableau Server for sharing among not only Tableau Desktop users, but also web-based users with web edit mode. Tableau Server actually makes the physical connection to the data source and acts as a "proxy," redirecting your browser requests to the actual data source.

When you initially log in to Tableau Server, look for the Data Sources option on the Content page. When you click it, you'll notice a list of published data sources (and you'll notice that a default filter appears on the left side of the screen limiting the list to just-published data sources). Select the data source you wish to use for your new web-based workbook, and select New Workbook from the Actions drop-down (only check one data source—multiple checkmarks will disable the option to create a workbook).

A new tab will appear in your browser using web edit mode. As discussed previously in this chapter, the Data and Analytics panes will appear and rows and columns shelves will be available, as will Show Me. Use these features to design one or more new worksheets using the selected data source. When you are finished, you may save your new workbook with Save options at the top of the screen. Clicking Done will close the tab and return to the previous Data Source list from the Content page.

Tip *Although the initial data source view shows just published data sources, you may change the filter to display* embedded *data sources. These data sources actually are embedded within an existing workbook on the server. They do not stand alone. You may perform some limited modifications on this screen; however, embedded data sources cannot be used to create new workbooks. If you need to use an embedded data source, navigate to a view (worksheet or dashboard) based on the embedded data source and edit that view.*

Publishing Data Sources to Tableau Server

Published data sources used for creating new workbooks directly from a web browser are initially created in Tableau Desktop. First, ensure that any database drivers required to connect to the database (such as an Oracle or Teradata client) are installed on the computer running Tableau Server, in addition to your computer running Tableau Desktop. If necessary, download drivers from tableau.com/Drivers.

Then, start Tableau Desktop and connect to the data source (corporate database in your network, desktop data file, cloud-based data source, and so forth) that you wish to base your Tableau Server–published data source on. Although you may create worksheets in the workbook you've created, you don't have to if your primary purpose is publishing the data source to Tableau Server. In the initial worksheet that appears (or in Metadata view in the Link screen when first connecting), make any desired "metadata" changes to the data connection, such as hiding or renaming fields. In a worksheet, use options in the Data pane to create calculated fields, adding parameter sets and groups, building hierarchies, or other options that add sections or dimensions and measures to the Data pane. These steps will build the ultimate "view" of the data that will appear to the Tableau designer using either web edit mode on Tableau Server or their own copy of Tableau Desktop. Chapter 3 discusses the myriad options for customizing the Data pane.

(*continued*)

Once you've finished designing the organization of the data connection, you may choose to extract the original data source to a Tableau Data Extract (some cloud-based data sources will require you to extract). When you do so, you may choose to set an incremental refresh field to permit Tableau Server to perform scheduled incremental and full data refreshes. If you don't create an extract, Tableau Server will connect directly to the data source to provide real-time results to web edit mode or Tableau Desktop users.

Tip *The "data proxy" feature of Tableau Server provides an additional benefit to Tableau Desktop for Mac users. Even though Tableau Desktop for Mac won't connect to all the data sources the Windows version will, non–Mac-supported data sources can be published to Tableau Server and then used on a Mac by selecting the Tableau Server connection option.*

When you're ready to publish the data source to Tableau Server, right-click the data source name in the Data pane (CONTROL-click on Mac) and choose Publish To Server from the context menu. You may also choose Data | *<desired data source>* | Publish To Server from the drop-down menus. The Publish Data Source To Tableau Server dialog box will appear. Select the desired project (similar to a folder) that you want the data source published in. Give it an appropriate name and, optionally, a description. You may also add one or more tag keywords, separating each by a comma or space (if you want the tag to include a space, surround the tag with quotation marks). Other tags already used on the server will also appear. To maintain consistency, you may click one or more to add them to the data source.

If the data source you are publishing requires authentication (such as a database user ID and password), select how you want Tableau Server to provide the credentials (such as prompting the user on Tableau Server or embedding the currently used credentials in the data source). If you are publishing a Data Extract, select the server-based schedule you wish to use to refresh the extract (these schedule options are pre-defined on the server, as discussed later in this chapter). You may see both incremental and full refresh options, depending on whether you specified an incremental refresh field when you created the extract. And finally, if you want to set specific permissions for the data source, such as who can view it, change it, and so forth, click the Add button at the bottom of the dialog box and specify desired permissions.

When the data source is uploaded to Tableau Server, you'll receive a confirmation message. You may wish to test the published data source with either Tableau Desktop or Tableau Server in web edit mode to determine if the data source is properly organized and returns reliable data. In Tableau Desktop, choose Tableau Server on the initial Connect screen, log in, and navigate to the project you uploaded the data source to. In Tableau Server, either select Data Sources from the main Content page, or select a Project from the main Content page and then select Data Sources in that project.

(continued)

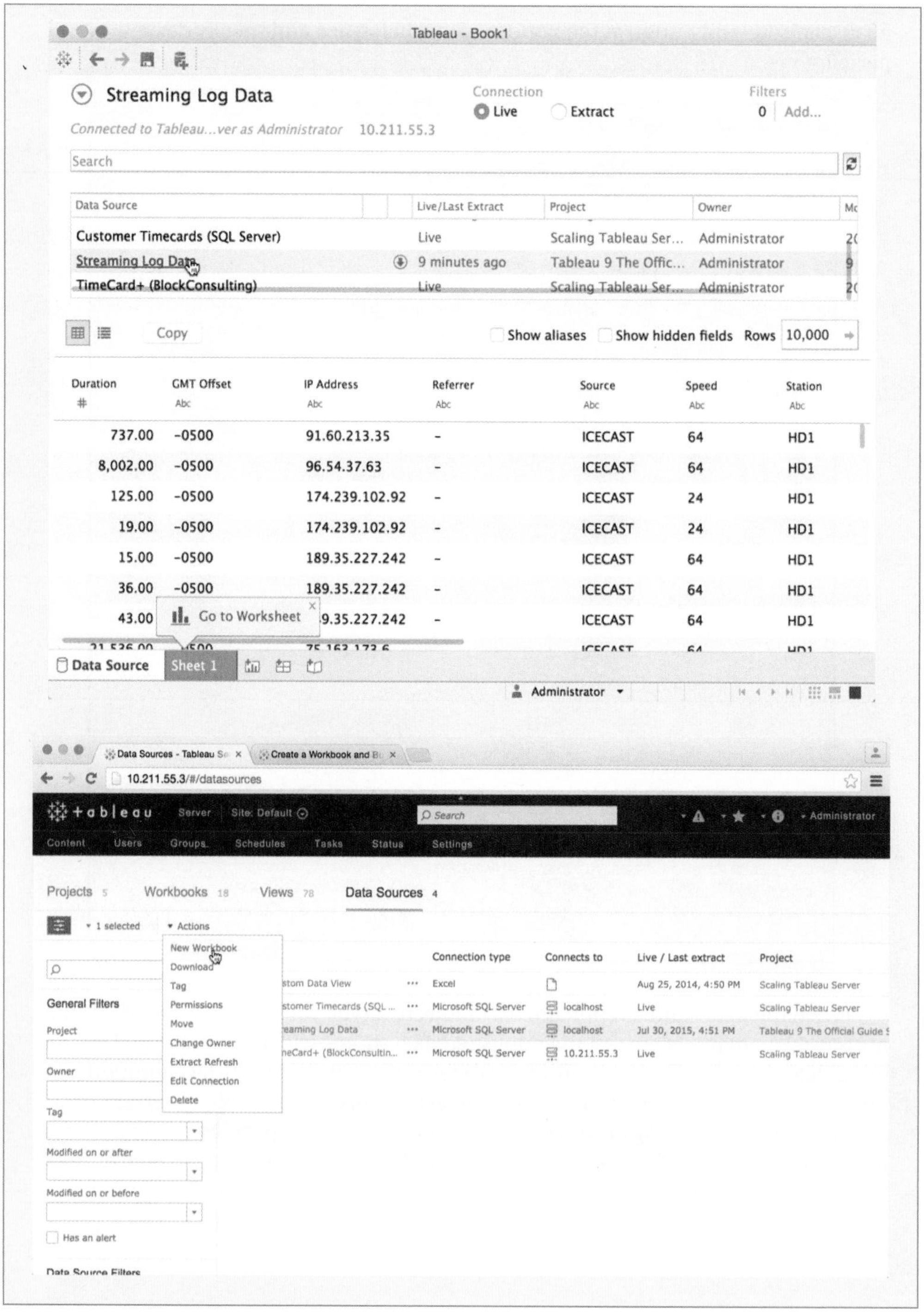
Tableau - Book1
Streaming Log Data
Connected to Tableau...ver as Administrator 10.211.55.3
Connection
Live
Extract
Filters
0 Add...
Search
Data Source
Live/Last Extract
Project
Owner
Customer Timecards (SQL Server)
Streaming Log Data
9 minutes ago
Tableau 9 The Offic...
Administrator
TimeCard+ (BlockConsulting)
Live
Scaling Tableau Ser...
Copy
Show aliases
Show hidden fields
Rows 10,000
Duration
GMT Offset
IP Address
Referrer
Source
Speed
Station
737.00 -0500 91.60.213.35 - ICECAST 64 HD1
8,002.00 -0500 96.54.37.63 - ICECAST 64 HD1
125.00 -0500 174.239.102.92 - ICECAST 24 HD1
19.00 -0500 174.239.102.92 - ICECAST 24 HD1
15.00 -0500 189.35.227.242 - ICECAST 64 HD1
36.00 -0500 189.35.227.242 - ICECAST 64 HD1
43.00
Go to Worksheet
Data Source
Sheet 1
Administrator
Data Sources - Tableau Se
Create a Workbook and Bu
10.211.55.3/#/datasources
+tableau
Server
Site: Default
Search
Administrator
Content
Users
Groups
Schedules
Tasks
Status
Settings
Projects 5
Workbooks 18
Views 78
Data Sources 4
1 selected
Actions
New Workbook
Download
Tag
Permissions
Move
Change Owner
Extract Refresh
Edit Connection
Delete
General Filters
Project
Owner
Tag
Modified on or after
Modified on or before
Has an alert
Connection type
Connects to
Live / Last extract
Project
Excel
Aug 25, 2014, 4:50 PM
Scaling Tableau Server
Microsoft SQL Server
localhost
Live
Jul 30, 2015, 4:51 PM
Tableau 9 The Official Guide
10.211.55.3

Note *As illustrated earlier in the chapter, many of these web-based edit, create, and server-based data source capabilities are also available to mobile devices via either dedicated iPad and Android apps, or HTML5 mobile browsers.*

Managing Tableau Server

Previous portions of this chapter discussed using the features of Tableau Server; however, you may find yourself in a position to manage some, or all, "back-end" portions of Tableau Server as a Tableau Server administrator. Although full coverage of all Tableau Server administrative topics is best left to the Administrator Guide portion of Tableau Server online help, some discussion of ways to organize Tableau Server users and content will be helpful as you approach day-to-day Tableau Server management. In order to perform most tasks in this section, your user ID will need to be granted the Server Administrator or Site Administrator role.

 Video *Managing Tableau Server*

Creating Sites

A Tableau Server *site* is, logically, an entirely separate Tableau Server system from the initial default site that is configured when Tableau Server is installed. It contains separate projects and content isolated from other sites and is logically separated completely from other sites. Physically, it exists on the same Tableau Server as other sites, using the same hardware resources, authentication method, and configuration. Some features are completely separated by site and cannot cross sites, such as workbooks and data sources. Some can optionally cross sites, such as users. Other items are common to all sites on the same server, such as schedules.

As a user, the first hint you'll have that you are using a multisite Tableau Server is if you're prompted to choose a site when you initially log in. In this case, your user ID is configured to use more than one site, and you need to select which site you want to use when you initially log in (you'll see this prompt in your browser, on your tablet, or in Tableau Desktop when logging in). If your user ID is only set to use one site, you won't be prompted—you'll simply go directly to that site. The URL in your browser will actually reflect the nondefault site you may be logged in to, but no other indicators within Tableau Server screens will indicate the site you're logged in to.

Assuming you are using the initial configuration of Tableau Server that only provides one site and you are one of the initial server administrators, click Settings at the top of the Tableau Server Content page. Select Add A Site from the menu that appears below. Then, click Add A Site. The New Site dialog will appear. Specify the site name and any configuration options, such as number of allowable users, maximum disk space allotment, site-wide options to use web authoring and subscriptions, and so forth, that you wish to specify just for this site.

Once you create an additional site, the top of the Tableau Server screen will change. Server and Site links will appear. Click Server to manage settings that are server-wide, such as schedules. Click Site to view or manage content or other items that are specific to a single site. You may change the site that you are managing from the small drop-down next to the current site at the top of the screen.

Creating and Grouping Users

When you initially install Tableau Server, you can choose from two broad methods of authenticating users: local authentication or Active Directory. Local authentication maintains a user database entirely on the Tableau Server itself. User IDs are created separately from any existing user database you may already have in use within your organization. Active Directory authentication will tie Tableau Server to an existing Microsoft Active Directory user database, permitting existing Windows users to be added to Tableau Server without re-creating their user IDs.

Caution   *If you are responsible for installing Tableau Server, consider this choice carefully, as you will be unable to change it after you initially make the selection at installation. If you later must change authentication methods, your only choice is to uninstall and reinstall Tableau Server entirely.*

This initial authentication choice determines how you add new users to Tableau Server. If your server is set to use local authentication, you will add all user information manually—either by adding users one at a time or importing a .csv file containing a list of users to add. If your server is set to use Active Directory authentication, you will add users one at a time by typing in their existing Active Directory user name, or select one or more Active Directory groups to add all at once.

Furthermore, if you have set up a multisite server (sites are discussed in the previous section), you have the choice of adding users at the server level, where they can be permitted to use more than one site, or at the site level, where they will be limited to using one site only. This choice is made by selecting either the server or an individual site from the options at the top left of the server (discussed in the previous "Creating Sites" section). If you create users at the server level, you'll be presented with a list of existing sites and you may assign the user to one or more, specifying a site role for each site. Or, you may click the Server Admin checkbox at the bottom of the Add User dialog box to permit them to administer all sites on the server. If you create users at the site level, the multiple site option won't appear. You may still choose to make the user a site administrator or server administrator, however.

When you add users, you must select a site role for the user, which sets a series of default permissions for the user. Available options appear in a drop-down list. If you click the small "i" information icon, a pop-up window will appear annotating the various permissions granted by each role. In particular, notice that site and server administrators appear to be granted the same permissions. The difference, however, is that server administrators may manage all sites on a multisite server, whereas a site administrator can only manage the specific site(s) that their user ID exists on.

Site role	Web access	Interact	Publish	Manage
Server Administrator	✓	✓	✓	✓
Site Administrator	✓	✓	✓	✓
Publisher	✓	✓	✓	
Interactor	✓	✓		
Viewer	✓			
Unlicensed				
Viewer (can publish)	✓		✓	
Unlicensed (can publish)			✓	

Tip *You may be somewhat confused by the various unlicensed options you see in the Site Roles drop-down list. An unlicensed role exists to permit you to maintain an existing user who no longer needs an active license, such as an employee who goes on extended leave, or an employee who is no longer involved with your organization but still has content on the server that they own. The Unlicensed (can publish) role is specifically provided for Tableau Desktop users who don't normally need to view content on Tableau Server. With this role, they don't use an active license, but still have the ability to publish content to the server from Tableau Desktop.*

If you are using Tableau Server core licensing (a licensing option based on the number of CPU cores being used by your server, rather than by the number of user IDs created on it), you may make use of the Guest user account. The Guest account is provided to allow Tableau Server content to be viewed without needing to be specifically authenticated to a user ID, such as with custom web-based systems that may embed Tableau Server content. Even if you are not using core licensing, you may still see the Guest account in the user list.

Placing Users in Groups

Grouping users into logical hierarchies is helpful for administration purposes, such as setting permissions and creating user filters (discussed earlier in this chapter). By being able to add multiple related users to groups, you can apply permissions to a group, rather than needing to apply permissions to each individual user. You have various group options, depending on whether you initially choose local or Active Directory authentication. If you chose local authentication, all groups are created and maintained manually, whereas Active Directory authentication will permit you to specify Active Directory groups, replicating them and the users they contain, on Tableau Server. Groups are maintained at the site level (there is no such thing as a "server" group on a multisite Tableau Server).

To maintain a group, click Groups at the top of the main Content view. A list of any existing groups will appear, including the All Users group, which cannot be deleted and includes all users on the site. If you wish to add a new group manually (regardless of whether you are using local or Active Directory authentication), click the New Group button and give the group a meaningful name. If you are using Active Directory authentication, you may choose Import Group. Once groups have been created, you may check one or more individual groups and make management choices from the Actions drop-down.

To add or remove users from manually created groups, click the group name on the Groups list. Any existing users in the group will appear. Check one or more of them and make management choices from the Actions drop-down. Click Add Users to add users to the group. A list of all users on the site will appear, where you may select as many users as desired to add to the group.

Add Users

Choose users to add to group "Central Region".

- [ ] Administrator
- [ ] Anna Andreadi
- [ ] Cassandra Brandow
- [ ] Chris
- [ ] Chuck Magee
- [ ] Denise Roberts
- [ ] Erin
- [ ] George Peck Test Account
- [x] Kelly Williams
- [x] Pat
- [x] Sam
- [ ] Tableau Software
- [ ] Trusted Ticket Test Account
- [ ] William

Cancel   Add Users (3)

Projects

A *project* is similar to a folder in other business intelligence (BI) toolsets. Unlike folders in some other tools, however, projects in Tableau Server cannot be nested (that is, projects cannot contain sub-projects—they can be only one level deep). All content in Tableau

Server (workbooks and data sources) are added to a particular project, and they can only reside in a single project. Projects are completely separated by site. If you have multiple sites, you will have a separate set of projects for each site. By organizing projects that match the business rules and processes of your organization, you are able to make navigating and managing Tableau Server more straightforward.

Tableau Server pre-installs a "default" project that can't be renamed or deleted in each site you create and (if selected during installation) a "Tableau Samples" project in the initial default site that you can rename or delete. Beyond those, you are completely free to create and manage as many projects as you choose.

From Tableau Server's main screen, select Projects. A list of existing projects in the site will appear. To add a project, click New Project. Give the project a descriptive name and, optionally, a description. Once the project has been created, Tableau Desktop users (based on permissions) will be able to save workbooks and data sources to it. From the Projects view, you can also select one or more projects and choose options from the Actions drop-down. Note that if you delete a project, *all content within the project is deleted.* Make sure you really want to do this before you proceed.

Moving content from one project to another can't be accomplished from the Projects view. You need to select one or more workbooks from the Workbooks view (you can only move entire workbooks, not individual views). Select one or more workbooks that you wish to move, and choose Move from the Actions drop-down. Select the destination project and click Move.

Permissions

Of course, Tableau Server users should be limited to seeing content that is required to meet their business needs. And only relevant users should be granted the ability to add, delete, or change Tableau Server content. For this key aspect of managing even the simplest of installations, Tableau Server *permissions* are used. Although the initial introduction to permissions may come from Tableau Desktop when you publish a workbook or data source to Tableau Server, many additional permission tasks are carried out in a web browser with Tableau Server itself.

An initial concept to consider when assigning permissions is that of object *ownership.* Initially, the user who creates the content (who publishes a workbook or data source from Tableau Desktop) or who creates a project is considered that project's owner. Ownership grants extended permissions to that object by default. Also, it's important to consider how to deal with members of your organization who may leave or move on to other tasks that no longer involve Tableau Server. You cannot remove a user who owns any content, but you can "unlicense" them. If you remove their content, then you may remove the user account. Or, you may change the owner from the Actions drop-down on the Projects, Workbooks, or Views view and assign a new one.

Although the owner of an object is given special consideration, so is a project leader. This permission permits the user to grant permissions for all objects within the project they are assigned to be a "leader" of. This permits administrators to create projects (discussed earlier in the chapter) and assign one or more users the Project Leader permission for that project. Then, that user can manage content within that project, while still having limited permissions for other content on the server outside of their specific projects.

Another important concept to grasp is that permissions are granted at the content level, not the user or group level. For example, you can't select a user or group and assign permissions that user or group has for a project, data source, workbook, or view. However, you can select the project, data source, workbook, or view; choose Permissions; and select users and groups to apply permissions for that project or workbook. Start permission assignment by clicking Projects, Workbooks, or Views on the main Tableau Server content view. Select the desired object (you can check multiple objects), and choose Permissions from the Actions drop-down.

The Permissions screen, illustrated in Figure 9-1, will appear. If any previous permissions have been assigned, additional lines below the All Users line will appear. Each line at the top of this screen is referred to as a *permissions rule*—a set of individual capabilities that can be granted, denied, or not specified (the relationship between these options is discussed later in this section). To add a permissions rule, click Add A User Or Group Rule just above the Resulting Permissions list. Then select either a group or user to assign the rule for. You may select the option for Group or User next to the drop-down arrow and then enter the first few characters of the group or user name to narrow down the list. Once you've selected the group or user to assign permissions to, you may select from a set of pre-defined permissions, such as Editor, Interactor, and so forth. A resulting set of capabilities will be granted (as indicated by the green checkmark), denied (as indicated by the red x), or not specified, as indicated by the small gray dot. You may also choose the

Figure 9-1   Permissions

Custom option and individually click a capability to cycle through granted, denied, and unspecified options.

Once you have specified permissions on one or more permission rule lines, you will want to ensure that the end result is, in fact, what you want. Because of overall permissions provided by a user's site role and other permissions that may be granted at higher levels (for example, a denial permission), the end result may be something different than you specified in this screen. Click either the All Users line or any permissions line you created to see users affected by that line. The Resulting Permissions portion of the Permissions screen will show the net permissions that are granted. For example, in Figure 9-1, note that some users match the set of permissions granted to the All Users rule. However, note that Cassandra Brandow is denied the ability to export an image because of the permission rule added just for her. And notice that Denise Roberts has no permissions at all, as she is a member of the Eastern Region group that has been denied all permissions to this content.

Tip *Although you don't set permissions for content at the user level, there is a basic set of permissions that a user gets based on the site role they are assigned when first added to the Tableau Server. This site role determines the maximum permissions you can assign to content for that user. For example, if you assign a user the Viewer site role, you may remove their ability to view certain content (you can reduce permissions below their site role). But if you attempt to assign permissions that are higher than their site role, the permissions still won't be granted (you cannot supersede the permissions provided by the site role).*

As you assign permissions, remember that there is a relationship (to a certain extent, an "inheritance") between groups and users. By default, if you assign permissions to an object for a group, users within the group are given the same permissions to the object. However, if a different set of permissions is assigned to a specific user, those permissions will take precedence over those specified at the group level.

With projects, workbooks, and the views (worksheets, dashboard, stories) they contain, a different relationship exists. If you assign permissions to a project, existing workbooks within the project *won't* automatically take on those permissions—only workbooks added after the project permissions are set will take on identical permissions. Assigning permissions to a workbook won't automatically set views within the workbook to the same permissions (workbooks with Show Views As Tabs selected being an exception). If, for example, you later add a new sheet to a view in web edit mode, the workbook permission will be applied. In each of these cases, to propagate the higher-level permissions to the lower-level contents, make sure to click the Assign Permissions To Contents button in the upper right.

There's also a relationship between granted, denied, and unspecified permissions and where they are specified. For example, if a permission is denied in one place and granted in another, the denial takes precedence—the user won't be able to perform that task. If a permission isn't specified anyplace, the user won't be able to perform the task. However, if the permission is unspecified in one place and granted in another, the user will be able to perform the task (granted supersedes unspecified).

Best Practice *Permissions are often the most confusing aspect of even a minimally complex enterprise system. Give yourself extra time to experiment with permissions before you roll major system or organizational changes out to production. In particular, TEST permissions before you roll out a major production system. Create several test accounts in various groups and assign desired permissions at user, group, project, data source, and workbook/view levels. Then log in with the test accounts to make sure you achieve the desired results.*

Schedules

As discussed earlier in several sections of this chapter, Tableau Server includes the ability to perform two general types of tasks on a schedule: Tableau Data Extract refreshes (both incremental and full) and subscription delivery (e-mail sent to users containing the most current representation of a view). Schedules for these two types of activities are maintained separately—any schedules that can be provided for extract refreshes won't be available for subscriptions, and vice versa. When Tableau Server is initially installed, there are a few "sample" schedules added for each type of activity, but you'll probably want to modify or remove these sample schedules and add your own.

Creating and modifying schedules is done slightly differently, depending on whether you are using a single-site or multisite server. If you are running a single-site server, all schedule choices are made from the Schedule option at the top of the screen. However, if you are running a multisite server, the options on the Schedules screen will vary, depending on whether you have selected Server (you are administering all sites) or have selected a specific site at the very top of the screen. Although you may create new schedules and run a schedule immediately in either case, you'll only be able to rename, remove, or modify schedules if you are administering the entire server.

Click Schedule. A list of existing schedules will appear. You may select one or more schedules and choose options from the Actions drop-down. If you wish to add a schedule, click New Schedule. Give the schedule a meaningful name, assign the schedule to either extract refreshes or subscriptions, select the priority of the schedule (this is relevant when multiple schedules may be running at the same time), choose whether to execute the schedule in a parallel or serial thread, and set the date/time specifics of the schedule. When you save the schedule, it will be available when extract refreshes are specified when publishing or when subscriptions are added from a view.

Command-Line Options

Although a fairly rich set of administrative and management options is available from your web browser when logged in to Tableau Server, there may be occasional features or requirements that aren't met with the web interface. Or, you may want to have several administrative or maintenance steps proceed one after the other without having to manually execute them one at a time in the web interface. And finally, you might benefit from a regularly required administrative feature running automatically on a schedule, such as nightly or weekly. For that, Tableau Server provides two command-line tools that can be run from a Windows command window. In addition, several of these commands can be combined in a Windows batch file. Either a single command or a batch file can be scheduled with the Windows built-in Task Scheduler.

Tip *If you wish to be able to run either of these commands from any directory, add the program files location of your Tableau Server installation (in particular, the "bin" subdirectory) to the Path environment variable in computer properties. Otherwise, you'll need to change to that directory before you execute either a tabcmd or tabadmin command.*

---

tabcmd

Tabcmd can perform general maintenance and content tasks, such as removing or adding content, adding sites, adding users en masse, and so forth. Because tabcmd can be run on any computer in your network, you must establish a valid Tableau Server session at the beginning of a series of tabcmd commands by logging in. Get specific options from Tableau Server online help, or type the following at the command line:

```
tabcmd --help
```

For example, a series of tabcmd commands can be used to log in, add a new site to the server, and log out.

Tip *Even though tabcmd is installed on the Tableau Server computer by default, you may install it on other computers on your network that don't have Tableau Server installed. This permits you to run maintenance tasks on any computer on the network. On the original Tableau Server, find the Extras folder within the original Tableau Server installation folder within Program Files. Find the TabcmdInstaller.exe file and copy it to, and run it on, the computer where you'd like tabcmd installed. Note that tabadmin can only be run from the Tableau Server computer.*

tabadmin

Tabadmin will perform a variety of administrative tasks, such as customizing some server behavior and appearance, resetting user passwords, and starting and stopping the server. Because tabadmin can only be run from the actual Tableau Server itself, you don't need to execute commands to log in to the server before executing tabadmin. Get specific options from Tableau Server online help, or type the following on the command line:

```
tabadmin help commands
```

For example, a series of tabadmin commands can be used to customize the logo and name of your Tableau Server. Once the customizations are applied, tabadmin is used to restart the server.

```
Microsoft Windows [Version 6.1.7601]
Copyright (c) 2009 Microsoft Corporation.  All rights reserved.

C:\Users\George>cd C:\Program Files\Tableau\Tableau Server\9.0\bin

C:\Program Files\Tableau\Tableau Server\9.0\bin>tabadmin customize name "Ablaze
Group Analytics"

C:\Program Files\Tableau\Tableau Server\9.0\bin>tabadmin customize logo "Y:\Clip
art\Ablaze Logo Square Small.png"

C:\Program Files\Tableau\Tableau Server\9.0\bin>tabadmin restart
===== Stopping service...
   -- Service stopped successfully
===== Starting service...
   -- Service was started successfully

C:\Program Files\Tableau\Tableau Server\9.0\bin>
```

10
CHAPTER

Custom Programming Tableau and Tableau Server

Tableau and Tableau Server 9 provide improved automation capabilities beyond previous versions with a series of application programming interfaces, or *APIs*, to permit developers to programmatically perform various Tableau tasks. Although most of these options apply only to Tableau Server, the Tableau Data Extract API creates Tableau Data Extract (.tde) files that are used by Tableau Desktop as a data source.

There are four approaches to adding Tableau resources to external third-party applications. One requires no custom coding or language implementation, whereas the other three are full APIs that you invoke within a custom application using JavaScript, Python, or another supported programming language.

- **Embedding a View**   This approach, used with Tableau Public, Tableau Online, or Tableau Server, permits you to embed an existing Tableau Server view (worksheet, dashboard, or story) into another web page separate from that coming from Tableau Server. Although you'll probably be required to design your own web page that embeds a Tableau Server view, no custom coding is required to embed—the code is provided from Tableau Server for you to cut and paste.

- **JavaScript API**   This approach, used with Tableau Public, Tableau Online, or Tableau Server, is designed to customize the *appearance of existing views*. The JavaScript API permits you to completely customize appearance and behavior, such as modification of filters, parameters, toolbars, and so forth, with JavaScript API calls. As the name implies, the JavaScript API is a pre-defined JavaScript library installed on Tableau Server by default that you may call from your custom JavaScript web applications.

Tip *Although there is no Tableau Desktop interface for legacy full-client application development, you may consider embedding a web browser object in a full-client application. You may then use the JavaScript API with a Tableau Server implementation to provide a custom Tableau interface in the application.*

- **REST API**   The REST (representational state transfer) API was originally informally referred to as the Tableau Server Administrator API, in that its primary purpose is modifying and adding content, users, and other "internal" resources on Tableau Server. Available for Tableau Server, and with some limitations for Tableau Online (this API is not available for use with Tableau Public), this API permits you to programmatically perform tasks similar to those provided by the tabcmd command-line utility (discussed in Chapter 9).

- **Tableau Data Extract API**   This API provides for programmatic creation of a Tableau Data Extract (.tde) file. Although you can also create .tde files with Tableau Desktop, this permits .tde manipulation from within a custom program, such as third-party data creation and maintenance utilities, or custom applications that connect to data sources not supported by Tableau Desktop.

The remainder of this chapter will cover the last three options. This is designed to introduce you to each API, providing an introductory look at techniques to perform common tasks. Each API has a complete set of online documentation that fully covers all objects, methods, requirements, and capabilities.

JavaScript API

The JavaScript API provides a complete object model for retrieving content from Tableau Server. Using the JavaScript API, you can augment or replace the standard Tableau Server interface in your own custom web applications.

Download *At www.tableaubook.com, download* JavaScript API Example.zip *for the sample application used in this section. Note that you will need access to Tableau Server to make use of the sample.*

Although full documentation is available on Tableau.com, the sample application illustrated here includes a common set of functions. This sample application is broken down into the following sections:

- Accessing and initializing the JavaScript API
- Navigating multiple sheets in a workbook
- Supplying values to parameters
- Changing filters
- Trapping events

Accessing and Initializing the JavaScript API

The JavaScript API is available on all versions of Tableau Server, including your own internal version, as well as Tableau Public and Tableau Online. Supply the server name or Internet Protocol (IP) address when initially referencing the library, followed by **/javascripts/api/tableau-2.0.0.min.js**.

To initialize the API, assign a series of variables for the actual view itself (**viz** in the following example), the workbook the viz object references (**workbook** in the following example), and the sheet (dashboard, worksheet, or story) being displayed from within the workbook (**activeSheet** in the following example). In addition, reference the placeholder in the underlying Hypertext Markup Language (HTML) where the view will actually display. In this example, a <div> tag in the underlying HTML page is referenced by name via a **placeholderDiv** variable. The actual view that you want to display is supplied to a variable as well (in this example, the **url** variable). Options for display of the view, such as width and height, whether to display the toolbar, and so forth, are placed in an **options** variable and included when the viz is instantiated.

Tableau Server will always require the JavaScript API to operate within the realm of a Tableau Server user ID. If your custom web application is making use of a Tableau Server–supported single sign-on approach, such as Kerberos or Security Assertion Markup Language (SAML) code to implement, it should precede instantiation of the viz object. If you have no single sign-on option in place, Tableau Server will prompt for a user ID and password the first time this code executes.

```
<script type="text/javascript" src="http://10.211.55.3/javascripts/api/tableau-2.0.0.min.js">
// Add your own Tableau Server name or IP address in place of 10.211.55.3</script>
var viz, workbook, activeSheet;
```

```
var placeholderDiv = document.getElementById("TableauViz");
var url = "http://10.211.55.3/views/SuperStoreAPIExample/SalesByYearCategory";
//Add your own Tableau Server name or IP Address to the var URL
//If not using a single sign-on method (Kerberos, SAML, etc.), you'll be prompted for log in
the first time

 var options = {
    width: "900px",
    height: "500px",
    hideTabs: true,
    hideToolbar: true,
    onFirstInteractive: function () {
      workbook = viz.getWorkbook();
      activeSheet = workbook.getActiveSheet();
    }
  };

  viz = new tableau.Viz(placeholderDiv, url, options);
<div id='TableauViz'></div>
```

Navigating Multiple Sheets in a Workbook

When viewing in Tableau Server, the intial "view" (worksheet, dashboard, or story) may be selected from the Content view. In the JavaScript API, the view you specify when initializing is what will be displayed by the viz object. However, the "parent" workbook will be placed in an object that can later be manipulated with calls to change sheets. The argument will be the actual name of the sheet within the workbook.

Note *activateSheetAsync is an example of one of several asynchronous methods supported by the JavaScript API. Online help provides more detail on the ability to chain events to permit handling of "promises" of completion of asynchronous API calls.*

In this sample code, the choice made with radio buttons on the source web page is used to navigate between two sheets. Although not related to actually changing sheets, notice use of an additional method in this code to turn an "event listener" on or off, which will fire an event if the viewer selects marks on the view. This event listener is discussed in more detail later under "Trapping Events."

```
function ChangeSheets() {
  if(document.getElementById('bars').checked) {
    workbook.activateSheetAsync("Sales By Year/Category");
    viz.removeEventListener(tableau.TableauEventName.MARKS_SELECTION, onMarksSelection);
  } else {
    workbook.activateSheetAsync("Sales/Goal By State");
    viz.addEventListener(tableau.TableauEventName.MARKS_SELECTION, onMarksSelection);
  }
}
```

Supplying Values to Parameters

One of the powerful capabilities of the JavaScript API is to supply values to parameters embedded within the source workbook. These parameters may be used within calculated fields and dialog boxes (such as the "N" value in a Top N filter) within the workbook. Unlike Tableau Desktop and out-of-the-box Tableau Server, a parameter does not have to be visible on a worksheet for it to be changed by the JavaScript API. By manipulating parameters from within the API, you have rich flexibility for controlling worksheet behavior without a parameter even being visible to the viewer.

In this example, a text box on the encompassing web form permits the viewer to specify a number, which is passed to a **goal** parameter used on both worksheets in the sample workbook.

```
function UpdateParameter() {
  workbook.changeParameterValueAsync("Goal", document.
getElementById("Goal").value);
}
```

Changing Filters

Although traditional quick filters will be fully functional within views exposed by the JavaScript API, you are free to change filter values with API code. If you change quick filter values, the quick filters will reflect the change. If you change filters that are not visible as quick filters, the worksheet will reflect the change. As an aside, filters that are set within the workbook to apply to more than one worksheet will propagate to all related worksheets when code changes one (as in the case of the two sheets used in this example).

An additional option permits specification of the filter update type, which permits specifying "All" (equivalent to checking All in the quick filter), "Remove" (equivalent to unchecking the value in the quick filter), "Add" (equivalent to checking the value in a quick filter), or "Replace" (replaces any existing filter value with that specified in the call).

In this example, a combo box on the encompassing web form is used to set a filter that applies to both worksheets within the sample workbook. As such, the filter will change whichever sheet happens to be viewed at the time. Because the filter is specified in the workbook to apply to both sheets, the alternative sheet will reflect the filter if the view changes to the other sheet, even though the filter is changed only once.

```
function ChangeFilter() {
  workbook.getActiveSheet().applyFilterAsync(
    "Region",
     document.getElementById("Region").value,
    tableau.FilterUpdateType.REPLACE);
}
```

Trapping Events

So far, examples covered in this section are the result of some action being performed by the viewer, such as changing radio buttons or specifying a new value in a text box. The JavaScript API has been called based on these actions. However, another capability of the JavaScript API is to "catch" events that may be "fired" by various behaviors of a workbook.

In this example, an event handler is enabled to trap the selection of marks on the worksheet. When a viewer selects one or more marks, the event code is executed.

This example shows an asynchronous call from the JavaScript API, which "chains" to a function when it is finished. The second function creates a variable to retain the collection of dimensions or measures and their values, which are included within the mark (an immediate way to confirm that multiple fields and values are on a mark is to hover over the mark and look at the fields and values that appear on the tooltip—the collection will contain the field/value pairs in the same order). As such, this example retrieves the state (the second member of the zero-based collection) and passes it to an external Wikipedia web search.

Note *Because the intent of the sample application is to only trap mark selections on one worksheet, notice removeEventListener and addEventListener calls that are executed when sheet navigation occurs. This is illustrated earlier in the section under "Navigating Multiple Sheets in a Workbook."*

```
function onMarksSelection(marksEvent) {
  return marksEvent.getMarksAsync().then(reportSelectedMarks);
}

function reportSelectedMarks(marks) {
      var pairs = marks[marks.length - 1].getPairs();
      var pair = pairs[1];
      window.open ("https://en.wikipedia.org/wiki/" + pair.formattedValue);
      //You may need to allow popups to see the resulting page
}
```

REST API

Although the JavaScript API (discussed previously in the chapter) is the key to a custom web interface to present content, the REST API permits custom approaches to administrative and maintenance tasks for Tableau Server. Tableau Server and the REST API are web-based;

however, the language and development environment you use need not be. The development tool used need merely support a standard REST HTTP/XML-based interface and does not have to present a user interface in a web browser.

The example described in this section, which is presented as a Python script, performs the following steps:

- Signs in to Tableau Server and retrieves an authentication token to use throughout the rest of the script

- Adds a new user account to Tableau Server

- Retrieves a list of workbooks on the server that the new user ID has rights to

- If a specified workbook is found in the list of workbooks, obtains the identifier of the workbook

- Using the workbook identifier, sets a series of permissions on the workbook for the new user ID

- Signs out of Tableau Server and releases the authentication token

Download *At www.tableaubook.com, download* Tableau Rest API Sample.py *for the sample Python script used in this section. Note that you will need access to Tableau Server to make use of the sample.*

It's helpful to understand several concepts that will present themselves throughout the sample code:

- The REST API makes use of HTTP URIs (universal resource identifiers) that are similar to those placed on a web browser address line when navigating the World Wide Web. For example, the URI to initially sign in with the REST API is **http://<*your Tableau server*>/api/2.0/auth/signin**. If you have implemented Secure Sockets Layer (SSL) support on your Tableau Server, or if you're using Tableau Public, the URI will begin with **https://**.

- HTTP calls fall into POST (to create new items), GET (to retrieve information), PUT (to update existing items), and DELETE (to remove items) categories.

- The REST API makes use of *tsRequest* XML "payloads" for certain calls to provide supporting data to the call and returns results in a block of XML text. Several libraries (such as ElementTree/ET) are used to form payload XML.

- The REST API returns a status code (such as 200 for "OK," 201 for "Created," and so forth) indicating the result of the API call. In addition, a block of XML is returned containing the results of the call, such as the LUID for a new user ID or a list of workbooks. An included library provides a utility for parsing and searching the resulting XML block.

Sign In to Tableau Server and Retrieve Authentication Token

Once utility libraries have been imported, a request is built to execute the auth/signin URI, which is submitted via a POST request. Items included in the XML payload are the user ID, password, and Tableau Server site to query (the default site is represented by an empty string).

If the call is successful (the response status code is 200), the returned XML is parsed to return LUIDs for the site that has been logged in to, as well as an authentication *token* that represents the Tableau Server sign-in session. The authentication token is used in subsequent calls (via an HTTP HEADER) to ensure that REST APIs are authorized by Tableau Server.

```
# Sign in to Tableau Server and retrieve a user LUID (Local Unique ID)
import math
import xml.etree.ElementTree as ET # Contains methods used to build and parse XML
import requests  # Contains methods used to make HTTP requests
# The following packages are used to build a multi-part/mixed request.
# They are contained in the 'requests' library.
from requests.packages.urllib3.fields import RequestField
from requests.packages.urllib3.filepost import encode_multipart_formdata

# The code extracts values from the XML response by using
# ElementTree. This requires using a namespace when searching the XML.
# For details, see:
#     https://docs.python.org/3/library/xml.etree.elementtree.html has more details
```

```
# The namespace for the REST API is 'http://tableausoftware.com/api'
xmlns = {'t': 'http://tableausoftware.com/api'}

#Replace localhost in URL with your own server name
url = 'http://localhost/api/2.0/'

### SIGN IN

NAME = 'George'
PASSWORD = 'George'
SITE = ''   #Empty for default site

# Builds the request
xml_payload_for_request = ET.Element('tsRequest')
# Change name, password and contentUrl for your individual environment
credentials_element = ET.SubElement(
    xml_payload_for_request, 'credentials', name=NAME, password=PASSWORD)
site_element = ET.SubElement(credentials_element, 'site', contentUrl=SITE)

xml_payload_for_request = ET.tostring(xml_payload_for_request)

# Send to server
server_response = requests.post(url+'auth/signin', data=xml_payload_for_request)
if server_response.status_code != 200:
    # Something went wrong
    print(server_response.text)
else:
    # Reads and parses the response
    xml_response = ET.fromstring(server_response.text)

    # Gets the token and site ID
    TOKEN = xml_response.find(
        't:credentials', namespaces=xmlns).attrib.get('token')
    SITE_ID = xml_response.find('.//t:site', namespaces=xmlns).attrib.get('id')
```

Note *Several API calls in this initial code return local unique identifiers, referred to as LUIDs (similar to, but shorter than, global unique identifiers, or GUIDs, that you may be familiar with). LUIDs are helpful in that they permit the REST API to refer to a specific workbook, user, Tableau Server site, and so forth, even if they are renamed on the server. LUIDs retrieved are then used in subsequent calls to identify specific resources, such as users and workbooks.*

Add New User Account

To add a new user to Tableau Server, a request is built to execute the sites/*<site signed into>*/users/ URI, which is submitted via a POST request. Items included in the XML payload are the user name of the new user and their site role (setting their password is accomplished with an additional Update call). The site the user will be created within is passed as part of the URI via the site LUID retrieved from the initial sign-in call.

If the call is successful (the response status code is 201), the returned XML is parsed to return the LUID for the just-created user.

```
### ADD A USER

# Username and Site Role of user to create
NEWUSER = 'Denise'
SITEROLE = 'Interactor'

# Builds the request
xml_payload_for_request = ET.Element('tsRequest')

user_element = ET.SubElement(
    xml_payload_for_request, 'user', name=NEWUSER, siteRole=SITEROLE)

xml_payload_for_request = ET.tostring(xml_payload_for_request)
```

```
# Send to server
server_response = requests.post(url+'sites/' + SITE_ID + '/users/', data=xml_payload_for_request,
                                headers={"x-tableau-auth": TOKEN})
if server_response.status_code != 201:
    # Something went wrong
    print(server_response.text)
else:
    # Reads and parses the response
    xml_response = ET.fromstring(server_response.text)

    # Gets new user LUID
    NEWUSER_LUID = xml_response.find('.//t:user', namespaces=xmlns).attrib.get('id')
```

Retrieve the List of Workbooks and Obtain a Workbook Identifier

To retrieve a specific workbook you want to set permissions for, the collection of all workbooks the new user can access must be queried. A request is built to execute the sites/<*site signed into*>/users/<*user account just created*>/workbooks/ URI, which is submitted via a GET request. Both the site and user accounts are included in the URI via their LUIDs.

If the call is successful (the response status code is 200), a loop searches the resulting list of workbooks for a match to the desired workbook (specified in the WORKBOOK_TO_LOOKUP variable). When the workbook is found, the LUID for the workbook is obtained.

```
### GET ALL WORKBOOKS NEW USER CAN READ

# Change this to the name of a workbook on your server
WORKBOOK_TO_LOOKUP = 'Science'

# Send to server
server_response = requests.get(url+'sites/' + SITE_ID + '/users/' + NEWUSER_LUID + '/workbooks',
                               headers={"x-tableau-auth": TOKEN})
```

```
if server_response.status_code != 200:
    # Something went wrong
    print(server_response.text)

else:
    # Reads and parses the response
    xml_response = ET.fromstring(server_response.text)

    # Cycle through workbooks -- match name to LUID
    workbooks = xml_response.findall('.//t:workbook', namespaces=xmlns)
    for workbook in workbooks:
        if workbook.get('name') == WORKBOOK_TO_LOOKUP:
            WORKBOOK_LUID = workbook.get('id')
            print ('Workbook ' + WORKBOOK_TO_LOOKUP + ' found with LUID ' + WORKBOOK_LUID)
            break
    else:
        print('Workbook ' + WORKBOOK_TO_LOOKUP + ' not found')
```

Set Permissions

Next, permissions are set on the desired workbook. A request is built to execute the sites/*<site signed into>*/workbooks/*<desired workbook>*/permissions/ URI, which is submitted via a PUT request. Both the site and workbook are included in the URI via their LUID. In addition, a block of desired permissions, organized as a *map,* is created with a series of permission capability/grant-or-deny pairs to use in the XML payload.

If the call is successful (the response status code is 200), the permissions were properly set and no response XML need be used.

```
### SET PERMISSIONS ON WORKBOOK FOR NEWUSER

#Permissions "map" of permission/allowance
permissions_map = {
        "AddComment": "Deny",
        "ViewComments": "Deny",
```

```
        "ExportData": "Deny",
        "ChangeHierarchy": "Allow",
        "WebAuthoring": "Allow"}

xml_payload_for_request = ET.Element('tsRequest')
permissions = ET.SubElement(xml_payload_for_request, 'permissions')
granteeCapabilities = ET.SubElement(permissions, 'granteeCapabilities')
user_xml = ET.SubElement(granteeCapabilities, 'user', id=NEWUSER_LUID)
capabilities = ET.SubElement(granteeCapabilities, 'capabilities')
for perm, mode in permissions_map.items():
    capabilities.append(ET.Element('capability', name=perm, mode=mode))
xml_payload_for_request = ET.tostring(xml_payload_for_request)
print(xml_payload_for_request)
server_response = requests.put(
    url+'sites/' + SITE_ID + '/workbooks/' + WORKBOOK_LUID + '/permissions', data=xml_payload_
for_request, headers={'x-tableau-auth': TOKEN})

if server_response.status_code != 200:
    print(server_response.text)
else:
    print('Permissions Set...')
```

Sign Out of Tableau Server

In order to release resources and licenses, REST API code should always sign out of Tableau Server and release the authentication token. A single line of code using the /signout URI, submitted via a POST request, accomplishes this.

```
# Sign Out
server_response = requests.post(url+'/signout', headers={'x-tableau-auth': TOKEN})
```

This code results in a new user named Denise being created and her account granted a separate permissions rule for the Science workbook.

Tableau Data Extract API

The *Tableau Data Extract API* (abbreviated to "TDE API" throughout the rest of this chapter) permits you to create Tableau Data Extract (.tde) files outside of Tableau Desktop. This can be used for your own custom data import or integration applications. These applications can be freely distributed either within or outside your organization. They can also be scheduled with internal application logic or with Windows Task Manager.

The TDE API is available in both 32- and 64-bit versions for Windows and Linux, supporting Python, C, C++, and Java. Get the desired version of the API from Tableau.com, ensuring that the version of the TDE API you download matches the "bitness" of your development tool (for example, if you are using 64-bit Python, make sure you download the 64-bit version of the TDE API).

Follow instructions within the API documents for configuring your development environment to use the TDE API (for example, for use with Python as illustrated here, you'll need to run the Setup.py script to add the TDE API module to Python).

Download   *At www.tableaubook.com, download* TDE API Sample.zip *for the sample Python script illustrated in this section.*

The TDE API example presented in this section as a Python script creates a .tde file and imports the contents of a .csv file into it. If the .tde file doesn't exist, it is created and data is added (much as in a full refresh from Tableau Server or Tableau Desktop). If the .tde file already exists, data is appended to the existing file (much as in an incremental refresh from Tableau Server or Tableau Desktop).

This is accomplished via the following steps:

- The desired .tde file is "opened" (if it doesn't exist, it will be created). The .csv file to import is opened.
- The schema (field names/data types) is retrieved from the existing .tde. If the .tde doesn't exist, the schema is defined from scratch.
- The .csv file is read row by row, with each .csv field being mapped to a commensurate .tde field. The .tde row is added to the .tde file.
- The .tde file is closed.

Open the .TDE and .CSV Files

After importing necessary Python modules, a **tdefile** object is created referencing the desired .tde file. If this file already exists, it will be opened. Otherwise, it will be created. The .csv file is opened as well.

```
# Import Modules
import dataextract   #Tableau Data Extract API
import os
import datetime
import csv

#Open end-result Extract file - will create if it doesn't exit
tdefile = dataextract.Extract('Sample Data Extract.tde')

#Open CSV
csvFile = csv.reader(open('Sample Source Data.csv', 'rb'), delimiter=',')
```

Define the Schema

The *schema* (field name/data type organization) must be defined for the .tde file. With the exception of the DateStamp field, which is created within the Python script, there is a one-to-one field match between the .csv file and resulting .tde file.

If the .tde file already exists, the existing schema is retrieved via a TableDefinition object. If the .tde file doesn't exist, a TableDefinition object is created, consisting of a set of AddColumn calls. Each AddColumn call includes the desired field name and data type for the .tde file. If not already found in an existing .tde file, the TDE API **table** object is created to reference the single "table" that will comprise the .tde file. The schema **tableDef** object that was defined earlier is supplied.

```
#Check for existing Table Definition
if tdefile.hasTable('Extract'):
    table = tdefile.openTable('Extract')
    tableDef = table.getTableDefinition()
else:
    #Create Table Definition from scratch
    tableDef = dataextract.TableDefinition()
```

```
tableDef.addColumn('DateStamp', dataextract.Type.DATE)
tableDef.addColumn('Customer Name', dataextract.Type.CHAR_STRING)
tableDef.addColumn('Order ID', dataextract.Type.CHAR_STRING)
tableDef.addColumn('Product Name', dataextract.Type.CHAR_STRING)
tableDef.addColumn('State', dataextract.Type.CHAR_STRING)
tableDef.addColumn('Quantity', dataextract.Type.INTEGER)
tableDef.addColumn('Unit Price', dataextract.Type.DOUBLE)
#Create extract Table object
table = tdefile.addTable('Extract', tableDef)
```

Cycle Through the .CSV File and Add Rows to the .TDE File

The TDE **newrow** object is created to represent the new row that will be written to the .tde file. Again, the previously referenced tableDef object, representing the schema, is supplied. The current date is added to a variable to add to the .tde file as the DateStamp field. The .csv file is advanced to the second record (via the next() method) to skip the header row.

A loop through the .csv file, one record at a time, is then established. Within the loop **line[*field order*]** data from the .csv file is passed to the **newrow** object via data type-appropriate **set** options. The **newrow** is added to the .tde file via **insert**.

Note   *An **if** test is provided in the sample script to test for the existence of data from the .csv file in the existing .tde. This logic may be used to perform the equivalent of a Tableau Server or Desktop incremental refresh, only adding data to the .tde file if it can be determined that the .tde doesn't already contain it. Your custom application must make this determination on its own without reading existing data in the .tde file (perhaps write a separate file containing a date stamp or last key field used that can be read later). This is required because the TDE API will only write data to a .tde file—it cannot read .tde file data.*

```
#Create extract row object
newrow = dataextract.Row(tableDef)


numrows = 0
currentdate = datetime.date.today() #Current Date
```

```
if True: #Potentially add logic to determine if data is new -- TDE API doesn't *READ* existing TDE
    #Process CSV record-by-record
    csvFile.next() #skip header row
    for line in csvFile:
        newrow.setDate(0, currentdate.year, currentdate.month, currentdate.day) #DateStamp
        newrow.setCharString(1, line[0]) #Customer Name
        newrow.setCharString(2, line[1]) #Order ID
        newrow.setCharString(3, line[2]) #Product Name
        newrow.setCharString(4, line[3]) #State
        newrow.setInteger(5, int(line[4])) #Quantity
        newrow.setDouble(6, float(line[5])) #Unit Price
        table.insert(newrow)
        numrows = numrows + 1
    print('Rows added to TDE: ' + str(numrows))
else:
    print('No new data to add...')
```

Close the .TDE File

Once all data has been "logically" written to the .tde file, the file must be explicitly closed. Not only does this release memory, but it physically writes all data to the .tde to prevent a possible corrupt .tde file.

```
#IMPORTANT! Close the TDE to fully write file
tdefile.close()
```

The result is the data in the sample .csv file being written to a Tableau Data Extract. If the script is run multiple times without deleting the .tde file, the .csv data is appended to the previous data in the .tde.

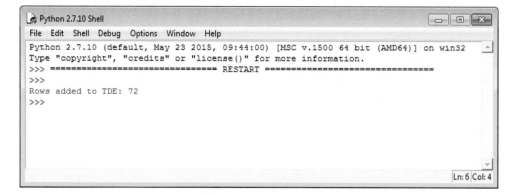

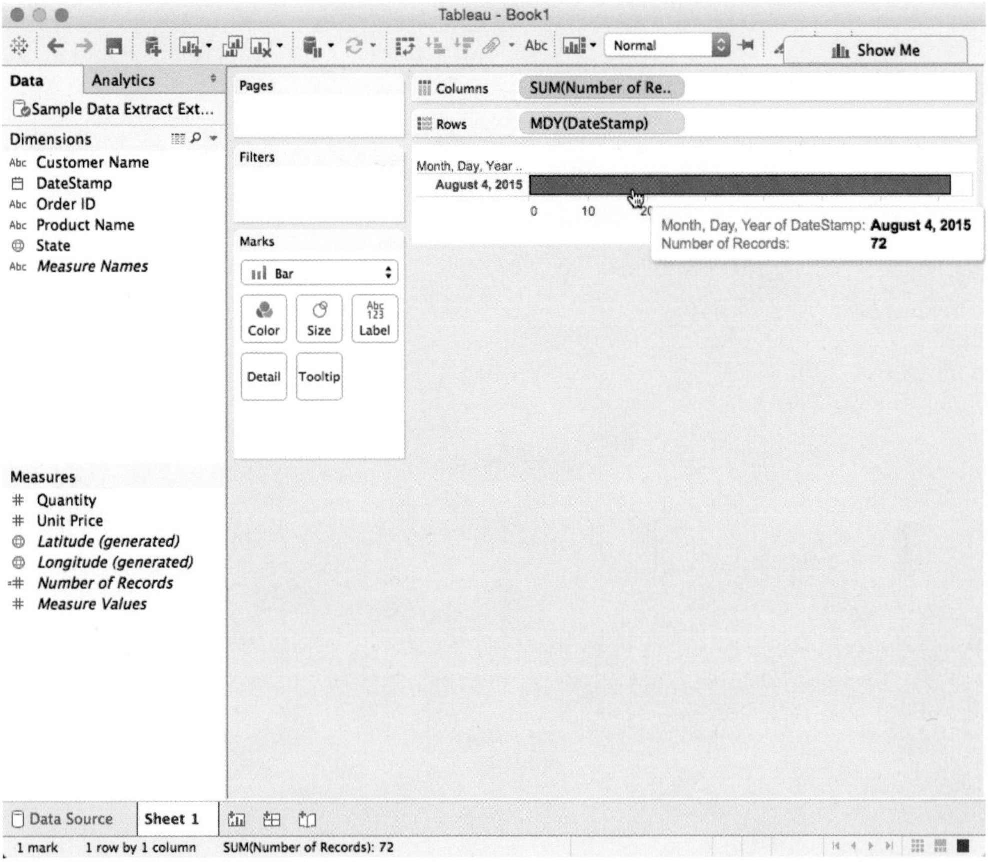
Tableau - Book1
Show Me
Data
Analytics
Sample Data Extract Ext...
Dimensions
Customer Name
DateStamp
Order ID
Product Name
State
Measure Names
Measures
Quantity
Unit Price
Latitude (generated)
Longitude (generated)
Number of Records
Measure Values
Pages
Filters
Marks
Bar
Color
Size
Label
Detail
Tooltip
Columns
SUM(Number of Re..
Rows
MDY(DateStamp)
Month, Day, Year ..
August 4, 2015
Month, Day, Year of DateStamp: August 4, 2015
Number of Records: 72
Data Source
Sheet 1
1 mark
1 row by 1 column
SUM(Number of Records): 72

Index